THE PLANTFINDER'S
GUIDE TO
DAISIES

THE PLANTFINDER'S GUIDE TO
DAISIES

John Sutton

 David & Charles

 Timber
Press

PICTURE ACKNOWLEDGEMENTS

All photographs are by Justyn Willsmore, except page 37 (bottom) and 79 by John Sutton,
and the plates, which are by Karl Adamson

Note: Throughout the book the time of year is given as a season to make the
reference applicable to readers all over the world. In the Northern Hemisphere the seasons
may be translated into months as follows:

Early winter – December	Early summer – June
Midwinter – January	Midsummer – July
Late winter – February	Late summer – August
Early spring – March	Early autumn – September
Mid-spring – April	Mid-autumn – October
Late spring – May	Late autumn – November

First published in the UK in 2001 by David & Charles Publishers
Brunel House, Newton Abbot, Devon
ISBN 0 7153 0973 0
A catalogue record for this book is available from the
British Library

First published in North America in 2001 by Timber Press Inc.,
133 SW Second Avenue, Suite 450, Portland, Oregon 97204, USA
ISBN 0–88192–497–0
Cataloging-in-Publication data is on file with the Library of Congress

Project editor: Jo Weeks
Book design by Ian Muggeridge
Printed in Italy by LEGO SpA

Photographs:
Page 1 The glowing deep orange *Gazania cookei* ♉ creates an illusion of tropical warmth.
Page 2 Flowerheads of *Aster* 'Little Carlow' ♉ and *Elaeagnus* × *ebbingei* 'Gilt Edge' ♉.
Page 3 The striking flowerheads of the cardoon, *Cynara cardunculus*, a most handsome ornamental thistle.
Page 5 A Mexican native, *Cosmos sulphureus* is a free-flowering half hardy annual.

Contents

Preface

There are books on ornamental grasses, on ferns, on bulb flowers, but there have been none, until now, on the garden plants of the daisy family. Given the almost universal popularity of the daisy flower form – which is perceived as a symbol for flowers in general – this is surprising. It is a rare mixed bouquet of cut flowers that includes no member of the daisy family.

The daisy family is the largest in the entire spectrum of families of flowering plants, and as might be expected the diversity of flowerheads within it is almost endless. There are colour and size, of course, but what gives individual character to the flowerheads is the almost endless variety of combinations of ray florets ('petals') and the central disc: there is the number of ray florets; there is their spacing and their shape – broad and rounded at one extreme, needle-fine and quilled at the other; there is their poise – reflexing or radiating horizontally; and there is the colour of the disc, its size relative to the length of the rays, and its shape – flat, convex or conical. Flowerheads of many species are borne singly on separate stems, but others form part of an inflorescence, and then how they are arranged in it, and how densely, may create very different visual impressions.

The daisy family by no means ends with what the person in the street might regard as daisies. The regal spikes of *Ligularia* 'The Rocket', the strange, flat, densely packed, umbel-like inflorescences of *Achillea filipendulina*, the spiky, metallic-blue globes of *Echinops*, the splendid, tufted flowerheads of the cardoon, and the pretty cornflowers, are all in the daisy family. So, too, is an extraordinarily rich assortment of plants grown primarily for their silver and grey foliage, much of it exquisitely divided.

At the end of the twentieth century, The Royal Horticultural Society decided to mark the dawn of the twenty-first with a millennium spectacular of yellow and golden flower trials. All the ten genera chosen were of the daisy family, including some of the best loved of its herbaceous perennials. The Society's decision paid tribute to the immense debt our gardens owe to this one group of flowering plants. This book extends that tribute.

Long-lasting and honey-scented, 'White Swan' is a much-admired cultivar of *Echinacea purpurea*.

(Opposite) The popular globe thistle, *Echinops ritro* ♔ with *Acanthus mollis* at Oxford Botanic Gardens.

Part One Introduction to Daisies

Daisies in the Garden

Where herbaceous perennials and annuals can be used in gardens – which is almost everywhere – some member or another of the daisy family can be placed. However, in my opinion, there are three particular situations in which the daisies excel to an extent unrivalled by other families. First is the irreplaceable contribution made by species in many genera to the silver- and grey-leaved flora of our gardens. Second is the remarkable wealth of long-lasting cut flowers included in the family. Third is the multitude of plants in the family that suit one specific garden environment: a site very well exposed to sun and with a freely drained soil. On this site, however its owner chooses to garden, a cornucopia of natives to the Mediterranean region and to southern Africa, for example, can be expected to thrive to the fullest extent. No one would make a selection of plants for such a situation without drawing on them to exploit to the full its potential to give the maximum pleasure.

Silverlings

Graham Stuart Thomas has extended the meaning of the word 'silverling' to encompass silver-leaved plants. In dictionaries, the definition is a silver coin, such as the biblical shekel, but the distinguished former gardens adviser to the National Trust has taken a useful initiative, and I will give it support by using the word in his sense here. Among the little-sung glories of the wealth of subshrubs and herbaceous perennials in the daisy family is silver and grey foliage – dramatic as in *Onopordum*, sharply cut as in *Senecio cineraria*, filigree-fine as in many *Artemisia*, exquisitely dissected as in *Tanacetum haradjanii* and *T. ptarmiciflorum*, woolly as in *Helichrysum* 'Schwefellicht' ('Sulphur Glow').

In a late 1990s catalogue, compiled by the discerning owners of one of England's leading nurseries for plantsmen, there is a list of over 30 genera of herbaceous perennials with notably fine grey and silver foliage – silverlings – among their species and cultivars. Fourteen plant families feature in this list, but over a third of the genera belong to just one, the daisy family. In her book *Grey and Silver Plants* (Collins, 1971), Mrs Desmond Underwood chose to write about 31 genera. Over half of these belong to the daisies. Below is a comprehensive list of genera in the daisy family that contain species with silver or grey foliage.

Silver- and grey-leaved daisies

Achillea	Celmisia	× Leucoraoulia
Ajania	Centaurea	Olearia
Anacyclus	Cynara	Onopordum
Anaphalis	Echinops	Othonna
Andryala	Eriophyllum	Ozothamnus
Antennaria	Galactites	Raoulia
Anthemis	Gazania	Rhodanthemum
Argyranthemum	Helichrysum	Santolina
Artemisia	Hieracium	Senecio
Brachyglottis	Leontopodium	Seriphidium
Cassinia	Leucogenes	Tanacetum

That the silverlings make a large contribution to the visual enjoyment of our gardens goes almost without saying. Unlike the short-lived floral displays of the vast majority of plants, the pleasures of fine foliage are there to enjoy for many months each year. Few gardens altogether lack silverlings, and few would not be impoverished if they were taken away. In Britain, their presence is one of the distinctive indications that gardening activity is taking place, because our native flora is relatively poor in them. Silver or grey foliage is among the most widespread of adaptations that plants have made in order to survive in areas of intense solar radiation: the silver or grey surface reflects radiant heat. Hence, the Mediterranean area is so often the natural environment of our silverlings – for example, *Senecio cineraria* and *Santolina chamaecyparissus*.

Like white, silver and grey bring their own calming contribution to the symphony of colour in the garden. Silver foliage excels as a foil for pinks and mauves, while greys are to be preferred where the flowers are blue, purple or white. Shrubs with reddish-purple foliage, such as *Berberis thunbergii, Prunus atropurpurea* and *P. × cistena* ♛ ,

Previous page: *Rudbeckia* 'Sonora' and *Bracteantha* Bright Bikinis are both perennials easily grown as annuals.

A contrast in flower form – *Rudbeckia fulgida* var. *deamii* and *Sinacalia tangutica*.

For its lovely foliage, *Artemisia* 'Powis Castle' is a garden favourite.

are strikingly complemented by silver-leaved *Artemisia* or *Santolina*. *Anthemis punctata* subsp. *cupaniana* and *Salvia officinalis* Purpurascens Group are pleasing companions, both thriving in a dry, sunny position. Other examples of satisfying associations with silver- and grey-leaved plants could be given almost interminably.

Both greys and silvers are invaluable for separating bright colours which if seen side by side would detract from one another, and may have a jarring effect even when they do not clash. Think of, say, neighbouring drifts of those two fine plants *Sedum* 'Herbstfreude' ('Autumn Joy') ♛ and *Schizostylis* 'Sunrise', and then think of them again, separated by *Artemisia* 'Powis Castle'.

Grey and silver foliage is seen at its best in full sun, and planting should take this into account so far as possible. However, unlike many other plants that also give of their best in such locations, silverlings perhaps come into their own most of all on dull, cloudy days, and as light fades in the evening. Then their pale foliage stands out, just as white flowers do, while darker colours — reds and blues — become dull.

Cut flowers

As a gardening activity, growing flowers specifically for cutting is like growing your own vegetables — done primarily for enriching the quality of life within the four walls of home, rather than enhancing the garden. After all, taking flowers off plants actually detracts from their garden value. Fortunately, many of those members of the

daisy family that particularly commend themselves as cut flowers are also exceedingly prolific. Once any of these are well established, it would be a rapacious filler of vases whose depredations would even be noticed. Gardening and domestic floristry can then go hand in glove.

There is, however, a good case for growing some daisies primarily for cut flowers, giving them space where their characteristics other than as vase fodder are not of importance. Quite apart from what heavy cutting can do to spoil plant appearance, separate provision opens up the possibilities of selecting plants entirely for their value as cut flowers. Pyrethrums (*Tanacetum coccineum*) are a good example. They are fine border plants while they are in flower, but their flowering period is short. It is largely for this reason that they have suffered a spectacular decline in popularity over the last few

decades. The shortness of their flowering period matters nothing like so much if a few plants are grown in an out-of-the-way corner or along with the vegetables, with a view to giving delight in the home for a few weeks early each summer.

For reasons other than the brevity of the flowering period, you may not be greatly enthused about giving space in bed or border to all manner of plants that could give great pleasure as cut flowers in the home. As examples, many owners of small gardens would not choose golden rod (*Solidago*), as a bed or border plant simply because other perennials give better value in a small space. Others might not particularly favour *Helianthus* – too big, or too invasive, perhaps – or *Liatris* or *Aster tongolensis*, and most would exclude from their choice the early-flowering cultivars of the florists' chrysanthemum,

typically stiff and leggy in habit as they are. They all have distinctive appeal as cut flowers, though, and all last long in the vase.

Annuals are often regarded as poor value in return for effort in comparison with shrubs and herbaceous perennials. Still, there are some that make pleasing cut flowers: in the daisy family, the China aster (*Callistephus chinensis*) and the annual cornflower (*Centaurea cyanus*) come to mind. So does the less known but distinctive safflower (*Carthamus tinctoria*), not to mention almost the entire gamut of everlasting flowers.

There are, of course, innumerable small gardens in which there are no out-of-the-way corners and in which

Osteospermum 'Weetwood' ♀ foiled by *Heuchera* 'Cascade Dawn' in the Cotswold garden of Bourton House.

Some gardeners prefer single-flowered French marigolds to the doubles: here is 'Disco Flame'.

vegetables and soft fruit find no place. If cutting flowers that you have grown yourself is, nevertheless, of importance, then your selection of garden plants ought to take this into account. The list of genera with long-lasting vase flowers, below, is a useful starting point.

Daisies suitable for cut flowers

Achillea	*Craspedia*	*Leucanthemum*
Amberboa	*Cynara*	*Liatris*
Ammobium	*Dahlia*	*Matricaria*
Anaphalis	*Doronicum*	*Petasites*
Anthemis	*Echinacea*	*Rhodanthe*
Aster	*Echinops*	*Rudbeckia*
Bracteantha	*Emilia*	*Solidago*
Calendula	*Erigeron*	*× Solidaster*
Callistephus	*Gaillardia*	*Stokesia*
Carthamus	*Gerbera*	*Tanacetum*
Centaurea	*Helenium*	*Xeranthemum*
Chrysanthemum	*Helianthus*	*Zinnia*
Cosmos	*Heliopsis*	

Dry, sunny sites

It is not just for gardeners in sunny places and on sandy soils that this group of plants has special interest. Even in cool locations, and even on heavy moisture-retentive soils, there are situations in many gardens where summer water supplies are sparse, and plants enjoy (or suffer) full sunshine. For example, unshaded, sloping sites inevitably have fast drainage and surface run-off of heavy rain, and, if their aspect is southerly, plants growing there will have high rates of transpiration from the foliage. Raised beds (see 'Cultivation' pp.16–19) are valuable for creating artificially a dry, fast-draining root environment in gardens where such conditions do not exist naturally. When they are sited in a sunny position, as is usually done, they provide a home for exactly the same range of plants as is adapted for naturally dry garden sites.

The rich flora of the daisy family from the Mediterranean area, southern Africa, Australia and the prairies of the USA provides a wealth of plants that will flourish in just such conditions. They are usually well represented in a development of recent years – the gravel garden. In Britain, the most famous and most visited gravel garden is probably Beth Chatto's extensive version near Colchester in Essex, created on the unshaded site of a former car park in an area with the lowest rainfall in the British Isles. In her catalogue, Beth Chatto lists over twenty genera in the daisy family that she commends as suitable for such an environment. These and others are listed below.

Daisies particularly suitable for dry, sunny sites

Those with ★ after the name are suitable for use in rock gardens, i.e. at least one species or cultivar is dwarf enough. The term rock garden should be taken to include scree beds and dry stone walls, both of which are characterized by free drainage and, therefore, by seasonal dryness, except in areas of high summer rainfall. Accordingly, most of the plants that thrive in dry, sunny sites will thrive here, too, though some simply grow too tall to be appropriate.

Achillea★	*Cotula*★	*Leptinella*★
Antennaria★	*Crepis*★	*Onopordum*
Anthemis	*Cynara*	*Othonna*★
Artemisia★	*Echinops*	*Raoulia*★
Carlina★	*Eriophyllum*	*Rhodanthemum*★
Centaurea★	*Gazania*★	*Santolina*
Chamaemelum★	*Haplopappus*	*Senecio*
Cichorium	*Helichrysum*★	*Serratula*★
Coreopsis	*Leontopodium*★	

Heavy, moisture-retentive soils

It is above all else for herbaceous perennials that the daisy family is best known and most appreciated. As already indicated, a wealth of members do best in light, free-draining soils of relatively low moisture retention. Nevertheless, many of the finest herbaceous plants in the family thrive in heavy, moisture-retentive soils. The list below should disabuse any gardener of the view that preference for the opposite accounts for nearly all the worthwhile species in the family. The daisy family is nothing if not versatile, after all, and on whatever soil the reader gardens there is more than a lifetime's worth of herbaceous perennials to enjoy.

A handsome plant for a large garden, *Telekia speciosa* does well in semi-shade.

Daisies for heavy, moisture-retentive sites

(Many species in other genera are also capable of a fairly good performance in such soils, provided they are well-drained.)

Anaphalis	*Eupatorium*	*Petasites*
Artemisia	*Helenium*	*Pulicaria*
Aster	*Helianthus*	*Rudbeckia*
Centaurea	*Kalimeris*	*Senecio*
Cirsium	*Leucanthemella*	*Silphium*
Craspedia	*Leucanthemum*	*Sinacalia*
Cynara	*Liatris*	*Telekia*
Doronicum	*Ligularia*	

Containers

Five genera dominate the container-plant scene in summer – *Begonia*, *Fuchsia*, the ivy-leaved and zonal geraniums (*Pelargonium*), *Impatiens* and *Petunia* – and none of them are daisies. In the runner-up category, however, the marguerites (*Argyranthemum*) and *Osteospermum* are among the most important. We can also be pretty confident that as the twenty-first century progresses, the second of these will rapidly become a good deal more popular still, especially if the already promising progress is maintained in breeding cultivars that less readily close up their flowerheads in cloudy conditions. Dwarf dahlias are likely to be seen more widely, too, thanks to the efforts being made to develop patio cultivars, tailored for container growing in terms of height, habit and flowering behaviour.

All the South African members of the daisy family (pp.120–129) have good potential as container plants, too. One often seen, and in some hard-to-define way presenting a rather classy image, is the *Arctotis* hybrid 'Flame' ♛.

A wide range of container plants is listed below. An ★ after a name indicates that the genus has one or more species that are important as foliage plants. Hence, in *Senecio* we find the prodigiously popular silver-leaved *S. cineraria*, and in *Helichrysum* what is arguably the best of the trailing foliage plants, *H. petiolare*.

Daisies particularly suitable for containers

Ageratum	*Brachyscome*	*Helichrysum*★
Ajania★	*Chrysanthemum*	*Leucophyta*★
Arctotis	*Cosmos*	*Osteospermum*
Argyranthemum	*Dahlia*	*Sanvitalia*
Artemisia★	*Euryops*	*Senecio*★
Asteriscus	*Felicia*	*Tagetes*
Bidens	*Gazania*	*Thymophylla*

2 The Cultivation of Daisies

Most members of the daisy family are very straightforward to grow: not a few are plain easy, with failure being unlikely in such accommodating genera as *Anthemis*, *Gaillardia*, *Helianthus* or *Solidago*, among the herbaceous perennials, or with that cheerful self-seeder *Calendula*, or with annual chrysanthemums species, now in the new genus *Ismelia*. There are, of course, challenges for those who seek them – *Celmisia* comes to mind – while among other genera there is a considerable number of attractive species for rock gardens that will not persist over damp winters (such as those of Britain) in circumstances much removed from the ideal. Otherwise, most of the disappointments from the daisy family arise from failing to match your choice of plant with appropriate conditions.

To take one well-known example, the range of daisies from South Africa demand sunshine. They give much the best account of themselves in light, fast-draining soil that is low in nutrients. If there is nowhere in your garden where such an environment is approximated, it is better to choose other plants to grow. At the other end of the scale, the herbaceous perennials *Helenium*, *Ligularia* and *Rudbeckia*, along with the Michaelmas daisies, are some of the most valuable members of the family that thrive in heavier, moisture-retentive and relatively fertile soil.

Attempting to fly in the face of hostile root conditions is unlikely to give satisfaction without special measures. As a whole, these are scarcely worth the taking, unless you have a passion for a particular group of plants or you have an unbounded enthusiasm for overcoming this sort of challenge. For those who qualify in one of these categories, the following paragraphs may assist.

Modifying your soil

Improving drainage

If you have naturally heavy, moisture-retentive soil and wish to provide a fast-draining, drier environment, poorer in nutrients, and therefore more conducive to flowering than to excessive leaf growth, it is not difficult to give helpful – albeit pretty obvious – advice: use containers and raised beds.

Containers of any and every sort will be well-drained, almost by definition, provided only that the drainage holes are sufficient in size and number and the escape of surplus water through them is not impeded. They are usually filled with a proprietary compost, which, without liquid feeding, may be counted on not to be very nutrient-rich after a very few weeks: watering and free drainage rapidly carry away any initial excess of plant food.

For a grander scale, any kind of raised bed, so long as it is not lined with plastic, will provide a well-drained environment – the higher the bed above the level of the adjacent ground or pathways, the sharper the drainage. There are many ways of retaining the soil in position round the edges. Dry stone walls are perhaps the most aesthetically pleasing and the most conducive to fast draining. They also provide a fine environment for a wealth of low-growing plants, both in and out of the daisy family. The downside is cost, and the fondness that snails have for this habitat.

The soil within the bed can be entirely artificial, just like the compost bought to put in containers. It can, indeed, be a purchased compost, a deluxe answer at a deluxe cost for all but the smallest beds. As a material to assist drainage and reduce the moisture-holding properties of the natural soil of your garden, sand is excellent, and comes at a very affordable price. Obtain it as coarse as possible.

Improving moisture retention

An altogether more difficult feat is to provide satisfactory conditions for plants that do best in clay soils, when your own is sandy and lets water pass through it like a sieve. The traditional advice is to add abundant organic matter, and this is entirely sound, though it cannot be a total answer. Compost, leaf mould and animal manure, if you can obtain it, are all fine. Peat is better for improving moisture retention than anything else, thanks to its naturally sponge-like qualities, but it adds virtually no nutrients. For environmental reasons, many gardeners now use it with reluctance, if at all. Although it is a good deal more expensive, coir (the husk material surrounding coconuts) can be substituted for peat.

Improving the moisture retention of your soil will go a long way towards providing the conditions the roots of some plants demand, but it needs to be complemented by supplying sufficient moisture, sufficiently often to replenish what is lost. Well worth a try here is the proprietary porous hose, which is designed to be buried in the soil: losses by evaporation or water running off the surface are eliminated, the hose is never anywhere else when it is wanted, and delivery is direct to the roots.

Mulching – covering the soil with a material that will, among other things, reduce evaporation from it – is useful, and depending on just what material is used, may help to control weeds and look good into the bargain. Chipped bark is perhaps the most attractive choice. Woven plastic soil covers, which let rain and overhead irrigation through, are very efficient, but a cover of grit or bark chippings or some other organic material is needed to conceal their starkly utilitarian appearance.

General cultivation

Little can be written about the cultivation of the members of the daisy family that applies more particularly to them than to plants from similar natural environments but belonging to other families. Nevertheless, some points are well worth the making because they have such a large bearing on the satisfaction that can be obtained.

Feeding

Herbaceous perennials and shrubs require annual feeding, even before the growing season gets underway. The easiest way of boosting the nutrient supply of established perennials is to scatter a general-purpose fertilizer over

Free-flowering, vigorous and easy to grow, *Helianthus* 'Lemon Queen' enjoys wide popularity.

the soil surface in late winter and let the rain do the rest of the work in taking it down to the roots. Although a large number of genera flower best in poor, fast-drained soil (see The Plants pp.34–181) and so do not require this type of feeding, the majority of perennial daisies do best with an adequate, balanced supply of nutrients, topped up annually.

The benefits of feeding apply with particular force where such plants have been in place for two or more years, and where the soil is naturally hungry and freely drained. Most soils of this description are sandy, and in them plant development will be checked without the help of fertilizer. If, for any reason, you decide to apply a dry feed well into the growing season (mid-spring or later), do water it in well: it is only useful once dissolved and actively feeding the roots. And, if you perceive a need for treatment in fire brigade-style of a plant you judge to be starving – most often this will be one in a container – a liquid feed is, of course, not to be beaten for speed of effect.

Support

With few exceptions, taller annuals and herbaceous perennials need support. So do a few shorter, weaker-stemmed plants like *Brachyscome iberidifolia*. More often than not it is entirely sufficient to provide it for the bottom half of the plant only. To avoid an unsightly appearance, support should be put in place as the plants attain about one-third of their final height.

Quite the most aesthetically satisfactory method, and one at least as good functionally as any alternative, is to use brushwood. The traditional peasticks – hazel, from coppiced plantations – are unrivalled for the purpose, but are now almost unobtainable. Prunings from shrubs and trees are an excellent alternative if available.

A variety of proprietary wire and plastic support material can be bought, or canes and garden twine can be put to effective use around and between stems to provide a firm support for their bases. I find the least obtrusive proprietary supports are the horizontal arcs of green plastic-coated wire with a leg at each end to push into the soil. Inserted around and, if appropriate, also within a clump or drift of plants, overlapping at their ends but with some variation in height, they provide unobtrusive and sufficient, and almost invisible, support. A dreadful trussed-up appearance can be produced by providing an uninterrupted surround to a uniform height, as by some sort of fence. Too few canes, too tall, augmented by twine, do plants a similar aesthetic disservice.

Routine chores

That weeding and deadheading well repay the time spent on them surely goes without saying. Mulching – mentioned previously in connection with reducing moisture-loss from the soil by evaporation – is also of value for weed suppression, and chipped bark is good for the purpose as well as being particularly pleasing to the eye. If it is to be used, early spring is the time to apply it.

Cutting down the flowering stems of herbaceous perennials, after flowering, is a classic autumn garden chore. In a few cases, no time should be lost in doing this as soon as flowering comes to an end. This will stimulate the development of a good early autumn flush of basal growth, which will do much to secure the survival of the plant over winter. In heavier, wetter soils, if cutting down is left until mid- or late autumn, the risk that there will be no plant alive in spring will be greatly increased. Notable plants in this connection are some *Anthemis* and *Coreopsis* species and *Gaillardia aristata* and its hybrids.

Pest and disease control

The daisy family presents no more problems than any other with regard to pests and diseases. The only pests

About half a metre tall, *Buphthalmum salicifolium* is an easy-going perennial with a long flowering period.

that are widespread — aphids and slugs — are no less so on plants outside the family. Powdery mildew is notably troublesome for many genera in the daisy family, although it is, of course, not confined to it.

Aphids

Greenfly and blackfly are a notorious scourge: for all the general lack of enthusiasm for spraying among gardeners, outdoors this is the pest for which the sprayer is most often reached. Fortunately, a very wide range of effective insecticides is available. Insecticidal soap solutions are very safe to use, and appeal to gardeners who avoid using synthetic chemical products. Pyrethrum and rotenone (derris) are plant-derived products, but both are dangerous to fish. Insecticides containing pirimiphos-methyl, heptenophos two and dimethoate are effective: the first also against a wide range of other pests, including the greenhouse summer nightmares — whitefly.

Slugs and snails

Slugs and snails are a particular cause of grief in wet weather in spring — either early, as the young shoots of hardy herbaceous perennials begin to push, or late, when half hardy plants are set out in their final positions.

Slug pellets containing metaldehyde, thinly scattered, are the commonest means of control. Used as advised by the manufacturers, it is claimed that there should be no risk to domestic pets or to wildlife that is predatory on the pests. There has, however, been long-standing concern about the effects of the chemical in the natural food chain. Biological control can work well on lighter soils. The control agents are microscopic nematodes, which are watered onto the soil. They are readily available, but treatment costs are quite high.

Apart from direct control, including frequent evening pest collection forays and the use of traps, there is everything to be said for reducing slug and snail numbers by eliminating their preferred resting and hiding places. Among these are decaying foliage, and stones and litter of all descriptions, especially polythene.

Capsid bugs

Capsid bugs are sap-sucking insects, particularly common on chrysanthemums and dahlias. The symptoms are misshapen young leaves, punctured by small holes. Watch for signs of damage from late spring onwards. If you want to spray, pirimiphos-methyl, dimethoate or fenitrothion all give control.

Earwigs

Earwigs are notoriously destructive on dahlias. Like slugs, these too can be trapped — the traditional straw-

A native of the eastern USA, *Heterotheca mariana* is uncommon in cultivation.

stuffed pots, inverted over the ends of the supporting stakes, work well. If spraying is resorted to, insecticides containing cypermethrin, dimethoate and pirimiphos-methyl are all effective, but all are dangerous to fish.

Powdery mildew

Powdery mildew is a notorious scourge of the best-known Michaelmas daisy group, the New York asters (*Aster novi-belgii*), and is widespread in the daisy family more generally. It is quite disfiguring, with the white powdery growth coating the upper surfaces of the leaves. Although new growth of perennials in spring will start disease-free, overall plant vigour will be seriously sapped over the years, if annual infections go unchecked. A humid atmosphere and dry roots predispose plants to infection. Nothing can be done outdoors about the former, but watering plants where infection is feared or has already begun probably does help plants cope better with the disease. Spraying is a near necessity with the New York asters, and may be needed for other daisies, too. A fungicidal spray containing triforine and bupirimate is usually very effective. So are dusts containing carbendazim or sulphur, but both are unsightly for a little while after application.

3 The Propagation of Daisies

There are few problems in propagating the members of the daisy family described in this book. A greenhouse is an asset for many, of course, but a sunny windowsill and a good coldframe, managed with a little care, usually make a successful alternative.

Annuals

Some of the most garden-worthy daisies grown annually from seed are perfectly hardy and, given accommodating soil, are about as easy to grow as any plant can be. Annual sunflowers, *Calendula*, the annual chrysanthemum species (*Ismelia*), annual cornflowers, *Coreopsis tinctoria*, and *Rudbeckia hirta* all come to mind.

You may be blessed with soil that can be forked, trodden and raked to a good seedbed tilth in all conditions other than completely sodden. If so, sowing hardy annuals in early or mid-spring where they are to grow is the convention because it requires a minimum of effort, and avoids the root disturbance usual with transplanting. The earliest flowering and the biggest plants, however, result from sowing early in the previous autumn. Where the objective is primarily to have cut flowers – perhaps growing them alongside vegetables – this is well worth trying if the soil is free draining. It is usually less practicable in other circumstances, often because free space, not overshadowed by neighbouring plants, is unavailable at the time. An alternative to autumn-sowing outdoors is to sow in a greenhouse or coldframe in early spring. This is also often the best thing to do if you ordinarily find it difficult to make a good seedbed. Even the humble coldframe provides a very much more friendly environment for hardy annuals than natural soil outdoors in spring. Of course, planting out can be done before the risk of spring frosts is at an end.

Most half hardy annuals need to be started under protection of some kind because sowing in the open in late spring is too late to give good results. Sowing outdoors any earlier fails because the plants are not hardy enough to germinate well in cold soil, or to survive any last frosts.

A heated greenhouse is the ideal place to sow, especially if it is equipped with an electric propagator. The warmth needed for fast, vigorous germination is also to be found on a windowsill indoors, or even in the airing cupboard. Unfortunately, living room conditions are not suitable for growing on the seedlings – there is not enough light and too much warmth. If you do not have a greenhouse, they can be grown on in a coldframe, or even a simple cloche or two, to protect the young plants from late frosts as necessary.

Raising the members of the daisy family in this way is no different from raising plants in any other family, and is no more difficult. The principal mistake is simply to sow too early, with the result that the plants become too big before they can safely be planted out. How big is too big depends on their spacing in the trays in which they are grown. In general, a useful guide is to sow six to eight weeks before the last date on which there remains a risk of late spring frost. If you do not have a greenhouse, sow a little later to allow for the more spartan conditions provided by a frame or cloche.

Most daisies are quite tolerant of some root disturbance at transplanting time, provided they are well watered in and not allowed to suffer moisture shortage until they are established. For these, the easiest and cheapest treatment is the best: prick out the small seedlings into a plain seedtray filled with potting compost. Do not bother with cell tray inserts as these demand more careful watering.

A small number of annuals do resent root disturbance, and may take a considerable time to recover if it is inflicted on them. The most important of these is *Zinnia*, which should be raised in cell trays or individual pots. Among the hardy species, if they are not raised by direct outdoor sowing where they are to grow, the annual chrysanthemums, sweet sultan (*Amberboa moschata*) and safflower (*Carthamus tinctoria*) need the same treatment.

As planting time approaches, hardening off should be put in hand. Ideally, young plants from a greenhouse should be transferred to a coldframe a fortnight or so before finally setting out in their flowering positions. In the frame, ventilation should be increased as weather conditions allow. In practice, you will find that you can get away without this traditional treatment if you have a sheltered spot in which to stand out the plants. Favourable weather for their removal from the green-

Among the most popular of the garden hybrids of *Anthemis* is 'Sauce Hollandaise'.

house to the open is obviously needed, but covering them overnight with synthetic garden fleece is then sufficient to protect them from slight frosts.

Herbaceous perennials
Seed

The cheapest and most productive method of raising herbaceous perennials is, of course, by seed, and this is easily done for almost all the hardy species in the daisy family. Many will produce a good show of flower in their first growing year, provided that it is possible to start them early in heat. The limitation is that the majority of cultivars, as distinct from species, do not come true from seed, and as these cultivars are often a real improvement on the nearest alternative that *can* be raised from seed it seems a pity to invest space in inferior plant material. For example, named cultivars of *Helenium autumnale* are a better proposition than the mixed bag that can be grown from seed. Likewise, vegetatively propagated clones of *Achillea ptarmica* The Pearl Group are better than the seed-raised equivalent, and garden pyrethrum cultivars like 'Eileen May Robinson' are better than anything likely to be had from a seed packet. Those cultivars that do come true from seed are mentioned in the plant directories (pp.34–181).

The traditional method of raising hardy herbaceous perennials from seed is to sow in an outdoor seedbed in very late spring or in early summer, thin the resulting seedlings as necessary, and transfer the young plants to their flowering positions in mid-autumn or in early spring the following year. If you have worries about slugs, weeds and cats, the deluxe version is to sow in a pot or seedtray, and prick out the seedlings 10–15cm (4–6in) apart in a prepared nursery bed. Nicer still is to do so in potting compost in a box 10–15cm (4–6in) deep, but this does mean that watering will be needed throughout the summer. The traditional seedtray, only 5cm (2in) deep, is much less satisfactory: such a limited volume of compost for the roots makes watering and feeding to the requirements of the plants difficult.

Just as with annuals, there are a few perennial daisy genera that do not respond well to root disturbance. If they are to be grown from seed, they really need to be sown directly into pots, 11cm (4½in) in diameter with say three seeds in each, thinning to one seedling if necessary. Members of the thistle tribe are the plants principally concerned – *Echinops* and *Onopordum* most notably.

For greenhouse owners there are alternatives to the traditional outdoor sowing and raising of herbaceous perennials. One is to sow in late summer, and to prick out the seedlings into boxes as described above. The plants are overwintered in the greenhouse – not necessarily heated, though frost exclusion is a definite advantage. They are then set out in the open in early or mid-spring. This method eliminates the inevitable risks of outdoor misadventure for the young plants, especially where the soil or the garden situation is unfriendly in winter.

The second alternative is to sow in heat in mid- or late winter, and treat the plants much like half hardy annuals. Quite a few perennials started in this fashion will flower usefully in the same year. Examples that respond particularly well to this treatment include *Gaillardia* and *Achillea millefolium*.

Division

For almost all perennials, in the daisy family and outside it, division is the most usual method of multiplying plants. The practice also has other important virtues, including the curtailment of any unwanted spread and the rejuvenation of established plants, where congestion and competition is impairing performance. If perennial weeds are present, lifting, dividing and replanting also provides an opportunity to remove their roots: otherwise the only possibilities for controlling the weeds are chemical, and necessarily on the basis of treating individual leaves and shoots with a substance like glyphosate ('Roundup'). The traditional interval between divisions is three years, but any enthusiast will be able to tell by observation whether an advantage is likely in dividing more or less frequently.

When to divide is a matter for careful thought. In warmer areas on light, free-draining soils, autumn is usually the best choice, especially for plants flowering in spring or early summer. Division should be carried out as soon after the end of summer as practicable, so as to allow re-establishment before the lower soil temperatures encountered later bring root development to a halt.

Division in early spring is the safer choice where winter soil temperatures are usually low for a long period or where the soil lies wet. Unfortunately, plants that flower before late summer are usually far short of their best in the first season after spring division. If you are prepared to go to the extra trouble, the advantages of autumn division may be had by dividing in autumn but planting the divisions in pots, with a view to setting the plants out into their final positions in mid-spring. There is no need to put these pots in a frame, but the plants would respond to the kindness.

One thing to beware of for plants in pots outdoors over the winter is the freezing of the roots: they are much more exposed to risk of this than if they are planted out in the garden. The pots should be protected by being plunged to their rims in chipped bark, sand or

Osteospermum 'Blackthorn Seedling' ♀ belongs to one of the hardiest species in its genus.

even soil; make sure they are stood on a surface that permits free drainage.

Spring-divided plants can profit from an initial period in pots, too. Certainly if you are keen to multiply your stock to the fullest possible extent, and therefore need to use very small divisions – perhaps just a single shoot and a few roots – this sort of deluxe start will pay dividends.

It is quite common for newly purchased herbaceous perennials to have enough shoots to allow division before planting. Spring is the most usual time to buy, and though good divisions may be put straight into their final quarters, they too are particularly likely to reward a period, say six weeks, in a comfortably-sized pot before setting out.

Summer division is excellent for a very few herbaceous perennials that flower relatively early in the year. Among the best-known examples are *Doronicum*, *Tanacetum coccineum*, *Aster alpinus*, *A. tongolensis* and *Leucanthemum* × *superbum*. Do the job as soon after flowering as possible, water in well, and be prepared to look after the newly divided plants with care for a week or two if the weather is dry and warm: water and temporary shade are, of course, what will be needed.

The best division technique varies according to the nature of the underground part of the plant. Once dug up, inspection of the roots will easily resolve the matter.

The use of a sharpened spade, a large sharp knife, a pair of forks inserted back to back (and the handles then pulled together), or a pair of strong hands are all appropriate over the range of herbaceous perennials. In any event, two guiding principles must be the selection of the most vigorous outer shoots, and the retention on the divided portions of as much root as practicable. Once divided, the sooner these are replanted the better, but if waiting there must be, protection from drying winds is important.

Stem cuttings

For gardeners anxious to multiply plants to the greatest possible extent, using some or all of the shoots as cuttings is the best way forward. Propagating herbaceous perennials in this way is less often done by amateur gardeners than it profitably might be. It is certainly the most effective method of multiplying the great majority of cultivars, which will not come true from seed. Taken as young shoots in early or mid-spring, cuttings of most herbaceous perennials root easily. The pleasure of the first good show of flowers from these is usually not until the year following propagation, as the initially small new plants need their first growing season simply to build up their root system.

In most cases, the cuttings will root readily enough in a coldframe, and certainly, greenhouse owners who can provide some bottom heat should seldom have problems. Usual practice in taking the cuttings is to ease soil away from around the shoots of the parent plant, using a handfork. Finger and thumb pressure will then normally suffice to remove the cuttings-to-be from their point of origin. Sometimes one or two very small roots are already in evidence, a fairly sure indicator of success. Use of a rooting hormone may help, though for many species it is unnecessary if good rooting conditions are provided. These are a humid atmosphere to protect against dehydration and a suitable warm, moist rooting medium.

Once the cuttings are rooted, it is best to plant them out into their permanent positions. If this is not possible, put them in a nursery bed outdoors, 15–20cm (6–8in) apart, and leave them weeded but otherwise in peace until their final planting out in autumn or the following early spring.

Cuttings are used not only for hardy perennials but also for propagating and overwintering those that are half hardy. The best-known examples are *Argyranthemum, Gazania* and *Osteospermum*. The timing differs with these, though, because the objective is to have nicely rooted, small plants by mid-autumn, suitable for overwintering in a frost-free greenhouse. Large plants at this time of year are usually unwelcome because of the amount of greenhouse space they would occupy until planting out time seven months or so later. Cuttings should accordingly be taken in late summer or early autumn.

Root cuttings

A small number of hardy herbaceous perennials may be propagated by root cuttings, taken in late winter. These consist of short lengths of root, inserted vertically and the correct way up in ordinary potting compost, with the top just covered. Root cuttings are usually taken from plants that have been dug up for the purpose. This is a most convenient and productive method when it works, but in the daisy family is confined to very few cultivated genera indeed. The two for which this method is most useful are *Centaurea* and *Echinops*. Others include *Gaillardia, Catananche* and *Cynara*, though the last is more usually, and very easily, propagated by using young shoots as cuttings.

Shrubs

Semi-ripe cuttings

Shrubs are most usually propagated by semi-ripe cuttings taken in early to midsummer. The term semi-ripe means that the bases of the shoots used have begun to harden. The most usual practice is to pull them off the plants where they arise from older wood, a treatment that results in a very small 'heel' of this remaining attached to the new season's growth. The cuttings are then treated just as for those of herbaceous perennials. Hormone-rooting powder is well worth using and has more of an influence on success with woody cuttings than it does with non-woody ones.

A common phenomenon encountered with this type of cutting is that large changes occur in the ease of rooting as the year's new shoots grow and the summer progresses. Knowing just what stage of development to wait for to ensure the best prospect of success requires experience. Some shrubby plants are notoriously tricky in this respect, *Artemisia absinthium* 'Lambrook Silver' among them. Fortunately, for the amateur gardener who simply wants one or two new plants, perhaps just for use in eventual replacement of the parent, a plan that is usually effective is simply to take a series of cuttings over a month or two. This should ensure sufficient success for the purpose in hand.

4 Botany

ven among the most dedicated gardening enthusiasts, botanical description is regarded with serious unease. At its worst and most detailed, it is heavy going indeed. For example, there are almost twenty adjectives in use to describe different types of bristliness and hairiness on leaves and stems – from 'arachnoid' and 'canescent' to 'velutinous' and 'villous', they all have distinct meanings.

My aim is to avoid using any more of this technical vocabulary than is necessary. To get the most from many of the plant descriptions though, it is necessary to be familiar with a few concepts and a small number of the specialized terms used to describe flowerheads and foliage. These are all defined in the glossary (p.182), but are also introduced here.

I promise that there will be no plant descriptions remotely similar to the one invented by the father of modern rock gardening, Reginald Farrer. In his *English Rock Garden* (1918) an imaginary plant is described, tongue-in-cheek, as 'an acaulescent herb of circinate vernation with the leaves imparipinnatipartite or uncinate-lyrate with mucronate-crenulate lobules, setulose-papillose, decurrent, pedunculate, and persistent'. He continues, in rather lordly style, with a partial justification of this formidable verbal battery as 'a method of shorthand to tell the initiated in quite a few words, what could otherwise only be conveyed to the profane in a great many'. Any reader confident of not being counted among Reginald Farrer's 'profane' may skip the rest of this chapter!

Flowerheads

The most significant feature shared by all the members of the daisy family is the structure of the flowerheads (*capitula*, singular *capitulum*). What is seen at first glance as a flower is in fact a composite of a number of very small and stalkless florets. These are all densely packed and attached at their bases to the swollen end of the flowering stem, the receptacle (see diagram A). The original name given to the family, the Compositae, marks the distinctive character of these flowerheads. In many species, the number of florets in each flowerhead is large, often running into three figures.

In the simplest type of flowerhead in the daisy family, all the florets are identical, small and have a tubular *corolla* (the fused petals). A typical floret of this kind is shown in diagram A, from which it can be seen that it is what botanists describe as perfect – with both male organs (anthers) and female organs (ovary, style and stigma).

Flowerheads in which only simple tubular, or disc, florets are present are called *discoid*, and lack any equivalent to the petals of flowers in other families. Common examples occur in *Ageratum*, *Eupatorium*, *Santolina*

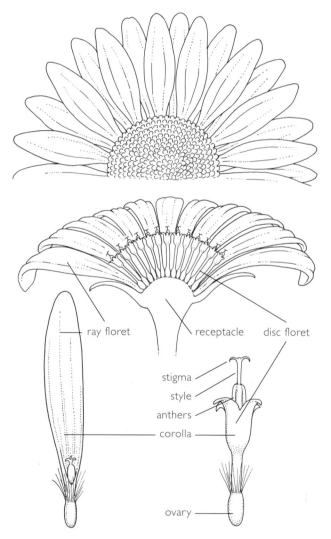

ray floret · receptacle · disc floret

stigma
style
anthers
corolla
ovary

A Flowerhead and flowerhead in section and the form of the individual ray floret and disc floret.

and the thistles such as *Cynara* and *Onopordum*.

The flowerheads universally regarded as of typical daisy form have two distinct types of floret – disc and ray – and are called *radiate* flowerheads. In them the simple, unshowy tubular florets form a central disc, surrounded by the ray florets. Although the ray florets are tubular at their bases, one side of the corolla is greatly lengthened and enlarged (see diagram A).

These comparatively large and showy florets are often loosely referred to as rays, or, quite incorrectly, as petals. Unlike the disc florets, they are symmetrical only in the limited sense that it is possible to cut them into identical halves along one specific line of bisection. Ray florets are seldom sexually perfect, being generally either without anthers, and therefore female, or without sexual organs altogether, and therefore sterile.

Disciform flowerheads also have outer florets that differ from those in the centre. These outer florets, however, are usually tubular and do not radiate outwards in the manner of ray florets. They are usually female, while the central florets are sexually perfect, i.e. have both anthers and stigma. Examples of *disciform* flowerheads are found in *Artemisia* and *Helichrysum*.

One other type of flowerhead – *ligulate* – is found only in one tribe of major importance outside tropical climates, the Lactuceae (see p.30).

Involucres and bracts

Surrounding the receptacle, and attached to it around the outer florets of the flowerhead, are the bracts, which collectively form the *involucre*. This is particularly conspicuous in the thistle tribe, the Cardueae, especially in such genera as *Cynara* and *Onopordum*. The bracts are commonly in several rows, and in the tribe Gnaphaliae – the 'everlastings' – the innermost are greatly enlarged, often coloured and in many cases radiate outwards. To these is owed the showiness of the flowerheads of genera such as *Ammobium* and *Bracteantha* (see diagrams C and D).

The pappus

In the flowers of most plant families, a *calyx* is found immediately below the petals, and surrounds their bases. This either comprises a number of separate green sepals or is a single, fused structure, often tubular or bell-

B Flowerheads of annual cornflower (*Centaurea cyanus*) with outer floret (left) and central floret (right).

C Flowerheads of blessed or holy thistle (*Silybum marianum*) with spiky elongated involucral bracts.

D The small flowerheads of strawflower (*Bracteantha*) are surrounded by greatly enlarged bracts.

shaped. In Compositae the calyx is absent, but instead a whorl or tuft of scales or bristles may surround the base of the floret. This is the *pappus*, and its detailed structure is botanically important in classification. It usually persists after the withering of the corolla, and in some cases develops to assist the dispersal of the one-seeded fruits by wind: the 'parachutes' of the dandelion are particularly well known. This type of fruit is known botanically as a *cypsela*, a form of *achene* (see diagram E).

Leaves

Only two important features of foliage in the daisy family need attention here. The first concerns their arrangement: very simply, alternate positioning of leaves along the stems is much the most usual in plants of the Compositae. Opposite leaves are commonly found in just three of the 11 tribes of genera that are important to gardeners in the British Isles – Eupatorieae, Helenieae, and Heliantheae. All 11 tribes are described in 'Classification' (pp.27–31).

The second foliage feature concerns leaf division. A very noticeable aspect of the leaves of many species is that they are partially divided in a pinnate fashion. The Latin *pinna* means feather; in pinnate leaves, entirely separate leaflets are arranged in two ranks, one on either side of the central leaf stalk (the *rachis*). A very familiar example of a pinnate leaf is that of the ash tree (*Fraxinus*), while in the daisy family the one best known is *Dahlia*.

While pinnately divided (compound) leaves are not widely found in the daisy family, *pinnatifid* and *pinnatisect* leaves are. A pinnatifid leaf is divided almost to the midrib into broad divisions. A pinnatisect leaf is likewise divided, but into narrower divisions. *Bipinnatifid* and *bipinnatisect* are used when the inital divisions of the leaf blade are themselves again divided in the same fashion (see diagram F). *Achillea, Argyranthemum, Artemisia, Brachyscome, Cosmos, Santolina* and *Tanacetum* are among the best-known genera exhibiting finely divided leaves – mostly bipinnatisect. Pinnately lobed leaves are also common in the family, as in *Chrysanthemum*.

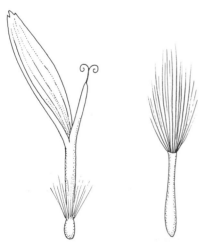

E Florets of the hawkweed (*Crepis rubra*), showing pappus at base of floret (left) and later (right), attached to the end of the 'seed' – correctly a single-seeded fruit, the cypsela.

F *Cosmos sulphureus* has bipinnatisect leaves.

5 Classification

What naturally interests gardeners most about plants is what they look like, when they are attractive, whether they are worth a place in the garden, and if so, what conditions suit them. How they fit into a scientific classification system and how closely they relate to other plants are secondary concerns. Even so, understanding something of how the huge daisy family is divided is interesting in its own right, contributes to the appreciation of the plants and, at least sometimes, serves as a helpful guide to growing some of them successfully.

With around 25,000 species in over 1,500 genera, the daisy family is the largest of all plant families and accounts for about 10 per cent of all flowering plants. Its traditional scientific name, Compositae, has been in use since the eighteenth century. The family name Asteraceae is also of very long standing and is now widely used by botanists in order to standardize all family names on the basis of attaching the ending *–aceae* to the name of an appropriate genus – hence Rosaceae for the rose family, Ranunculaceae for the buttercup family and so on. The name Compositae nevertheless continues to be scientifically acceptable as an alternative to Asteraceae.

Origin and distribution

Members of the Asteraceae are distributed worldwide, and include plants of almost all habits of growth. Gardeners in cool temperate climates, such as the British Isles, are particularly conscious of the wealth of herbaceous perennials and annuals in the family. Shrubs are less well represented, there are very few climbers and, in effect, no trees, though woody genera and climbers are much more strongly in evidence in warmer climates. None of the very few climbers included in the plant directories are entirely hardy (see *Mutisia*, p.181, and *Senecio*, p.130). The family also includes a very few aquatics and even some epiphytes – plants growing on other plants (usually trees) but not parasitic on them: neither of these categories are in evidence in gardening in Britain.

The age and area of origin of the family can only be hypothetical, partly because the fossil record is more or less confined to pollen. The first plants recognizable as daisies are thought to have emerged roughly 50 or 60 million years ago. It is thought likely that these primitive ancestors were woody plants with comparatively large flowerheads. They would not have had the classic daisy appearance because ray florets would have been lacking. The flowerheads would instead have been discoid (see p.24), with all florets identical, forming a tuft on the receptacle, just as in present-day thistles.

Tribes and genera

In large and diverse plant families like the Compositae, it is usual to group genera into tribes. As the daisy family has over 1,500 genera, grouping is invaluable botanically, in order to study the relationships between them and, at least sometimes, very useful horticulturally also. Before trying to come to terms with what kind of plant group a tribe is, some understanding of what a genus is will be helpful. In turn, a start should be made with the species, the building blocks of a genus.

Of all the units of classification, the species is the easiest to comprehend, perhaps because we all relate personally to the concept, as members of the species *Homo sapiens*. The species is the basic unit of classification of living organisms. All individuals in a plant species share a number of features, particularly in the flower, which distinguishes them from members of all other species. These individuals are usually capable of cross-fertilization, and are usually unable to produce seed if pollinated by another species.

The concept of a genus is harder to grasp. It is a group of species that share important common characteristics, sufficient to distinguish them from other plants in the same family. In practice, professional botanists commonly disagree about the limits for membership of a genus. Hence the dividing of one genus into two or more is a common event, as is the re-positioning of species into different genera. This reorganization has been going on since the nineteenth century, if not before, and can confidently be expected to do so into the indefinite future.

Classification into tribes is carried out on the basis of certain features shared by a group of genera, indicating that their relationship is particularly close. A fundamental aim of professional botanists in grouping genera in this way is to do so in reflection of their evolution from a common ancestral stock. At the present stage of knowledge this must be an imperfect enterprise, but as techniques and methodologies advance, a closer approach to this goal becomes possible. Genera in a given tribe will resemble each other in most important features. Given the huge natural variation in the plant kingdom, exceptions in respect of some characteristics are almost the rule: determining which tribe a genus properly belongs to is seldom on the basis of just one or two individual characteristics. Some judged to be of particularly key importance relate to very detailed features of floral parts – anthers and styles, for example. These require some specialist knowledge and training to detect, and for this reason are not described in detail here. In practice, the concept of a tribe is a great deal easier to understand by examples than by definitions. The descriptions that follow should go some way towards demonstrating this fact.

Daisy tribes

According to the most recently published comprehensive scientific study of the daisy family there are 17 tribes, although not all botanists agree on this number. Many of the tribes were recognized and described very early in the nineteenth century, by the French botanist Cassini. Eleven of the 17 are horticulturally important. Of the six remaining, three comprise only tropical genera and, in northern temperate areas, none of these is likely to be seen outside the greenhouses of botanic gardens. The other three contribute between them just six genera of horticultural importance in temperate climates.

Each tribe is named after a genus within it that possesses all the characteristics that typify the tribe. The names characteristically end with *eae* – a not always readily pronounceable convention when the stem name itself ends in 'i', as in Helenieae.

The plant directories (pp.36–181) are, to a large extent, divided on the basis of the division of the daisy family into tribes, for example, the sunflowers, tribe Heliantheae (pp.36–43), the genus *Aster* and its close relatives in the tribe Astereae (pp.64–81) and so on. Although gardening considerations have set a limit to this approach, it is still invaluable to be able to profit from the work of botanists in finding our way through the prodigious wealth of plants in the daisy family.

Anthemideae

Tribe Anthemideae has as its best-known garden genera *Anthemis, Achillea, Artemisia, Chrysanthemum, Santolina* and *Tanacetum*. From this list alone its garden importance is

Aster × *frikartii* has an exceptionally long flowering period. Its most popular cultivar is 'Mönch' (above).

immediately obvious. *Chrysanthemum* and its most closely related genera have a directory to themselves (pp.82–91).

The hundred-odd genera of this tribe are herbaceous plants, shrubs or subshrubs (like some of the best-known *Artemisia* species). Aromatic finely dissected foliage is widespread among them. The flowerheads are mostly radiate and white or yellow, but in some important genera are instead discoid, as in *Santolina*. Anthers and styles are of very characteristic structure, and the involucral bracts have thin, dry, more or less translucent edges. Distribution in the wild is worldwide, but genera are especially abundant in the Mediterranean area and Central Asia. There are few in Australia and South America.

Astereae

Tribe Astereae obviously includes the genus *Aster*, along with *Brachyscome*, *Callistephus* (the annual China aster), *Erigeron*, *Olearia* and – less obviously – *Solidago*. Like the previous tribe, it is horticulturally of front rank importance.

Most of the 174 genera within the tribe are annuals or herbaceous perennials or shrubs. The leaves are commonly undivided. Though there are genera with discoid and disciform flowerheads, those known to gardeners have radiate flowerheads (in *Solidago* with very short and inconspicuous rays). The ray florets are often numerous and slender, as in *Aster*, *Brachyscome*, *Erigeron* and *Felicia*. The structure of the style is very characteristic, and has been much used by botanists to separate members of the tribe from non-members. Members are distributed worldwide, but predominantly in areas round the Pacific and Indian Oceans.

Calenduleae

Tribe Calenduleae is much the smallest in the entire family, with only eight genera. Three of these are well known – *Calendula*, *Dimorphotheca* and the currently very fashionable *Osteospermum*.

In this tribe the flowerheads are always radiate, with the ray florets well developed. The tribal distribution is strongly centred on Africa, and all but one genus is represented in South Africa. The habitats are mainly arid. At the edges of its distribution in the wild, species are also found in the Atlantic islands, south and central Europe and western and south western Asia.

Cardueae

Cardueae is the tribe of the thistles and cornflowers. The most important genera horticulturally are *Centaurea* (Cornflower), *Cynara* (Cardoon and Globe artichoke), *Echinops* (Globe thistle) and *Onopordum*. In the plant directory these and other members of the tribe are on pp.92–96 and pp.97–103. They are mainly herbaceous perennials, very commonly spiny and usually with dissected leaves. The flowerheads are predominantly discoid. The detailed features of the style and anthers are seldom found outside it.

The cornflowers – *Centaurea* and closely related genera – constitute a sub-tribe, differing from other members in a number of botanically important respects. The genera concerned mostly have entire leaves, and the species described in the plant directories are without spines. Many of them also have enlarged marginal florets, radiating strongly outwards from the flowerhead centre. True ray florets are not found in this tribe.

The Cardueae are predominantly found in Europe, Asia and North Africa.

Eupatorieae

The Eupatorieae is known for two fine genera of herbaceous perennials, *Eupatorium* and *Liatris*, and for one widely grown annual, *Ageratum*. It is a large tribe with 170 genera, of which some are shrubs, trees and vines that are not fully hardy.

Distinctive features of members of this tribe include opposite leaves and discoid flowerheads with blue, reddish-blue or white florets. A fine detail of the floral structure contributes to the character of the flowerheads – the long filamentous extensions to the styles (see diagram G). It is the profusion of these above the corollas that give the typical fuzzy appearance of *Ageratum* and *Eupatorium* inflorescences. Members of the tribe are almost entirely native to the Americas, predominantly in Mexico and Central and South America.

Gnaphalieae

Gnaphalieae (silent 'G') is the tribe of the everlasting flowers. As such, *Helichrysum*, *Ammobium*, *Anaphalis* (Pearl everlasting) and *Rhodanthe* are well-known genera (see pp.104–112). Others widely appreciated are the rock garden plants *Antennaria* and *Leontopodium* (Edelweiss), and the shrubby genera *Cassinia* and *Ozothamnus*.

Flowerheads in the great majority of genera are discoid or disciform. What they might lack in showiness because of the absence of ray florets is often compensated for by the often coloured, inner bracts of the involucres, which are enlarged, papery, and extend outwards around the flowerhead. It is because they dry well, without losing shape or colour, that so many members of this tribe are valuable as everlasting flowers. The tribe is distributed worldwide, but is particularly well represented in Australia and South Africa.

Helenieae

Tribe Helenieae is well known among gardeners for the fine herbaceous perennial hybrids of its type genus *Helenium*. *Tagetes* (French and African marigold) is even more

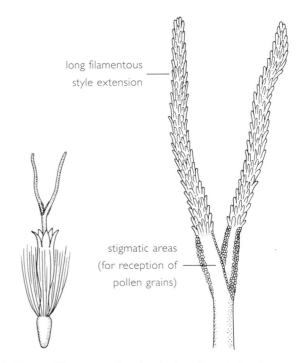

long filamentous style extension

stigmatic areas (for reception of pollen grains)

G Floret of *Eupatorium* showing the long, branched style (detail right).

widely known, and has in full measure the showiness that also characterizes *Gaillardia*, and the more refined *Eriophyllum*.

Members of the Helenieae are mostly annuals and herbaceous perennials with opposite leaves and yellow-rayed flowerheads. The Helenieae are closely related to the sunflower tribe, Heliantheae: among other differences, one that is botanically important is the absence of small, dry bracts called *paleae* among the florets. Most genera of this tribe are North American.

Heliantheae

Tribe Heliantheae makes a massive contribution to the garden flora worldwide. *Cosmos* and *Zinnia* belong here, as well as benchmark herbaceous perennials, such as *Coreopsis, Echinacea* and *Rudbeckia*. The genus of the sunflower itself, *Helianthus*, takes pride of place in the directories (p.36). The most horticulturally celebrated genus of the tribe, *Dahlia*, is dealt with separately (pp.113–119).

Members of the tribe that are important in temperate-zone horticulture are herbaceous perennials and annuals, but tropical natives include shrubs, trees, vines, lianas and aquatics. Leaves are generally opposite, at least on the lower parts of stems. Flowerheads are most often radiate and often solitary. Yellow is much the most common ray floret colour, followed by white. Anthers are usually more or less black, as are the fruits (cypselas). Most genera are native to the Americas, with Mexico particularly significant as a homeland: important *Dahlia* and *Zinnia* species are Mexican natives, for example.

Inuleae

Inuleae is among the smallest tribes, with under 40 genera. It is mainly known for its type genus, the herbaceous perennial *Inula*, and for *Buphthalmum* and *Telekia*, both very closely related. A most useful plant for containers, not yet widely known, is *Asteriscus maritimus*.

Despite the small size of the tribe, members display a range of habits – herbs, shrubs and small trees. Flower-head form likewise varies, but botanically close relationship is established by what are known as floral microcharacters. These concern the styles, anthers and cypselas. Inuleae is almost entirely found in the northern hemisphere, particularly in Europe, North Africa and central and western Asia.

Lactuceae

Lactuceae is the lettuce tribe, which in itself secures its horticultural importance. Of ornamental plants, however, the tribe's contribution is small: only *Catananche* (cupid's dart), *Cichorium* (chicory), *Microseris* and *Tolpis* are partic-

ularly notable. *Taraxacum* (dandelion) and *Sonchus* (milk or sow thistle) are other genera unfortunately well known to gardeners.

Members of the tribe are mostly herbaceous, and are characterized by their milky latex. The flowerheads differ from those of all other tribes, since all the florets are identical, except in size, and are a variant of ray florets, making the flowerhead appear double. This condition is not found in nature in other daisy tribes, where doubleness is only achieved by selection and breeding. In them it normally results in infertility because disc florets are replaced by ray florets, which either have no stamens, or are sterile. In Lactuceae, they are perfect, producing both pollen and seeds.

In the wild, members of the tribe are mostly found in the northern hemisphere, notably in western North America, southern Europe and North Africa.

Senecioneae

In Senecioneae there are over 3,000 species, a greater number than in any other tribe of the daisy family. The genus *Senecio*, itself, is the largest in the family, with over a thousand species. Horticulturally, the tribe is otherwise most notable for the florists' cineraria, *Pericallis*, the shrubs *Brachyglottis* and *Euryops,* and for two herbaceous genera, *Doronicum*, the yellow daisy of the spring, and the imposing *Ligularia*. *Senecio* and some other herbaceous genera in the tribe, such as *Petasites*, are dealt with on pp.130–136.

The diversity of garden use represented by the six genera mentioned reflects the variety of habit and flowerhead type found in the tribe. Many genera are shrubs, some are trees, and the climbing habit is quite common. Two distinguishing features widely shared are a single row of involucral bracts and a peculiar chemistry: certain alkaloids and other characteristic chemical compounds are synthesized by the plants. These are of value in protecting them from grazing. The European native *Senecio jacobaea* (ragwort) is notoriously dangerous to livestock, and this and other *Senecio* species have been claimed to account for more deaths than all other poisonous plants together.

The tribe has a worldwide distribution, but South America and tropical and South Africa account for most species.

Re-naming of plants

One of the major activities of the present-day botanists who specialize in classification is to re-examine the very

large important genera first described in the eighteenth and early nineteenth centuries. Examples in the daisy family are *Centaurea*, *Chrysanthemum* and *Senecio*. As these activities progress, some plants known to and loved by generations of gardeners under long-familiar names re-emerge under others that are entirely unfamiliar and often new. The former *Centaurea moschata* (sweet sultan) has become *Amberboa moschata,* for example, and *Chrysanthemum frutescens* (marguerite) has become *Argyranthemum frutescens*. *Chrysanthemum maximum* has become *Leucanthemum × superbum* and *Senecio laxifolius* has become *Brachyglottis*. The travails surrounding the botanical naming of the florists' chrysanthemum have become notorious in gardening circles worldwide. The dust has not entirely settled on this particular scene as the new millennium dawns.

In fairness to the botanists responsible, they are valuably developing the legacy left by their predecessors. These were relatively few in number and lacked many of the concepts and techniques of classification developed in the twentieth century. They achieved, nevertheless, a near miracle in creating some sort of rational order among the prodigious numbers of plant species – something like 250,000 for flowering plants alone. It is scarcely to be wondered at that some of their groupings were large and unsatisfactorily defined. For all their industry, they inevitably left much for their successors to do. If the results of very recent and current efforts sometimes annoy, say, because there is a new name to register, reflect that in 25 years' time a new generation of gardening enthusiasts and professional horticulturists will take for granted names that are new and confusing to most of us now. They will be puzzled that anyone should ever have wanted to retain *Leucanthemum*, *Argyranthemum* and *Rhodanthemum* in the genus *Chrysanthemum* as it was in my student days – large, shambling and unconvincing as a unit of plant classification at the level of a genus.

Finally, let us not imagine that the latter-day classifiers of plants are soul-lessly dedicated to advanced techniques of molecular biology, the microscope and the computer. They have humour, too. What otherwise is the explanation for three recently named small genera in the sunflower tribe, Heliantheae – *Damnxanthodium*, *Oblivia* and *Zyzyxia*?

The annuals *Rudbeckia* 'Toto' and *Cosmos* 'Sonata Pink' are both much dwarfer than their parental species.

Part Two The Plants

Introduction to the Plants

The following plant directory is divided into 13 chapters, each devoted to a specific group of genera. Within most chapters, the genera are arranged according to their horticultural value, with the most important and best-known taking pride of place. In Ornamental Thistles (pp.97–103), for example, *Echinops* is the first mentioned, simply because, in gardens, it outdoes any other genus in this group. *Cynara* and *Onopordum* follow as the two other widely seen genera. The remaining five genera in the chapter all contain garden-worthy species and cultivars, but must rank as 'also-rans' in terms of popularity.

A common exception to this scheme occurs where a genus of lesser value is closely related to another, more important one. Accordingly in Cornflowers (pp.92–96), *Amberboa* follows the more diverse, popular and horticulturally significant *Centaurea*. There are a few chapters, for example Some Key Annuals (pp.162–173), where the genera are arranged alphabetically. In these chapters, any assessment of the overall garden value of each genus is very much a matter of individual taste and there is no generally accepted consensus of opinion on the matter.

Hardiness

For every species described, an indication of hardiness, based on British gardens, is given. Readers in Canada and much of the USA need to bear in mind that winters in all the more populous areas of Britain are relatively mild. They are situated in hardiness zones 8 and 9, and thus have average annual minimum temperatures of between $-12°C$ ($10.5°F$) and $-1°C$ ($30°F$).

Perennials in most British gardens rarely experience temperatures lower than $-10°C$ ($14°F$), and then only for one or two very short periods in midwinter. In the USA, only the Pacific seaboard and Florida and Louisiana, as well as parts of other southern and south-eastern states, experience similar conditions. Areas with more snow-cover in winter have the benefit of its valuable insulating effect. This can rarely be relied upon in Britain, which typically has quite wet winters. Among some perennial species, prolonged wet soil conditions cause more winter losses than low temperatures. In the case of any doubt, it is wise to consult owners and managers of local plant nurseries as they are commonly a valuable fount of experience and advice on plant hardiness in their own areas.

Height and spread

Approximate plant heights are given in all plant descriptions. Wide variation occurs, depending largely on soil fertility, water supply, shelter from wind, or lack of it, and nearness to taller plants. For this reason, I have opted for no more precision than 25cm (10in) steps in indicating heights above a metre (3ft).

Awards

Two types of major awards to individual species and cultivars are recorded in the plant descriptions. The better known is the long-established Award of Garden Merit ♚ from the Royal Horticultural Society. The majority of these awards are given after careful comparative trials at Wisley, the society's garden 30km (19 miles) southwest of London. Some are also made as a result of decisions by consensus of the trials committee members, on the basis of their experience and observation.

Of more recent inception are the Fleuroselect Gold Medals. The first of these was awarded in 1992, and up to now they have been given only to cultivars normally raised from seed. The award-giving body is an international organization of breeders and distributors of ornamental plants, founded in 1970. New introductions are rigorously trialled on 20 European sites. So far, just 40 Gold Medals have been awarded. Medal winners in the daisy family are in the genera *Ammobium*, *Centaurea*, *Gazania* and *Zinnia,* among others.

Previous page: *Heliopsis helianthoides*, the parental species of fine cultivars such as 'Sommersonne'.

A parent of the Galaxy Hybrids, *Achillea* 'Taygetea' also has a unique character of its own.

6 Sunflowers

For the most part tall, large-flowered and bristly-haired, the sunflowers scarcely need introduction. The four genera in this group are similar in appearance and culture. Their appraisal by gardeners is scientifically confirmed by botanists, who place them in the same tribe, one of just three in which the leaves are usually opposite (i.e. in pairs, at least on the lower parts of the stems).

HELIANTHUS Sunflower

For gardeners in northern temperate zones, this North American genus is one of the four best-known genera in the entire daisy family, along with *Aster*, *Chrysanthemum* and *Dahlia*.

There are about 70 species of sunflower. Those described here are herbaceous plants of erect habit. Except for *H. salicifolius*, the leaves are simple and ovate or lance-shaped. The flowerheads are solitary, as in *H. annuus*, or in few-flowered loose corymb-like clusters. The ray florets are sterile.

Helianthus is economically the most important member of the daisy family, as its annual species *H. annuus* is one of the world's great sources of vegetable oil and animal feedstuff. The same species, in its smaller-flowered forms, became a fashionable cut flower during the 1990s. One other species of some economic significance is the Jerusalem artichoke, *H. tuberosus*, grown for its distinctively flavoured but notoriously knobbly tuberous roots.

In gardens, it is yet again *H. annuus* that is the best-known species, for its arsenal of cultivars. Much more interesting horticulturally are the hardy herbaceous perennials, all of them smaller-flowered than *H. annuus*. *Helianthus* is a genus for relatively large beds and borders, and some of the perennial species are more appropriate for naturalizing. Sunflowers are attractive to bees, and the flowerheads of *H. annuus*, if left to ripen, encourage seed-eating birds. All species last well in water as cut flowers.

Cultivation is easy in almost any reasonable soil, and in the case of aggressive spreaders like *H. decapetalus* and

H. × laetiflorus, the principal problem may be curtailing the area of occupation: lifting and replanting every other year is wise practice for these. Otherwise, ordinary culture as hardy perennials, or for *H. annuus*, as a hardy annual, is sufficient. Most of the perennials thrive in dry soils and full sun. *H. atrorubens* and its cultivars tolerate partial shade. All are hardy to −15°C (5°F), except perhaps *H. atrorubens*. Tall plants may need support, particularly in the first year after planting.

Propagation of *H. annuus* is by seed, but the perennial species rarely produce seed in Britain, and some are sterile. However, all perennials, species and cultivars alike, are ordinarily propagated by division in autumn or spring. Where rapid multiplication is needed, basal cuttings taken in spring root readily.

Rabbits and slugs may be troublesome.

Perennials

In British gardens, the perennial sunflowers are mainly represented by about nine cultivars. 'Loddon Gold' is double-flowered and 'Lemon Queen' is distinctive in the comparatively pale colour of its ray florets. The remainder, all but two single and yellow-rayed, are unintentionally but very frequently sold under other names. For example, several distinct cultivars are sold by different nurseries under the name 'Capenoch Star'. The resulting confusion has long since spread to photographs in gardening books and magazines. Fortunately, in the 1990s the German nurseryman, Rolf Offenthal, carried out some painstaking investigations into the classification of the garden perennials and their cultivars. The 1999–2001 *Helianthus* trial at Wisley will probably also bring about some improvements in the reliability of naming, so there is likely to be less uncertainty about names in the future.

All the plants described below flower from late summer to mid-autumn unless otherwise stated.

H. atrorubens (Dark-eye sunflower) is a native of woodlands in the south-eastern states of the USA. This invasive species is little grown as a garden plant in Britain, but

Sometimes sold under the name 'Capenoch Star', this *Helianthus × multiflorus* cultivar is 'Major'.

Dwarf enough for use as a novel short-lived container plant, the annual sunflower cultivar 'Pacino'.

three popular cultivars are hybrids between it and either *H. × laetiflorus* or *H. pauciflorus* (itself one of the parent species of *H. × laetiflorus*). **'Gullick's Variety'** grows to about 1.5m (5ft) and has flowerheads up to 12cm (5in) across. These have several rows of medium yellow ray florets and a dark disc. Although vigorous, it spreads less aggressively than **'Monarch'**, which is taller at up to 2m (6½ft) high, and needs some support. This has flowerheads up to 15cm (6in) across, but with fewer ray florets than 'Gullick's Variety'. **'Miss Mellish'** is of similar height to 'Monarch', with flowerheads about 10cm (4in) across. Each comprises a double row of florets, in form similar to those of a cactus dahlia. It is not listed in the *RHS Plant Finder 2000–2001*, but in the nursery trade is sometimes sold as 'Gullick's Variety'.

Like *H. atrorubens*, 'Monarch' may not prove reliably hardy in the coldest areas of the British Isles.

H. decapetalus, to 1.5m (5ft) tall, has small flowerheads, up to 8cm (3in) across, with comparatively few pale yellow ray florets. It spreads aggressively by rhizomes, thrives in moist soils, and is best used for naturalizing.

H. × multiflorus is a hybrid of *H. decapetalus* and the annual sunflower, *H. annuus*. It origins are a mystery, the hybrid being first reported in Spain late in the sixteenth century. Its cultivars are well-behaved as border plants, bushy and vigorous without being invasive. A large num–

ber were introduced during the nineteenth and twentieth centuries, and three are deservedly in widespread cultivation. A welcome influence from *H. annuus* is apparent in the larger number of ray florets in the flowerheads. In all the cultivars described here, except 'Major', these are pleasingly poised, facing sideways rather than skywards.

'**Major**' has large, single golden flowerheads which face upwards, on plants of moderate height – 1.25–1.5m (4–5ft). It is not listed in the *RHS Plant Finder 2000–2001*, but is sometimes sold as 'Capenoch Star', which is similar, although 'Major' has rather pointed rays.

'**Capenoch Star**' ♧ grows to about 1.5m (5ft) with single flowerheads, usually over 10cm (4in) across. These are on long stems, making it an excellent cut flower. The ray florets are light yellow and each has a characteristic notch in the rounded tip, not found in other *H. × multiflorus* cultivars. The disc is dark yellow. This cultivar sometimes sports to an anemone-flowered form, similar to 'Meteor' (see below). '**Triomphe de Gand**' is similar, but dwarfer, to 1.25m (4ft), and has larger flowerheads, about 15cm (6in) across. The double-flowered 'Loddon Gold' is often mis-sold as this variety.

'**Loddon Gold**' ♧ bears fully double, golden-yellow flowerheads to 15cm (6in) across on plants up to 1.75m (6ft) tall. '**Soleil d'Or**' is also double, slightly deeper in

The double-flowered perennial sunflower 'Loddon Gold' ♧ was found as a sport around 1920.

colour, but smaller-flowered. '**Meteor**', which arose in the nineteenth century as a sport of 'Soleil d'Or', has anemone-centred, deep yellow flowerheads, 10cm (4in) across, on plants to 1.5m (5ft) tall. It is not listed in the *RHS Plant Finder 2000–2001*, but is often sold as either 'Capenoch Star' or 'Triomphe de Gand', which are not anemone-centred. Expert Rolf Offenthal believes that because of the confusion in names, the AGM given to 'Capenoch Star' was really awarded to 'Meteor'.

H. × *laetiflorus*, another natural hybrid that has been known for many years, arose in the wild in the northeastern USA. The parental species are *H. pauciflorus* and *H. tuberosus* (Jerusalem artichoke). It reaches a height of up to 2m (6½ft), and bears flowerheads up to 10cm (4in) across. Both the ray florets and the discs are yellow. An invasive species, spreading by rhizomes, it is usually confined to wild garden situations. Although a hybrid, it comes true from seed.

H. '**Lemon Queen**' is a widely grown cultivar of quite recent introduction and of uncertain parentage, though *H. microcephalus* is authoritatively suggested as a candidate. It is deservedly popular for its long-lasting and very profuse display of flowerheads up to 12cm (5in) across, with pale yellow ray florets and dark discs. The plants are bushy with hairy leaves and reach 1.75m (6ft). It is rhizomatous and vigorous, but not an aggressive spreader.

H. occidentalis, which I have only recently acquired, may have a place where the larger-flowered and more assertive species and cultivars are unwanted. Its slender branching stems usually attain 1.25–1.5m (4–5ft). The freely produced flowerheads, up to 6cm (2½in) across, have deep yellow ray florets and a yellow disc.

H. quinquenervis. See *Helianthella quinquenervis* (p.43).

H. salicifolius (Willow-leaved sunflower) is remarkable in this genus for being grown primarily for its foliage. An established clump is an impressive sight, of distinctive architectural value in the garden. It makes a fine specimen in a lawn, and looks particularly good positioned near to a pool, though it actually grows best in dry soil.

The plants are very tall, up to 3m (10ft), though some clones are shorter. It has erect, unbranched stems – stout on well-grown plants – densely furnished with very narrow, gracefully drooping, deep green leaves, up to 20cm

'Lemon Queen' is unusual among the perennials in *Helianthus* for the colour of its rays.

(8in) long. They are almost hairless. The golden-yellow flowerheads are quite small, 5cm (2in) across, and are not produced until autumn.

Annuals

H. annuus needs no introduction, as the sunflower of both agriculture and children! Found in the wild over much of the USA, it is a rough, hairy, stout-stemmed but branching plant, up to 3m (10ft) tall but varying considerably in height. In the wild its flowerheads are up to 15cm (6in) across. Greater size and unbranched stems are hallmarks of the tall, cultivated varieties. The dwarfer, smaller-flowered cultivars retain the original branching habit and are very much more valuable, both as garden plants and as cut flowers. Some have ray florets of an almost sumptuous deep velvety red.

A selection follows of the large number of cultivars available, given in order of height. Where not otherwise stated, these have a branching habit, and single flowerheads generally between 10cm and 15cm maximum diameter (4–6in), with medium to deep yellow rays. ★ denotes a Fleuroselect award.

'Pacino' is very dwarf (30–40cm/12–16in) and is suitable as a container plant. 'Teddy Bear' (40cm/16in) is double flowered. 'Music Box'★ (75cm/30in) has flowerheads in a range of colours from cream to mahogany, including bicolours. 'Floristan'★ (1m/3ft) has reddish-brown rays tipped yellow. 'Sonja'★ (1m/3ft)

has rays of a very deep yellow, bordering on pale orange. The sister cultivars 'Prado Red' and 'Prado Yellow' are 1.25–1.5m (4–5ft) tall. These produce little pollen, an asset when they are used as cut flowers. The larger-flowered 'Soraya'★ (1.5m/5ft) is similar in colour to 'Sonja'. 'Valentine'★ (1.5m/5ft) has lemon-yellow rays. 'Velvet Queen' (1.5m/5ft) and 'Moulin Rouge' (1.75m/6ft) both have deep crimson rays. 'Sun King' (1.75m/6ft) has large, double flowerheads. 'Autumn Beauty' (2m (6½ft) has large flowerheads in a colour mixture similar to 'Music Box'.

H. debilis is the only other annual species ordinarily cultivated. Native to the southern USA, it is relatively small-flowered and is good for cutting. The plants grown in gardens are of the variety *H. debilis* var. *cucumerifolius*, the cucumber-leaved sunflower. An erect, branched plant, about 1.5m (5ft) tall, it has flowerheads up to 8cm (3in) across, with brownish-purple centres. The rays are yellow, but other colours are found in cultivars, just as in *H. annuus*. Some of these may, in fact, be hybrids between the two species. 'Vanilla Ice' has cream rays.

SILPHIUM

Silphium has female ray florets and male disc florets, a clear botanical difference from *Helianthus* in which the ray florets are purely for show, pollen and seed alike coming from the central disc.

Tall, coarse, and stiffly erect herbaceous perennials, the cultivated *Silphium* species are suitable only for very large beds or for wild gardens. The sparsely branched stems bear large, rough-hairy leaves, and are crowned in late summer and early autumn by open inflorescences reminiscent of the better-known *H. salicifolius*.

Silphium does best in moisture-retentive soils, and *S. laciniatum* prefers shade. Despite the height of the species, support is usually unnecessary. They are very hardy. Propagation is best by seed, but division is an alternative.

Species

Both species below are about 2m (6½ft) and flower in summer and early autumn. The disc florets are a deeper yellow than the fairly narrow but quite numerous rays.

S. laciniatum (Compass plant) produces flowerheads about 12cm (5in) across, quite widely spaced in a narrow, raceme-like inflorescence. Flowering commences in late summer. The leaves are deeply pinnately cleft into

PLATE I
Sunflowers

Helianthus atrorubens
'Miss Mellish'

Helianthus annuus
'Autumn Beauty'

Helianthus
'Lemon Queen'

*All plants shown at
approximately half lifesize*

Helianthus
atrorubens 'Major'

Helianthus
× *multiflorus*
'Soleil d'Or'

Helianthus
annuus
'Valentine'

Helianthus
occidentalis

Helianthus
× *multiflorus*
'Meteor'

Helianthus annuus
'Sun King'

rounded lobes – in younger plants they are erect and poised so that the edges point north and south. This shields the surfaces from the force of the midday sun, and from this feature the plant has its common name.

S. perfoliatum is rather earlier to flower and has smaller flowerheads, about 8cm (3in) across, in greater numbers. Each of these is on a long stalk but borne in a loose corymb-like inflorescence. The leaves on the upper part of the stem are perfoliate – the bases of the leaf blades in each pair are fused, so that the stem passes through them.

HELIANTHELLA

Like those of the cultivated species of *Silphium*, the flowerheads of *Helianthella* are sunflower-like, but *H. quinquenervis* has the advantage of being modest in size and suitable for gardens of all sizes. The ray florets, 15–20 per flowerhead, are narrower than in most perennial garden cultivars of *Helianthus*. *H. quinquenervis* is drought-tolerant, and readily propagated by seed or division.

H. quinquenervis grows to 1–1.5m (3–5ft) tall and produces solitary pale yellow, nodding flowerheads up to 10cm (4in) across, on long stalks. The flowering period is late summer to early autumn. Some nurseries inadvertently offer *Helianthus* 'Lemon Queen' as this species.

HELIOPSIS

Another sunflower look-alike, the single species of this genus in cultivation may be thought quite lacking in any touch of elegance, but it is a veritable model of undemanding culture: robust, long-lived, extremely cold-hardy, flowering over a long period from midsummer to early autumn, drought-tolerant and not invasive. It is also a good cut flower, especially in its single-flowered versions such as 'Sommersonne' ('Summer Sun').

Native to the Americas, the genus has fifteen species, differing from the sunflowers, *Helianthus*, in having fertile ray florets that wither but do not fall from the flowerheads as the seeds set and ripen. Cultivation is without problems, other than slugs as growth commences in early spring. Support is ordinarily necessary only for the little-grown taller cultivars. *Heliopsis* will thrive on any reasonably fertile soil, and does best in full sun. Lifting and dividing every third year is desirable.

Heliopsis helianthoides (left) is best known for its showy cultivar 'Sommersonne' ('Summer Sun').

Best used in a semi-wild setting, *Silphium perfoliatum* here thrives in Oxford Botanic Garden.

Propagation is by division in spring or, on lighter soils, in autumn if more convenient. If much multiplication is sought, cuttings in early spring root readily.

H. helianthoides is from the eastern USA, typically growing in a dry woodland or prairie environment. It is a stiff-stemmed, branching herbaceous perennial, up to 1.5m (5ft) tall, of dense, upright habit. The stems, and frequently the leaves, are more or less smooth. The leaves are up to 15cm (6in) long and ovate to lance-shaped. The flowerheads, very freely produced over a long period, are solitary, and up to 7.5cm (3in) across.

var. *scabra* is a rough-hairy plant. **'Sommersonne'** is a cultivar of it. Not exceeding 1m (3ft) in height, its single flowerheads have deep golden-yellow florets, surrounding a darker disc that becomes hemispherical as the flower matures.

'Lorraine Sunshine' introduced in 2000, has cream and green variegated foliage (the colour reverts if plants are grown in the shade). It grows to 60cm (24in) and has relatively small flowers, 5cm (2in) across.

A number of other cultivars, almost all of German origin, are available. Examples are **'Goldgefieder'** ('Golden Plume') ♔, which is double-flowered and 1.25–1.5m (4–5ft) tall, and **'Hohlspiegel'** ('Reflection'), about 1.25m (4ft), with orange, semi-double flowerheads.

7 Yellow Daisies

Little claim to botanical propriety can be made for the composition of this chapter. The 16 genera included are drawn from no fewer than six tribes. Their grouping together is unashamedly horticultural, the qualification for inclusion being that the greatest garden interest lies in the yellow-flowered species or cultivars. Only the sunflowers have been placed in a separate group (see pp.36–43), for their distinctive shared characteristics. *Balsamorhiza*, *Coreopsis* and *Rudbeckia*, though all in the sunflower tribe, are placed here because no gardener would regard them as sunflowers. *Helenium* has been included, somewhat marginally, because yellow is just about the predominant colour in the genus, despite the popularity and excellence of its orange- and red-flowered hybrids.

Coreopsis and *Rudbeckia*, together with *Anthemis, Doronicum* and *Helenium*, are among the mainstays of the hardy herbaceous perennial garden flora. Each of the others has an important contribution to make, too, in some cases of just a single species, but not necessarily falling short of excellence even then: *Buphthalmum speciosum* and *Eriophyllum lanatum* are cases in point. Very few species grown as annuals feature in this group, but *Coreopsis tinctoria* and *Rudbeckia hirta* are examples of starring quality.

ANTHEMIS Dog fennel, Chamomile

Very few of the hundred or so species of this genus are commonly seen in cultivation, but a handful are enormously popular, as they fully deserve to be. All of these are perennial and are characterized by finely divided hairy, aromatic foliage and solitary flowerheads, with white or yellow ray florets and yellow discs, which are produced with prodigious freedom.

Anthemis is mostly found in southern Europe, western Asia and North Africa. Its natural habitat is predominantly sunny with fast-draining soil, and in cultivation it does best and flowers most freely in comparable situations. Of those described below, the two dwarfest species are fine rock garden plants.

A. tinctoria and its taller cultivars benefit from some support, especially in an exposed situation. Together with *A. sancti-johannis*, they must be cut back hard when flowering is nearly over, in order to encourage a vigorous late-summer development of basal shoots. Both species tend to be short-lived, and failure to overwinter is commonest where this treatment is neglected.

Propagation of the species may be by seed, otherwise basal cuttings taken in late summer or spring root readily, while division in spring is the most-used method for *A. tinctoria*.

Slugs, aphids and powdery mildew may all attack members of the genus.

Species and cultivars

A. sancti-johannis, which is native to a limited area in Bulgaria, bears its flowerheads on stems up to 1m (3ft) tall, from early summer onwards. The flowerheads are up to 5cm (2in) across. The blunt-ended, orange-yellow ray florets are markedly shorter than the diameter of the yellow disc, around which they create an almost ruffed effect. The foliage grows in tufts, the individual leaves being hairy, oblong, and bipinnatisect, with a white tip to each lobe. The stems are usually slightly branched.

A. tinctoria (Dyer's chamomile) is a very similar species, much more widely distributed in the wild in Europe, the Caucasus and in western Asia and Iran, and rather later to flower. It has become naturalized in Britain and parts of North America. To 60cm (24in) tall, it has flowerheads to 3.5cm (1½in) across, with the length of the golden-yellow to cream ray florets about equal to the diameter of the golden-yellow disc. A yellow dye can be obtained from the flowerheads. The leaves are finely divided.

A fine early summer show of *Anthemis* 'E. C. Buxton' in a border at Bourton House.

Hybrids Much more widely grown than either of the above species are their popular hybrids, all flowering over an extended period from early to late summer. They are good cut flowers as well as deservedly popular border plants. All have a yellow disc; the colour given in the selection below is of the ray florets. Stems, though stiff, curve outwards from the base of the plant.

'**Alba**', white, 45–60cm (18–24in). '**Beauty of Grallagh**', deep golden-yellow, 60–90cm (2–3ft). '**E. C. Buxton**' pale lemon-yellow, 50–60cm (20–24in). '**Grallagh Gold**' golden-orange, 60–90cm (2–3ft). '**Kelwayi**' mid-yellow, 60cm (2ft). '**Sauce Hollandaise**' very pale yellow, changing to creamy-white, 60cm (2ft). '**Wargrave Variety**' pale yellow, 75cm (30in).

A. punctata **subsp.** *cupaniana* ⚘ is an evergreen perennial with woody-based stems, reliable and popular as the earliest large white daisy to flower each year. Native to Sicily, it sometimes dies back in winter. The branched, leafy stems form a spreading mat about 30cm (12in) high and up to 1m (3ft) in width. The leaves, up to 12cm (5in) long, are pinnatisect or bipinnatisect, grey-green in win-

'Beauty of Grallagh' is another popular *Anthemis* cultivar derived from crossing *A. tinctoria* and *A. sancti-johannis*.

The earliest flowering large white daisy *Anthemis punctata* subsp. *cupaniana* is native to Sicily.

ter but silvery-grey otherwise. Numerous flowerheads, up to 6cm (2½in) across, are held well above the foliage on wiry stems about 15cm (6in) long. The discs are yellow. The flowerheads are produced from late spring; I have observed that there is considerable variation within the species in the earliness at which flowering commences. As earliness in this plant is usually valued, propagating from appropriate parents should be worthwhile.

This is ideally a plant for a large rock garden, or a sunny position near the edge of a bed or border. On heavier soils it will do best in a raised bed.

A. carpatica and **A. marschalliana** are two dwarf species definitely most at home in a rock garden or trough. *A. carpatica* (syn. *A. cretica* subsp. *carpatica*) is a cushion-forming plant, not more than 25cm (10in) high, with white-rayed flowerheads, up to 4cm (1½in) across, in late spring. It hates lime. *A. marschalliana* (syn. *A. biebersteiniana*, *A. rudolphiana*) has ascending stems, up to 30cm (12in) high, with silvery-grey foliage and yellow flowerheads in early summer. Both are best protected from winter rains.

ARNICA

The two cultivated species of this genus are both entirely hardy herbaceous perennials, one from continental Europe and the other found in the Rocky Mountains of western North America. Both bear yellow daisies of rather starry appearance on stiff, few-leaved stems, arising from basal clusters of hairy foliage. The flowering period is summer, mid- to late for *A. chamissonis*, and a few weeks earlier for the European *A. montana*.

Although *Arnica* has been used for a very long period in medicine, it is dangerous to consume it without medical supervision. Medical herbalists still use it externally for treating sufferers from rheumatism and arthritis. It has also been used as a tobacco substitute. In the garden, these are plants for the front of a bed or border or, for *A. montana*, in a large rock garden. Both plants are rhizomatous, and *A. chamissonis* tends to spread rapidly on my own clay loam, which obviously suits it well. They are easy to grow in moisture-retentive soil, though *A. montana* thrives only in acid conditions. Propagation is by seed or division. They are susceptible to slug attack.

A. chamissonis is found along the length of the Rocky Mountains from Alaska to New Mexico. Plants at flowering are usually 60–70cm (24–28in) tall, with pale yellow flowerheads, up to 5cm (2in) across, borne in very open cyme-like inflorescences.

A. montana is found over much of continental Europe, and makes a notable contribution to the Alpine mountain flora. Usually 40–50cm (16–20in) tall, its flowerheads are up to 8cm (3in) across and either solitary or in inflorescences of just two or three. The ray florets are golden-yellow or orange-yellow, the disc orange-yellow.

BALSAMORHIZA

A member of the sunflower tribe, this small genus is native to western North America. Although some species are much admired, even in most parts of its own continent *Balsamorhiza* is almost unknown as a garden plant. Its species have proved hard to cultivate successfully outside their native area, though the reasons for special difficulty are unclear. Perfectly drained soil does seem either essential or at least very advantageous.

B. sagittata is possibly the member of the genus most worth attempting to grow. A very hardy perennial, up to 60cm (24in) tall and flowering in late spring and early summer, it is found in the wild on dry slopes in Canada and the north-west USA. In flower it is a handsome plant: the bright yellow flowerheads, up to 10cm (4in) across, are borne singly or in twos or threes on almost leafless stalks above clusters of large, hairy, long-stalked leaves.

Propagation is by seed. As the genus is tap-rooted, plants may suffer from disturbance at planting and seedlings are best grown individually in pots.

CHRYSOGONUM Golden star

An accommodating groundcover plant for moisture-retentive soils, **C. virginianum**, the only species in this genus, is native to the eastern USA. It is hardy, often evergreen, and usually flowers for four months or more, starting in late spring. Growing to about 30cm (12in) high, it spreads by leafy runners. The solitary flower-heads, up to 4cm (1½in) across, have just five (occasionally six) ray florets around a small, yellow disc. The branched stems are furnished by hairy leaves in pairs.

The plant will do well either in full sun or partial shade. Propagation is by division or fresh seed.

COREOPSIS Tickseed, Golden marguerite

There is a special quality of glossy intensity of colour about the flowers of *Coreopsis*. For free-flowering over a long period, the popular perennial species are matched in performance by few other plants. There are about 114 species, native to the Americas and to Africa; the genus contains species from the now obsolete genera *Calliopsis* and *Leptosyne*.

Only the one annual and six herbaceous perennial species are much grown. The distribution of these in the wild is an area stretching from Nova Scotia down through the eastern and central states of the USA to Florida. Of these seven species, one is of large stature, while the others are medium to small. All are fully hardy. Typically, all the single flowers have eight ray florets and, in all the species described here, except *C. verticillata*, these are blunt-ended but toothed, to give a characteristic slightly ragged edge. The leaves – opposite in this genus – add valuably to the attractiveness of *C. verticillata* and *C. tinctoria* but in other species are unremarkable.

They are all easily grown plants for beds and borders, where the length of the flowering period is a particular commendation. Dwarf cultivars, such as *C. lanceolata* 'Goldfink', *C. grandiflora* 'Baby Sun' and *C. verticillata* 'Zagreb', are suitable for front edges; they are also well worth a trial for gardeners looking for a different pot plant to flower in spring in a cool greenhouse. Apart from such short-stemmed varieties, all *Coreopsis* are good cut flowers, with *C. grandiflora* possibly the best of all.

Any well-drained soil is suitable; flowering will be at its most free where soil nutrient levels are no more than moderate. *C. rosea* is happy in moist soils. All but *C. tripteris* are sun-lovers, though all will do in partial shade. Attention during growth is normally confined to dead-heading, though some do require support. In particular the annual *C. tinctoria* is weak-stemmed, and if the dwarf form is not grown, the display may be spoilt by flopping.

Propagation of all perennials may be by division or basal cuttings in spring. All species and many cultivars are readily propagated by seed. Sown in winter in a heated greenhouse, they will usually come into flower in their first season. *C. tinctoria* may be sown out of doors where it is to grow, in mid-spring, or – better on heavier soil types – in a greenhouse or frame in early spring and planted out at 6–8 weeks old.

Species and cultivars

C. auriculata makes a bushy, leafy plant with stems arising from a woody, stoloniferous rootstock, which spreads only slowly. The flowering stems, extending to 75cm (30in), are slender and rather lax. The solitary flower-heads, up to 5cm (2in) in diameter, are freely borne throughout the summer. Each deep yellow ray floret has a basal purple blotch. The plant needs cutting back in early autumn to promote young growth for overwintering safely. 'Superba' is a selection of the species. 'Schnittgold' ('Cutting Gold') has vivid golden rays and is the most widely seen of this species.

C. grandiflora is the species most valued as a cut flower, with bare, wiry stems, up to 60cm (24in) long, rising from a low clump of foliage. The solitary flowerheads are up to 6cm (2½in) across. The long flowering period extends from late spring or very early summer to early autumn. Although perennial, it tends to be very short-lived, and is sometimes deliberately grown as a biennial.

The species itself is not widely cultivated, but there are several cultivars that come true from seed: '**Early Sunrise**' (45cm/18in) has semi-double, light golden flowers; '**Mayfield Giant**' (1m/3ft) has large, single, bright yellow flowers; '**Sunburst**' (about 60cm/24in) has large, semi-double golden-yellow flowers; and '**Sunray**' (75cm/30in) is a deep yellow double.

Like most other perennial *Coreopsis* cultivars, the popular 'Sterntaler' comes true from seed.

The single-flowered **'Badengold'** and **'Flying Saucers'** are both sterile, so can only be propagated vegetatively. They are much more reliably perennial than the other cultivars described. 'Badengold', up to 1m (3ft) tall and polyploid, has the largest flowers. Though they are rather less freely produced than those of other varieties, its performance has been a talking point among visitors to the recently opened National Botanic Garden in Wales. 'Flying Saucers', also bright yellow, is quite compact, not exceeding 40cm (16in). Its flowers, 8cm (3in) across, are very freely produced over a long period.

C. lanceolata is similar in flowerhead characteristics, but more graceful in habit than *C. grandiflora*, again with most of the foliage at the base of the plant. In flower a height of about 60cm (24in) is attained. As for *C. auriculata*, cutting back in early autumn is advisable. It is the cultivars that are usually seen, and as with those of *C. grandiflora*, they will come true from seed.

'Goldfink' ('Goldfinch') is very dwarf at 25cm (10in); **'Sonnenkind'** ('Baby Sun', 'Sun Child') is similar but slightly taller – 30cm (12in); **'Sterntaler'** is taller again, 40cm (16in), and has a brown blotch at the base of each otherwise golden-yellow ray floret, giving the effect of a dark basal ring around the yellow disc.

C. rosea differs from all other species ordinarily cultivated in having pale rose-pink flowerheads. At 2.5cm (1in) in diameter these are a good deal smaller than those of the other species described, but very freely produced throughout summer. It spreads by runners and grows to 60cm (24in) high. It is usually grown as the cultivar **'American Dream'**, which comes true from seed. There is a white form, rarely seen.

C. tinctoria (syn. *C. marmorata*) is an annual species, and in full flower is one of the most eye-catching of hardy annuals. It has upright stems, 1m (3ft) tall, that are leafy and branched. The finely cut foliage, quite similar to that of *C. verticillata*, contributes greatly to its appeal. The flowerheads, up to 5cm (2in) across, have ray florets that are yellow at their outer ends with a reddish-brown basal area. This basal marking varies from being very short, creating a narrow ring round the dark red disc, to extending along most of the length of the floret, thus leaving only the tip yellow. Entirely crimson-brown variants are also found. Seed is usually sold as a mixture of these colours. Support is needed, except for the dwarf version **'Nana'** (up to 40cm/16in), which has the same range of colours.

C. tripteris is alone among the species described here in being relatively tall, reaching about 2m (6½ft), and in flowering in late summer and early autumn. It bears its pale yellow flowerheads, up to 5cm (2in) in diameter, each on its own short stalk in corymb-like inflorescences. It is an easily grown and long-lived species which thrives in partial shade.

C. verticillata is a favourite, and first choice among *Coreopsis* species for garden effect, as distinct from value as cut flowers. The flowers, up to 6cm (2½in) across, have a star-like appearance because the ray florets are more or less pointed, rather than blunt-ended as in the other species described. Flowerheads are very freely produced over a long period throughout the summer on numerous sparsely branched or unbranched, closely spaced stems.

They are foiled by a dense filigree of pinnately divided leaves with very narrow segments. The upright plants accordingly have the appearance of small bushes supporting a closely packed display of flowers. The rootstock is spreading. The plants are dependably perennial, and very drought tolerant.

'**Golden Gain**' (50cm/20in) has golden-yellow flowerheads; '**Grandiflora**' (syn. 'Golden Shower') ♛ is slightly taller (60cm/24in), and its deep yellow flowers are rather larger than the species; '**Moonbeam**' (50cm/20in) has lemon-yellow flowers; '**Zagreb**' (25–30cm/10–12in) is a gold-flowered dwarf, reputedly particularly drought resistant.

DORONICUM Leopard's bane

The special glory of the genus *Doronicum* is its earliness to flower. There are few enough herbaceous perennials of any kind that brighten the garden before late spring. Flowering two or three months later than it does, *Doronicum* would be but another yellow daisy: in spring it enjoys the stage unchallenged.

The 35 or so species are natives of Europe, south-west Asia and Siberia. Two are native to Britain – *D. plan-*

tagineum and *D. pardalianches*. They are all herbaceous perennials, and all are hardy in Britain and most of the USA. From the basal leaf clusters, erect leafy stems arise, bearing yellow flowerheads, either solitary or in few-flowered corymbs. The basal leaves are long-stalked, simple and mostly ovate or elliptic, with heart-shaped bases.

Relatively undemanding plants, they thrive in most soils, some species doing particularly well in heavier ones. They do best in partial shade, and the first three species described below are fine plants for naturalizing in a wild garden. In most gardens, they are grown as bed or border plants, and are good as cut flowers. Support is unnecessary, even for the taller species. Dead-heading is often rewarded by a second – though lesser – display of flowers in late summer.

Propagation of the species is by seed, and of both these and cultivars by division. Traditionally this is done in early autumn, but if carried out just after flowering and the divisions not allowed to dry out, there will be a better flower display in the following spring. In any event,

The annual *Coreopsis tinctoria* here creates a minor spectacle in a border at the Oxford Botanic Garden.

PLATE II
Yellow Daisies I

Gaillardia 'Kobold'

Helenium 'Coppelia'

Helenium 'Moerheim Beauty'

Helenium 'Wyndley'

All plants shown at approximately half lifesize

Helenium
'Chipperfield Orange'

Telekia speciosa

Coreopsis
lanceolata
'Sterntaler'

Leontodon rigens

Senecio lineariifolia

Buphthalmum
salicifolium

Arnica
chamissonis

division is best carried out fairly frequently – say every third year.

Some species are susceptible to powdery mildew and root rot may occur in wet soils. However, the genus is not attractive to slugs and snails.

Species and cultivars

D. austriacum is native to mountainous areas of central and south Europe and Turkey. Usually growing to about 75cm (30in) but occasionally much more, it flowers late for this genus – the end of spring and early summer. The slender stems are branched, and the flowerheads, which are up to 6cm (2½in) across, are produced in few-flowered corymbs. From a rhizomatous rootstock, leaves arise at about the same time as the flowering stems.

D. pardalianches (Great leopard's bane) is native to northern England, Scotland, and elsewhere in western Europe. Reaching a height of slightly less than 1m (3ft), it too flowers in late spring and early summer, starting just after *D. austriacum*. The branched stems each bear a considerable number of small flowerheads, not more than 5cm (2in) across. It spreads vigorously by rhizomes and, like the previous species, is best used for naturalizing.

D. × excelsum 'Harpur Crewe' (syn. *D. plantagineum* 'Excelsum') has another British native species, *D. plantagineum*, as one of its parents. It is an old garden hybrid, raised in 1876 and of uncertain origin.

It usually grows to about 60cm (24in), though it is taller in damp, shady conditions. Three or four flowerheads, up to 10cm (4in) across, are borne on each stem in mid- to late spring. Although preferring some shade, it can do well also in a sunny situation. For gardeners wanting to grow more than one *Doronicum*, it complements *D. columnae* and *D. orientale* and their cultivars in terms of height (taller) and flowering season (later).

D. columnae is a native of European mountains, like *D. austriacum*. The flowerheads are solitary, on stems up to 60cm (24in) tall, and open in mid- to late spring.

The species itself is little grown, but the hybrid **'Miss Mason'** ♛ is better-known. Long in cultivation, its parentage is uncertain, but *D. columnae* is probably involved. 'Miss Mason' would be my first choice if I could grow only one *Doronicum*. With dark green, glossy leaves, its flowerheads, several to each stem, are up to 8cm (3in) across.

D. orientale (syn. *D. caucasicum*) is a native of southern Europe, Lebanon and the Caucasus. It is quite similar to the previous species, but somewhat shorter (40cm/16in) and earlier to flower. The flowerheads, usually solitary, are up to 5cm (2in) across, and have characteristically narrow ray florets. Those of its cultivar **'Finesse'**, which comes true from seed, are narrower still, because the florets are curled into fine quills. Flowerheads are up to 8cm (3in) across, on plants about 50cm (20in) tall.

'Frühlingspracht' ('Spring Splendour') has double flowerheads of rather smaller diameter. It flowers freely, and has enjoyed considerable popularity, though not with me, because the rather blowsy flowers lack the straightforward appeal of the singles.

'Little Leo' is notably dwarf, just 25cm (10in) tall. The flowerheads are about 5cm (2in) across, with a double ring of ray florets. It comes true from seed, as do the following two cultivars. Both **'Goldcut'** and **'Magnificum'** have larger flowers than the species, and are 50cm (20in) tall. 'Goldcut', with long, stiff stems, is outstanding as a cut flower, while the multi-branched 'Magnificum' is probably the most popular and widely available *Doronicum*.

D. orientale, with its cultivars, is less tolerant of excessive soil moisture than most other species; it is susceptible to root rot and powdery mildew.

ERIOPHYLLUM Woolly sunflower

For all the summer wealth of other free-flowering, hardy herbaceous perennial yellow daisies, *E. lanatum* deserves much wider uptake. It is a vigorous front-of-border plant that produces a stunning display of small, all-yellow flowers of a starry appearance. This they owe to each flowerhead having just 8–10 ray florets, broad at the base but narrowing more or less to a point. Contrary to its common name, it is not closely related to *Helianthus*.

The plant performs best with full exposure to sun, and on dry, hungry soil: this said, I have known it to do impressively well on a fairly fertile clay loam. Where it is happy with conditions, it tends to be invasive. Its habit tends towards the sprawling. The dwarf form 'Pointe' is a good plant for a large rock garden.

Cultivation is without particular problems, except where roots are too wet and too cold for too long in winter. Propagation is by seed, division or cuttings in spring. The young shoots are susceptible to attack by slugs and snails, and by birds, which use the woolly foliage for their nests.

Less widely known than it deserves, *Eriophyllum lanatum* does particularly well on dry, hungry soils.

E. lanatum, native to western North America, is a generally grey-hairy plant. It grows to about 50cm (20in) with branched, quite stout stems. The cultivar **'Pointe'** is just 30–40cm (12–16in) tall. The flowerheads, about 4cm (1½in) across, are solitary or in loose few-flowered corymbs and open throughout summer. The foliage adds to the attractiveness of the plant; the basal leaves are lobed and the lower stem leaves are pinnatifid.

GAILLARDIA Blanket flower

Flamboyant, garish and untrendy are all epithets recently heaped on the head *Gaillardia* by distinguished garden writers from both sides of the Atlantic Ocean. When it comes to the popular red and yellow bicolours, I have to agree with them. The self-coloured cultivars are another story – for an appropriate position, they are fine, showy plants, long-lasting in flower. Containing almost 30 species, native to the southern USA, Mexico and South America, *Gaillardia* is closely related to *Helenium*. Its natural habitats are sun-exposed places – prairies and hillsides – and in gardens the genus does well on poor, dry soils and in sunny positions.

Two species, *G. pulchella* (annual) and *G. aristata*

(perennial), are cultivated, but hybrids between the two are much more widely grown. The half a dozen or so of these, such as 'Dazzler' ♥ and 'Kobold' ('Goblin'), account for the vast majority of the blanket flowers offered for sale by garden centres and nurseries. Both species and their hybrids are hardy and have grey-green leaves, often lobed or toothed. The flowerheads are solitary, and borne on long leafy stalks. The broad, showy ray florets are sterile, yellow, red or bicoloured, and at their tips often attractively lobed or toothed. The notably long flowering period extends from early summer to early autumn. All the taller *Gaillardia* are good cut flowers.

Cultivation is usually without problems, though all but the dwarfer cultivars look better for some support. Deadheading is a worthwhile chore, to maintain the long succession of flowerheads. Plants of *G. aristata* and the garden hybrids should be cut back hard in late summer to encourage a vigorous basal growth of shoots before cold weather brings growth to a halt. This improves the prospects of winter survival.

Propagation is most often from seed, which comes true to variety. Sown the previous summer, or even in the preceding winter in heated greenhouse conditions, the perennials come into flower in their first full year. The garden hybrids are sometimes intentionally treated as annuals. An alternative to propagation by seed is root cuttings. A lazy gardener's method is to slice the top off an established plant in early spring by using a spade or hoe a few centimetres below the soil surface. New top growth arises from the upper ends of the roots left in the ground. Once this is securely established, the mass of plants needs lifting, separation and planting out.

Gaillardia is subject to slug attack on new growth in autumn and spring, and to downy mildew.

Species and cultivars
G. aristata is a hardy perennial, growing to 75cm (30in) and bearing flowerheads up to 10cm (4in) across, with yellow ray florets and an orange-red disc. Plants are often reasonably long-lived but, nevertheless, *G. aristata* is little grown, and is important principally as a parent of the garden hybrids.

G. pulchella is the only widely cultivated annual species. It grows to 60cm (24in) and produces flowerheads up to 6cm (2½in) across. The ray florets are purplish-red either throughout or, more often, in their basal part, with the tips yellow. In the cultivar **'Lorenziana'** the disc florets

The perennial gaillardias are short-lived but flamboyant: here are 'Burgunder' (left) and 'Dazzler' (right).

are enlarged and tubular, and the double flowerheads assume a nearly spherical shape. **'Red Plume'** is a compact double-flowered, deep-coloured cultivar, 30–35cm (12–14in) high.

It is very easy to grow. On fast-draining soils in areas with mild winters, the best results are obtained from sowing in the very early autumn where the plants are to grow. Otherwise, sowing should be in spring. This may be done in the open, or treatment as a half hardy annual may be more convenient especially if the soil lies wet.

G. × grandiflora (*G. aristata* × *G. pulchella*) Even on the standards of freedom of flowering common in the daisy family, these hybrids are outstanding. Similar in size to those of *G. aristata*, the flowerheads have larger numbers of ray florets, forming an uninterrupted ring of vivid colour round the discs, which are usually a shade of reddish-brown. The untrammelled vigour of flower production undoubtedly owes something to these hybrids being tetraploid – having double the number of chromosomes normal for the genus. They have a strong

tendency to a short life span, especially on heavier soils. They differ from one another most significantly in height and, of course, flower colour. Heights are in the 60–90cm (2–3ft) range, except where shown. The following all have yellow-tipped ray florets of varying shades of orange and red: **'Bremen'**, **'Dazzler'** ♛, **'Fackelschein'** ('Torchlight'), **'Kobold'** ('Goblin') (30–35cm/12–14in) and **'Mandarin'**. Other cultivars include my own personal favourite **'Burgunder'** (30–35cm/12–14in), which has deep wine-red flowers, **'Goldkobold'** ('Golden Goblin') (30–35cm/12–14in), with both ray florets and disc golden-yellow, and **'Tokajer'** ('Tokay'), which is bright orange-rust.

GRINDELIA Gum weed

The sixty or so species of *Grindelia* are found in the wild from the southern tip of South America to Canada. Just two are of any note as garden plants – *G. chiloense* from Patagonia and *G. camporum* (syn. *G. robusta*) from California, which have quite showy yellow flowerheads from midsummer onwards.

Both species, like most in the genus, are resinous, and the flowerheads particularly often glisten with a gummy, white exudate. They are of borderline hardiness, and in

These *Helenium autumnale* hybrids were raised from seed, an inexpensive method of stocking borders.

colder areas need a foot-of-wall situation to ensure survival. In any event a sunny spot on well-drained soil is ideal. They do well on poor, dry soils. Propagation is by seed or cuttings.

G. chiloense (syn. *G. speciosa*) is an evergreen subshrub of rather sprawling habit, attaining a height of up to 1m (3ft). The long-stalked, bright yellow flowerheads have orange-yellow discs and are up to 7cm (3in) across. They are borne singly.

G. camporum (syn. *G. robusta*) is rather taller at up to 1.25m (4ft), and has stout, erect stems, but the flowerheads are somewhat smaller, not above 5cm (2in) across.

HELENIUM Sneezeweed

Helenium is poetically supposed to have sprung from soil watered by the tears of Helen of Troy, but as all species of this genus are American natives, the 'helenion' of the Greeks was perhaps *Inula helenium*.

A characteristic feature of the genus is the reflexing of the ray florets very soon after the opening of the flowerheads, so that their profile is rather like an upside-down shuttlecock. There are about 40 species, all annuals and herbaceous perennials. Of these, only one annual, *H. amarum*, and two perennial species are much cultivated. A third perennial, *H. bigelovii*, has been importantly involved in the parentage of the garden hybrids by which the genus is best known. Like their parent species, these are hardy, vigorous, clump-forming, fibrous-rooted plants with stiff stems furnished by alternate leaves.

All four species and some of the garden hybrids are yellow-flowered. It is, however, for the depth, intensity and warmth of the oranges and reds in cultivars such as 'Coppelia' and 'Moerheim Beauty' that the genus is most valued. Individually, plants stay in attractive condition in full bloom – which is profuse – for up to two months. The total flowering period for these hybrids extends over at least four, from early summer to early autumn. They are very attractive to bees as well as making very good cut flowers. Wearing gloves when handling the plants is prudent for sufferers from skin allergies, since *Helenium* foliage may aggravate these.

All species are fully hardy and do best in full sun. *H. autumnale* and the garden hybrids do best in moist soils, and commonly fail to thrive in very fast-draining soils in low rainfall conditions. In these, a late winter fertilizer application and watering if and as necessary, especially in late spring and early summer, may easily make the difference between a good outcome and a poor. *H. hoopesii* and the annual *H. amarum* are more tolerant of dry soil. *H. autumnale* and the taller hybrid varieties need support. With these, it is possible to pinch out the growing point of the shoots during late spring or early summer to produce a shorter, better-branched plant with a less leggy appearance. Dead-heading prolongs the flower display.

Perennial species and the garden hybrids rapidly form large clumps, and need division and replanting in spring every second or third year to maintain full vigour. It is best to replant pieces with only two or three shoots. If larger numbers of plants are needed, the species are readily raised from seed, and species and hybrids can be propagated by basal cuttings taken in spring.

Unsightly damage to foliage may result from leaf spot fungi. The lower stems and leaves tend to die before flowering commences in any case, and should be masked from view by appropriate associated planting.

'Chipperfield Orange', one of the *Helenium* cultivars remarkable for their intense orange and red colours.

Species and cultivars
Other than *H. amarum*, all those described are herbaceous perennials.

H. amarum (syn. *H. tenuifolium*) (Bitterweed, Sneezeweed) is a strong-smelling, showy annual with bright yellow flowerheads; its common name celebrates its use by the early US colonists to make snuff. The slender stems are densely leafy, up to 75cm (30in) tall, and bear many-flowered corymbs from midsummer to early autumn. Individual flowerheads are small, to 2.5cm (1in) across. Give some support. Native to south-eastern USA.

H. autumnale, widespread in the USA and southern Canada, attains a height of up to 1.5m (5ft) and has branching stems with almost hairless leaves, up to 15cm (6in) long and more or less lanceolate. The leaves have no stalks; the blades extend down the plant stems from their bases, forming leafy wings a few millimetres wide. The yellow flowerheads are up to 5cm (2in) across and each has between 10 and 20 ray florets. They are borne in corymb-like clusters.

The species is variable in height, flower colour and size. Although plants can easily be raised from seed, garden space is better devoted to hybrids (see opposite).

H. bigelovii is a shorter and larger-leaved plant than *H. autumnale*. Its stems attain about 60cm (24in), are unbranched or little-branched, and bear the flowerheads – yellow ray florets, dark brown centres – either singly or in few flowered inflorescences. The flowering period is earlier than for *H. autumnale* and its hybrids. It is a native of Oregon and California.

The species itself is rarely grown, but **'The Bishop'** is deservedly quite popular. It has clear golden-yellow flowerheads in early to midsummer and, at 60–70cm (24–28in), is the dwarfest perennial helenium cultivar.

H. hoopesii, like both the previous species, is a parent of some of the modern hybrids. It is quite often grown in gardens, and flowers freely from seed sown the previous year. At 1m (3ft) or just over, it is dwarfer than *H. autumnale*, and has larger leaves, which form rosettes at the base of the plant. The flowerheads, produced in early to midsummer, are also larger, up to 8cm (3in) in diameter. The ray florets are yellow or orange, and narrow in relation to their length. It is native to the southern USA.

Hybrids In vegetative features, these generally conform most closely to those of one of the parent species, *H. autumnale*, but most are a good deal shorter. The colours given are of the ray florets, the discs being yellow-brown to brown. In the 'Season' column, the figures refer to when flowering commences with 1 being early summer and 3 being late summer.

Name	Height	Colour	Season
'Bruno'	1.25m (4ft)	Deep crimson or reddish-brown	3
'Butterpat'	75cm (30in)	Rich yellow	2
'Chipperfield Orange'	1.25m (4ft)	Orange	1
'Coppelia'	1m (3ft)	Warm copper-orange	2
'Crimson Beauty'	75cm (30in)	Mahogany	3
'Moerheim Beauty'	75cm (30in)	Velvety copper-red	1
'Pumilum Magnificum'	1m (3ft)	Golden-yellow	3
'Rotgold'	1.25m (4ft)	Varying shades or combinations of red and yellow	3
'Waldtraut'	1m (3ft)	Tones of golden-brown	1
'Wyndley'	75cm (30in)	Yellow, overlaid dark orange	2
'Zimbelstern' ('Cymbal Star')	1.25m (4ft)	Gold, brown-highlighted	2

Among the earliest heleniums to flower, *H. bigelovii* 'The Bishop' is also of relatively short stature.

HETEROTHECA Golden aster

The 20 species of annuals and herbaceous perennials in this genus are native to southern North America; just two are notable for garden use. Both are hardy perennials.

H. villosa (syn. *Chrysopsis villosa*) is a useful mid- to late summer flowering plant for a large rock garden or a dry, sunny bank. The yellow flowerheads, up to 4cm (1½in) across, are borne in loose few-flowered clusters on branched stems. The most desirable version of the plant is the dwarf, relatively large-flowered **var. rutteri**, which is only about 20cm (8in) tall. The leaves and stems are densely covered in very short silver hairs.

Golden aster requires a well-drained, naturally dry soil and is propagated by seed or division.

H. mariana is uncommon in cultivation, but may well prove a useful addition to the late summer garden flora. Of upright habit, it grows to 1–1.25m (3–4ft) tall, and bears corymbs of yellow flowerheads. These are narrow-rayed and up to 6cm (2½in) across.

INULA

The fineness of the ray florets is the glory that distinguishes *Inula* from almost all the other yellow-daisy perennials of summer and autumn, and make the flower-

PLATE III
Yellow Daisies 2

*Rudbeckia
fulgida
'Goldsturm'*

*Rudbeckia
subtomentosa*

*Rudbeckia
triloba*

Rudbeckia hirta 'Sonora'

Rudbeckia occidentalis
'Green Wizard'

Rudbeckia fulgida
var. *deamii*

Rudbeckia hirta
'Marmalade'

Heterotheca
mariana

Sinacalia tangutica

All plants shown at
approximately half lifesize

heads of this genus, and its close relatives *Bupthalmum* and *Telekia*, very different in appearance to those of, say, *Helenium* or *Rudbeckia*.

Of the hundred or so species in the genus, the few of real garden worth fall into two groups, differentiated by height. It is the dwarfer species that are likely to interest most gardeners, two of them being deservedly popular – *I. hookeri* and my own favourite, *I. ensifolia*. The three tall species described below are for large gardens that provide both the growing space needed and the viewing distance necessary to appreciate them. All three may need support if grown in exposed situations. Like other cultivated *Inula* species, they are native of regions from Eastern Europe through the Caucasus to the Western Himalayas.

All species described are fully hardy herbaceous perennials with leafy stems. The flowerheads have numerous female ray florets, characteristically narrow because they are tubular. The flowering period is from mid- to late summer unless otherwise stated. Easy to grow in almost any reasonable soil, they are, indeed, often quite invasive. *I. helenium* will tolerate shade, but other species do best given reasonably good exposure to sun. Propagation is by seed or division.

Species and cultivars up to 75cm (30in)

I. dysenterica. See *Pulicaria dysenterica* (p.61).

I. ensifolia grows up to 50–60cm (20–24in) in height and produces small, golden-yellow flowerheads, up to 4cm (1½in) across, very profusely. They are solitary, on thin stems. The leaves are narrow. This is a fine, easy plant for a position at or near the front of a bed or border. Its cultivar **'Gold Star'** is a dwarfer version, about 30cm (12in) tall. The very similar but rather larger-flowered *Buphthalmum salicifolium* is an equally garden-worthy alternative.

I. hookeri is probably the most widely grown species of the genus. At up to 75cm (30in), it is taller than *I. ensifolia*, and has much larger flowerheads, to 8cm (3in) across. The greenish-yellow ray florets are fine to the point of being needle-like, and surround an orange-yellow disc. Leaves and stems – simple and little branched – are hairy. This rhizomatous plant is very attractive in flower but is invasive.

I. orientalis (syn. *I. glandulosa*) is similar to *I. hookeri*, differing most in the orange-yellow colour of its ray florets, which are also wavy. Its flowering period is earlier and – unfortunately – shorter.

I. royleana is a Himalayan native, and for a plant of its height – 60cm (24in) – has a commanding presence. It bears golden-yellow flowerheads, 12cm (5in) across, on unbranched stems furnished with large, hairy, ovate leaves. Unlike other species, it needs fertile soil to do well.

Species over 75cm (30in)

I. magnifica is also commanding, but on a much bigger scale. It flowers in late summer, is up to 2m (6½ft) tall, and bears deep yellow flowerheads up to 15cm (6in) across in few-flowered corymbs. The stout leafy stems arise from a basal cluster of very large, ovate, dark green, toothed leaves. (*Telekia speciosa*, see below, is quite closely similar.)

I. helenium (Elecampane) is similar but smaller-flowered. It is a Central Asian native, naturalized very widely in Europe – including Britain – and will thrive in shady, wild garden conditions. Its claim for attention is its very

Very narrow, tubular ray florets are a feature of *Telekia speciosa* and its relatives.

long history of uses in herbal medicine – Hippocrates wrote of them – rather than for its ornamental value, in which it is outdone by the previous species.

I. racemosa is an imposing plant, like *I. magnifica*. It differs importantly in having comparatively small flowerheads (up to 6cm/2½in across) on long racemes, occupying the upper part of stems that may exceed 2.5m (8ft). Flowering sometimes continues into the autumn. This Himalayan species, like *I. helenium*, has medicinal uses.

TELEKIA

A crowning display of fine-rayed yellow flowerheads is a feature that the fully hardy herbaceous perennial *T. speciosa* shares with the closely related *Inula magnifica*. To this it is very similar in both appearance and garden use. The only other species in the genus is not widely cultivated.

T. speciosa (syn. *Buphthalmum speciosum*) is an erect plant, up to 2m (6½ft) tall at flowering, with large, broadly triangular, pointed leaves with deeply toothed margins. The stems start to branch as flowering approaches in summer and early autumn. Each branch bears a loose terminal cluster of yellow flowerheads, up to 10cm (4in) across, each on its own stalk and clearly separate from its neighbours. The numerous ray florets are very narrow.

This handsome plant is for larger gardens, and is seen at best advantage where it is foiled by nearby trees or large shrubs. Its easy culture and propagation is basically as for *Inula*. It does best in semi-shade and in moist soil.

BUPHTHALMUM

This small genus is very closely related to *Inula*, differing only in details of floral structure. Horticulturally, it is only *B. salicifolium* that is of interest. A native of central Europe, it is often found on limestone soils.

B. salicifolium is very close to *Inula ensifolia* (p.60) in most respects. It is of similar height, at about 50cm (20in), but has considerably larger flowerheads – up to 6.5cm (2¾in) in diameter as against 3–4cm (1¼–1½in). Although the golden-yellow ray florets are of very similar colour, there are fewer in each flowerhead. They are noticeably broader in relation to their length, and are blunt-ended, rather than pointed as in *I. ensifolia*. The flowering period is also rather longer, usually commencing in early summer and continuing until early autumn. **'Dora'** is dwarf, about 30cm (12in) tall.

Cultivation is easy – as for *I. ensifolia*. The plant can be quite invasive if grown in fertile soil. Some support may be appropriate for its slender stems, though it can look good when allowed to sprawl naturally.

B. speciosum. See *Telekia speciosa*.

PULICARIA Fleabane

A free-flowering herbaceous perennial with small, yellow flowerheads from midsummer to early autumn, ***P. dysenterica*** is not uncommon as a wild flower in Britain. It is native to much of Europe, and to North Africa. For collectors of herbs, the plant has a history of medicinal use, to which it owes both its specific and its common names.

Pleasing enough that it is as a garden plant, this species is quite outclassed by its close relatives *Buphthalmum salicifolium* and *Inula ensifolia*. It has horticultural interest, though, for introduction in a semi-wild environment where the soil is particularly moist. The erect, branched stems reach a height up to about 75cm (30in). The bright yellow flowerheads are up to 3cm (1¼in) across, the relatively short ray florets surrounding a golden-yellow disc. Propagation is by seed or division.

RUDBECKIA Coneflower

This small, North American genus makes a rich contribution of showy plants to our garden flora in the second half of summer and the first half of autumn. In common with the closely related genus *Echinacea*, and with *Helenium*, the appearance of the flowerheads is often likened to a shuttlecock. This is due to the markedly conical outline of the central disc, surrounded by reflexed ray florets. Coneflowers are very free-flowering over a long period, are easy to grow and make good cut flowers, which is a useful enough list of attributes to earn serious consideration for the genus in most gardens.

The name of the genus commemorates the eighteenth-century Swedish botanist who taught Linnaeus at the University of Uppsala. There are only about 15 species in all. All the seven species ordinarily seen in cultivation are hardy herbaceous perennials, though the very popular *R. hirta* is short-lived and almost always cultivated as an annual. The plants are erect, mostly freely branched and bear large solitary flowerheads with sterile ray florets, which are yellow except in some cultivars of *R. hirta*. *R. laciniata* and its cultivars have divided leaves, but most species have simple leaves of no particular note horticulturally.

In the garden, the coneflowers are suitable for any position that receives most of the day's sunshine. They are also quite robust enough to be suitable for naturalizing, with *R. fulgida* and *R. laciniata* to the forefront in this respect. *R. hirta* cultivars are widely used in summer bedding and as a valuable gap filler, particularly in the first two or three years after planting shrubs.

Rudbeckia species generally do best on heavier soils because of their moisture-retaining qualities. Where the soil is naturally dry, liberal use of garden compost or peat in preparation, and generous watering in midsummer, are likely to pay good flowering dividends. Species tolerant of drier conditions are *R. hirta* and *R. fulgida* var. *deamii* In very moist soils, it is *R. maxima* and *R. subtomentosa* that are likely to be particularly at home.

R. hirta is normally treated as an annual, but other species are usually propagated by division in spring, every fourth or fifth year being sufficiently frequent unless there is a need to curtail the spread of a drift of plants. Where the greatest multiplication is wanted, cuttings taken at the same time of year are easy to root. All species are readily raised from seed sown in late spring or very early summer, and will flower freely the following year. Sowing in a heated greenhouse in late winter is also possible, and flowering the same year can then be expected. *Rudbeckia* is subject to aphid attack and infection by powdery mildew. All the plants described below commence flowering in mid- to late summer and continue through early autumn unless otherwise indicated.

Species and cultivars

Of the species treated as perennial, **R. fulgida**, native to south-eastern USA, is among the most popular of border plants. They are rhizomatous with hairy stems and leaves. The stems are usually branched in their upper halves, bearing flowerheads in profusion. These have deep yellow ray florets and a relatively small, almost hemispherical purple-brown disc.

In **var. deamii** the stems are either simple or slightly branched, reach a height of about 60cm (24in), and have flowerheads up to 6cm (2½in) across with 12–14 narrow ray florets. In the rather taller **var. speciosa** (syn. *R. newmannii*), which reaches 75cm (30in) or more, there may be up to 20 ray florets in each flowerhead, slightly longer and rather broader in relation to their length.

The cultivar **'Goldsturm'**, about 60cm (24in) tall, has larger flowerheads than either of the two varieties. They are up to 12cm (5in) across, with the ray florets up to

5cm (2in) long. It comes true from seed. If only one version of *R. fulgida* is to be grown, this outstanding herbaceous perennial is arguably the best of a good bunch.

R. hirta is sometimes known as black-eyed Susan (as is the unrelated greenhouse climbing plant *Thunbergia alata*). Unlike *R. fulgida*, it is short-lived if grown as a perennial, and is almost always treated as an annual, or occasionally (and successfully) as a hardy biennial. Again unlike *R. fulgida*, the central discs are markedly conical, and the ray florets are broader and, in most single-flowered cultivars, fewer. The species itself, native to the central USA, is not in cultivation, but the cultivars are very popular. In addition to other garden uses mentioned, the long-stemmed taller ones are good as cut flowers.

In order of height, among the better cultivars are:

Name	Height	Flowerhead (max diameter)
'Toto'	20–25cm (8–10in)	Single, golden-yellow, large disc, 5cm (2in)
'Sonora'	40cm (16in)	Single, golden-yellow with mahogany central zone, 15cm (6in)
'Marmalade'	50cm (20in)	Single, golden-orange, 8cm (3in)
'Goldilocks'	60cm (24in)	Semi-double, gold, 8cm (3in)
'Rustic Dwarfs'	60cm (24in)	Shades of yellow, bronze, red and mahogany, with some bicolours, 8cm (3in)
'Chim Chiminee'	60–75cm (24–30in)	Semi-double with quilled rays, shades of yellow, bronze and mahogany, 8cm (3in)
'Gloriosa Daisies'★	75–100cm (30–40in)	Single, golden-yellow, mahogany and well-defined bicolours, 18cm (7in)

★ tetraploid

R. laciniata (Cut-leaved coneflower). Native to Quebec and most of the eastern and central USA, the branching wiry stems of this species reach 2m (6½ft) and sometimes more. The handsome leaves are dark grey-green, the basal ones pinnate, with their pointed segments themselves deeply lobed and toothed. Also deeply lobed, with pointed segments, the strongly reflexed yellow ray florets are up to 6cm (2½in) long, and surround a deep yellow-green conical disc. This species is rhizomatous, and can be quite invasive.

'Goldquelle' ('Golden Fountain') ♈ is more compact,

Rudbeckias generally thrive in heavier soils, but *R. fulgida* var. *deamii* grows well in drier conditions.

grows to about 1m (3ft) tall, and has double flowerheads with lemon-yellow ray florets and a green centre. **'Juligold'** ('July Gold') is a tall single, originating as a chance seedling, and may be an interspecific hybrid. Up to 2m (6½ft) high, it is earlier flowering than the parental species. **'Herbstsonne'** ('Autumn Sun') is a favourite tall perennial for late summer and autumn. It is probably a hybrid between *R. laciniata* and *R. nitida*, a non-hardy species not in cultivation. It is 1.5–2m (5–6½ft) tall and has flowerheads up to 12cm (5in) across, single and bright yellow, with markedly tall green cones. The ray florets are broader than in *R. laciniata* and make a better show, although the oval leaves are less interesting. (The frequently encountered varietal name 'Herbstone' is simply a spelling mistake.)

R. maxima, 1.5m (5ft) or more tall, is a large-flowered species, remarkable for the height – up to 4cm (1½in) tall – of its blackish cones. The drooping ray florets are yellow and about 5cm (2in) long. It does well in moist soil, but may not be fully hardy in colder areas of the British Isles.

R. occidentalis is another tall species, up to 2m (6½ft), with very long cones, up to 6cm (2½in). The species is little grown, but its more widely seen cultivar **'Green Wizard'** has novelty value. Its dark cones are offset by a basal ring of elongated green bracts, in full view because of the absence of ray florets. The flowerheads appeal particularly to flower arrangers.

R. pallida. See *Echinacea pallida* (p.150).
R. purpurea. See *Echinacea purpurea* (p.150).

R. subtomentosa (Sweet coneflower) is distinguished partly by its anise-like scent. Its stiff-branched stems grow to about 1m (3ft), and bear flowerheads up to 10cm (4in) across. The disc florets are deep purple-brown, and the bright yellow ray florets are up to 4cm (1½in) long. It does well in moist soil.

R. triloba (like *R. hirta*, also known as Black-eyed Susan) would certainly be more popular if it were not so short-lived, often to the extent of behaving as a biennial. It is a much-branched plant, up to 1.5m (5ft) in height, and has a profusion of short-stalked flowerheads up to 8cm (3in) across. The deep yellow ray florets are few in number but broad; they are only slightly reflexed and surround a brown-purple disc. Some of the stem leaves are three-lobed, and give the plant its name. The flower display is long-lasting, and it is a favourite in my own garden.

Rudbeckia hirta cultivars are almost always grown as annuals: 'Marmalade' is my favourite.

8 Michaelmas Daisies and their Allies

The seven genera in this section are botanically closely related, all being members of the same tribe, and their flowerheads bear out the relationship by their quite evident similarity. It seems fitting that *Aster*, the genus to which the Asteraceae family owes its modern name, is among the few genera within the family that contain over 20 species of notable garden value. The common name Michaelmas daisy applies to a mere two of these species – *A. novi-belgii* (New York Michaelmas daisy) and *A. novae-angliae* (New England Michaelmas daisy).

Boltonia, *Kalimeris* and *Heteropappus* are botanically very closely related to *Aster*, and in flower particularly look the part because of their numerous slender ray florets. The single species of *Callistephus* is the plant known in everyday parlance as the aster. Correctly and fully the China aster, it is notable for the size of the flowerheads of most of its cultivars, and for being annual where all the cultivated *Aster* species of any note are perennial.

The popular *Erigeron* and the little-known *Townsendia* are both notable in this group for flowering mainly in early and midsummer, rather than autumn. The garden species of both have flowerheads of particular daintiness.

ASTER

To the genus *Aster* – the Greek word for 'star' – we owe more species of garden distinction than to any other genus in the daisy family. Between them they flower for half the year, from late spring to mid-autumn, not just the two months in which its best-known members, the Michaelmas daisies, are in their autumnal glory. Though some Awards of Garden Merit have been made to these, over 20 have gone to other *Aster* species.

Despite the recognition of garden excellence liberally bestowed on its members, I think that *Aster* is still under-rated among gardeners at large. This is partly because it is too closely identified with Michaelmas daisies alone, the fame of which as autumn-flowering plants is unfortunately twinned with their notoriety for being so susceptible to powdery mildew and Michaelmas daisy mite. Few other *Aster* species much in cultivation are liable to these troubles, but too many gardeners quite wrongly tar them all with that particular brush.

The 250 or so species of the genus are found on all continents except Australia, although they are predominantly plants of the northern hemisphere. Those of most horticultural significance – all herbaceous perennials – are almost all native to North America and to temperate areas in Europe and western Asia. Almost all are fully hardy. They range in height from around 25cm (10in) in *A. alpinus* to about 2m (6½ft). The leaves, usually dark green, are alternate and simple.

Flowerheads range in diameter from little over 1cm (½in) in *A. ericoides* to as much as 8cm (3in) in some cultivars of *A. amellus* and *A. × frikartii*. Colours are mainly in the range from mauve to lilac and deep blue, but there are whites and pinks, and among the Michaelmas daisies many cultivars have purple-red ray florets.

Aster species are generally easy to grow and to propagate and they will tolerate a good deal of neglect. Nevertheless, if division and replanting is not carried out often enough, plant performance far below potential will result. The desirable frequency varies widely from species to species.

Soil preferences also vary, and are mentioned in the species descriptions. As in gardening generally, it is wise to pay heed by growing most what best suits your soil. The true Michaelmas daisies, derived from *A. novae-angliae* and *A. novi-belgii*, are happiest on heavier, more moisture-retentive soils. Naturally less suitable soils need special preparation to give these plants a fair chance. Rather than making that effort, it might be better to choose one of the many *Aster* species that prosper in relatively dry soils like sandy loams. These include *A. amellus* and *A. × frikartii* as well as most of the valuable and under-appreciated small-flowered species, such as *A. ericoides*, *A. lateriflorus* and *A. sedifolius*.

As already mentioned, susceptibility to the disfiguring

disease powdery mildew varies widely in the genus. If you are not prepared to do some spraying, you are probably best advised to exclude from your planting plans any of the numerous cultivars of *A. novi-belgii*.

The only other serious disease is aster wilt, caused by a soil-borne fungus that infects the lower parts of the stems. At first, upward sap flow is reduced, leading to wilting, and the older leaves turn yellow, then brown. The fungus produces toxins that kill the leaves. Often only one or two stems in a clump are affected. They can be pulled out and destroyed; the rest can be allowed to flower, after which the entire clump should be destroyed. There is no cure or chemical preventative available to

Vigorous Michaelmas daisy 'Sonata' with *Helianthus* 'Lemon Queen' at Paul Picton's Old Court Nurseries near Malvern.

amateur gardeners. Affected plants must not be used for propagation. Avoid planting again in infected soil. Fortunately, the disease does not spread rapidly from one garden site to another.

As well as the ubiquitous aphids, slugs and snails, pests to watch for include the Michaelmas daisy mite (*Tarsonemus pallidus*). This is a serious and widespread problem on cultivars of *A. novi-belgii* but not on *A. novae-angliae*, nor most other *Aster* species.

The mites, too small to be seen by the naked eye, feed on the surfaces of stems, foliage and flower buds. Growth becomes distorted and stunted, stems show rough, brown scars and flowerheads fail to develop ray florets, turning into rosettes of small green leaves instead. An important alternative host plant is the strawberry, from which infestation can spread.

Unfortunately, there are no very effective chemical controls available for use by amateur gardeners. Therefore, during the spring and summer, all infested shoots should be removed promptly, and burned straightaway. If any signs of attack are apparent later, as flowering approaches, affected clumps should be dug up and burned as soon as the flower display comes to an end.

There are over 20 widely available *Aster* species, most of them with at least a few cultivars and some with many.

Aster novi-belgii 'Marie Ballard' named for his wife by the famous Michaelmas daisy breeder, Ernest Ballard.

To simplify this wealth of material, I have divided it into four groups: *A. novae-angliae* and *A. novi-belgii*; a group of 14 small-flowered species, all North American natives; six large-flowered species from Europe and Asia; and finally, two others that do not otherwise fit in elsewhere.

The Michaelmas daisies

In Britain alone there are well over 300 cultivars currently in commerce of the two very hardy North American species, *A. novi-belgii*, the New York Michaelmas daisy, and *A. novae-angliae*, the New England Michaelmas daisy. Included among those of *A. novi-belgii* – the great majority – are many in which other North American *Aster* species have been involved in the parentage. Most important among these are *A. laevis*, *A. lanceolatus* and, particularly in the case of dwarfer cultivars, *A. dumosus*.

The stems and leaves of *A. novi-belgii* are hairless, providing an easy means of distinction from *A. novae-angliae*, which is covered with fine short hairs. It is possibly this hairiness that makes the second species resistant to powdery mildew infection, as *A. novi-belgii* is not.

A. novi-belgii cultivars range in height from 15cm (6in) to 1.5m (5ft). Up to about 1m (3ft) tall, they are mostly compact and bushy, but even so plants attaining more than about 60cm (24in) need support to prevent collapse under heavy rain and strong winds while in flower.

In *A. novae-angliae*, the range of height is quite limited, all widely available cultivars being 1–1.5m (3–5ft) tall, with the solitary exception of the compact 'Purple Dome'. Plants are generally very stiff-stemmed, and given a sheltered garden and the support of neighbouring plants, the less tall cultivars (say 1.25m/4ft or less) may prove more or less self-supporting.

Frequent division (or propagation by cuttings and replanting) is needed for both species to achieve the best results: for ordinary garden purposes every other year should be the target.

A. novae-angliae flowerheads generally have narrower ray florets than those of *A. novi-belgii*. This enhances their attractiveness, but nevertheless, for dependable flower display in poor weather conditions, and for cut flowers, *A. novi-belgii* is the better of the two species. In overcast and damp weather, its flowers remain open while those of many older cultivars of *A. novae-angliae* tend to close up, and to behave likewise when they are used as cut flowers.

The very short selection of cultivars which follows scarcely does more than illustrate the range of heights and colours available. Flowerhead diameters range from 2.5cm (1in) to almost 6cm (2½in).

A. novi-belgii In the following list: early means flowering begins in late summer or very early autumn; late means it begins in mid-autumn; flowerheads are single and their diameter is usually 4–5cm (1½–2in) unless otherwise mentioned. Under height: A denotes shorter than 40cm (16in), B denotes 40–80cm (16–32in) and C denotes above 80cm (32in).

Flowering	Cultivar	Height	Flower colour, size and form
Early	'Alice Haslam'	A	Pale red, small
	'Dandy'	B	Purple-red, small
	'Ada Ballard'	C	Lilac-blue, large
	'Eventide'	C	Lavender-blue, large, double
	'Freda Ballard'	C	Purple-red, large, double
	'Patricia Ballard'	C	Mauve-pink, large, double
Mid-season	'Audrey'	A	Mauve-blue
	'Little Pink Beauty'	A	Mauve-pink, large
	'Snowsprite'	A	White, double
	'Chequers'	B	Violet
	'Jenny'	B	Purple-red, large, double
	'Blandie'	C	White
	'Coombe Rosemary'	C	Purple, double
	'Marie Ballard'	C	Lavender-blue, large, double
		C	
	'Raspberry Ripple'	C	Mauve-pink, double
	'Sonata'	C	Lavender, large
	'Winston S. Churchill'	C	Purple-red
Late	'Kristina'	A	White
	'Professor Anton Kippenburg'	A	Lavender-blue
	'Rose Bonnet'	A	Lilac-pink, large, double
	'Crimson Brocade'	C	Purple-red
	'Fellowship'	C	Pink, large, double
	'Climax'	C	Lavender-blue, large

A. novae-angliae has flowering periods as for *A. novi-belgii*. Unless otherwise shown, plant height at flowering is 1.25–1.5m (4–5ft), and flowerhead diameter 4–5cm (1½–2in).

Flowering	Cultivar	Height, flower colour and size
Early	'Barr's Blue'	Purple-blue
Mid-season	'Andenken an Alma Pötschke' ('Souvenir of Alma Pötschke')	1m (3ft), pink, smallish
	'Herbstschnee' ('Autumn Snow')	White
	'Lye End Beauty'	Purple-pink
	'Rosa Sieger'	Pink, large
Late	'Septemberrubin' (September Ruby')	Purple-red, large
	'Harrington's Pink' ♔	Pink, small
	'Purple Dome'	50cm (20in), violet-purple, small
	'Kylie' ♔	Pale pink, very small

Small-flowered American species

These 14 species, all native to North America, are broadly like the Michaelmas daisies (above) in most respects except the size of the flowerheads. The smallest within this group are little over 1cm (just under ½in) across, and the largest just over 3cm (1¼in). Trying to describe the garden effect the smaller-flowered species create calls into mind words like 'mist', 'clouds' and 'spray'. Among the species are some of the finest of all

The New England Michaelmas daisy 'Rosa Sieger' was raised by the famous German nurseryman Karl Foester.

PLATE IV
Michaelmas Daisies and Other Asters

A. novi-belgii
'Jenny'

A. linosyris

A. novae-angliae
'Barr's Blue'

A. × commixtus
'Twilight'

A. thompsonii
'Nanus'

A. × frikartii
'Mönch'

All plants shown at
approximately
three-fifths lifesize

A. × *frikartii* 'Jungfrau'

A. 'Little Carlow'

A. *sedifolius*

A. *novae-angliae*
'Herbstschnee'

Among the latest-blooming asters is the small-flowered
A. cordifolius 'Elegans', which is pretty and easy to grow.

late summer and autumn-flowering plants in any genus, in or out of the daisy family, and this is well borne out by the number holding an AGM ♔.

If the description following does not give contrary information, they all do well in any well-drained soil, including light, naturally dry ones, they are resistant to powdery mildew, need no support, and are good as cut flowers. Again, unless otherwise stated, division and re-planting at intervals of three years is sufficiently frequent.

For some species, after descriptions of cultivars more follow for hybrids. These have the species in question as one of the parents, and are broadly similar to it.

A. acris. See *A. sedifolius* (p.76).
A. × *commixtus* is probably synonymous with the culti-var **'Twilight'**. Free-flowering in late summer and early autumn, this grows to about 1m (3ft) in height and has violet-blue flowerheads about 3cm (1¼in) across. It is easy to grow and plants spread rapidly.

A. cordifolius flowers in mid-autumn, has heart-shaped

lower leaves, and the cultivars and hybrids by which it is known in gardens are about 1.25m (4ft) tall. The flower-heads, lavender-blue unless otherwise stated, are usually less than 1.5cm (just over ½in) across. Disc florets are yellow at first but soon darken to purple.

'Chieftain' ♔ is relatively large-flowered and about 1.5m (5ft) tall. **'Elegans'** is white and very late flower-ing. **'Silver Spray'** is pale lavender.

A. **'Little Carlow'** ♔ and *A.* **'Photograph'** ♔ are *A. cordifolius* hybrids. 'Little Carlow' flowers earlier than the other cultivars described, from very early autumn, and has larger flowerheads, about 2.5cm (1in) across. 'Photograph' is late-flowering and has flowerheads about 1.5cm (just over ½in) across. The discs retain their origi-nal yellow colour well. Although only about 1m (3ft) tall, its thin stems are best given some support.

A. divaricatus (White wood aster), a lovely plant, is a woodland native and thrives in shade. In late summer and early autumn, it is covered in a veritable starburst of

'Little Carlow' ♔, an *A. cordifolius* hybrid, is among the many perennial asters with an AGM.

The purple colour of the spring foliage of *Aster lateriflorus* persists through summer in its cultivar 'The Prince'.

pink. **'White Heather'** (1.25m/4ft) has large, white flowerheads and is late-flowering.

A. laevis (Smooth aster) flowers in early to mid-autumn and was extensively used in the past in breeding work for the development of *A. novi-belgii* cultivars. Compared with these, *A. leavis* cultivars have smaller flowers, and differ usefully in their resistance to powdery mildew and their ability to thrive in dry soils. Flowerheads are borne in an open panicle, and are widely spaced.

'Arcturus' has rosy-lilac ray florets in flowerheads 3cm (1¼in) across, and is about 1.25m (4ft) tall. **'Calliope'** grows to 2m (6½ft) or more, with rather larger flowerheads of lilac-purple. Both are late nineteeth-century introductions.

A. pringlei is closely similar to *A. ericoides*, and is known in gardens almost solely for its white-flowered cultivar **'Monte Cassino'** ♔. Flowerhead diameter approaches 2cm (¾in), and its height is around 1m (3ft). It is of less robust constitution than *A. ericoides*, and needs well-drained soil to overwinter dependably. It is known as 'September flower' to florists, and is grown commercially in greenhouses on a huge scale.

A. lateriflorus flowers late, in mid- to late autumn. A characteristic is the positioning of the small flowerheads along the upper sides of the long inflorescences. Those at the base of the large flower sprays are at a wide angle to the central stem. The flowerheads are less than 1.5cm (just over ½in) across in the species, with short, white, reflexed ray florets. The disc florets are yellow at first, but as in *A. ericoides*, change to purple. In spring, the young stems and foliage are also purple, the coloration persisting into summer. It fades to green in shaded situations.

The species itself is quite widely grown, is about 1m (3ft) tall, and there are several popular varieties. **'Horizontalis'** ♔ is dwarf (50cm/20in), compact and late flowering. The branches of its inflorescences are particularly widespreading. **'Lady in Black'** has larger flowerheads and is tall, at 1.25m (4ft). Stems and leaves hold their dark colour well. **'Prince'** is short (60cm/24in) and retains its dark foliage colour throughout the summer.

The *A. lateriflorus* hybrid **'Coombe Fishacre'** ♔ differs from the cultivars above in having flowerheads that are showier because of their relatively long ray florets of pale purple-pink. The foliage is green. Height is around 1m (3ft).

white flowerheads, about 2.5cm (1in) across, borne well above the foliage in airy corymbs. Plants are around 60cm (24in) tall, and the flowering stems arch over in delightful fashion almost to ground level. The leaves, heart-shaped and toothed, are distinctive in the genus.

A. eatonii is little grown, but deserves mention for being quite the earliest-flowering species in this group, and for remaining in bloom for a long period. Growing to about 1m (3ft) tall, its small sky-blue flowerheads from early to late summer.

A. ericoides is particularly easy to grow, produces well-branched flowering sprays in mid-autumn and has flowerheads 1.25cm (½in) across or less. The discs are yellow as the flowerheads open, but later change to purple.

'Blue Star' ♔ (1m/3ft) is lavender and comparatively late. **'Cinderella'** (75cm/30in) is white. **'Erlkönig'** (1.25m/4ft) is lavender-blue. **'Esther'** (50cm/20in) has relatively large pale purple-pink flowerheads to 2cm (¾in) across. **'Pink Cloud'** ♔ (1m/3ft) is pale purple-

The *Aster lateriflorus* hybrid 'Coombe Fishacre' ♀ approaching full flower at Old Court Nurseries near Malvern.

A. macrophyllus makes an interesting groundcover plant for dry, semi-shaded conditions. A fast-spreading plant with stiff stems, and up to 1m (3ft) high, it has large, heart-shaped leaves. The lavender-rayed flowerheads, 2.5cm (1in) across, are borne in late summer in open sprays.

A. pilosus is known in British gardens by one variety, **A. pilosus var. dentatus** ♀. This narrow-leaved plant, about 1.5m (5ft) tall, branches from near the bases of the stems. The flowerheads, about 1.5cm (just over ½in) across, are very freely produced in early autumn. The ray florets are white when young, but turn to purple-pink as they age. The discs are yellow.

A. ptarmicoides flowers in late summer. About 75cm (30in) tall, it has flowerheads 2cm (¾in) across with narrow white or cream ray florets, surrounding pale yellow or cream discs.

A. schreberi, a white-flowered species, is of similar habit and garden use to *A. macrophyllus* and like it, tolerates dry, semi-shaded conditions. Usually shorter, it has larger flowerheads, some exceeding 3cm (1¼in) across.

A. sedifolius (syn. *A. acris*). See p.76.

A. turbinellus hort ♀ is, with *A. × commixtus*, the largest-flowered of this group of species, with flowerheads up to 3cm (1¼in) across, each with up to 30 ray florets. The thin-stemmed plants reach up to 1.5m (5ft) in height, and need support. The flowering period is mid-autumn. This garden hybrid is thought to be the result of a cross between *A. novi-belgii* and *A. turbinellus* Lindl. It is mildew-susceptible.

Small-flowered cultivars

This group also contains a number of small-flowered cultivars, many of which have unknown or undisclosed parentage. In habit they are similar to *A. ericoides*. **'Herfstweelde'** ('Autumn Abundance'; 1.25m/4ft) flowers from mid- to late autumn, producing lavender-blue flowerheads, which are 3cm (1¼in) across. **'Hon. Vicary Gibbs'** (1.5m/5ft) has pale lavender-blue flowerheads, 2cm (¾in) across, from mid- to late autumn, and needs support. **'Ochtendgloren'** (syn. 'Pink Star') ♀ (1.25m/4ft) has mid-purple-pink flowerheads, 2.5cm (1in) across, in early to mid-autumn. **'Ringdove'** ♀ (1m/3ft) flowers from mid- to late autumn, producing flowerheads that are pale lavender and about 2cm (¾in) across.

Large-flowered European and Asian asters

It is not only the large size of the flowerheads that distinguishes the species in this group. Their combined flowering period extends over half the year, from the opening of the first *A. alpinus* in late spring to the time when the first hard frost of autumn curtails the display of other species. Among them, *A.* × *frikartii* is the most widely grown, but all are species of serious garden merit. *A. alpinus* and *A. thompsonii* var. *nanus* are fine rock garden plants.

All need a reasonably sunny situation and good soil drainage, the latter being particularly important for *A. amellus* and the two rock garden candidates. Support is not essential for any species, though for taller cultivars of *A. amellus* and *A.* × *frikartii* the effect of giving it might be preferred to letting the plants sprawl naturally. All should be divided and replanted every third year, immediately after flowering for *A. alpinus* and *A. tongolensis*, but in spring for others. Because *A. amellus* is particularly susceptible to aster wilt, it is best to replant on fresh soil. None of these species is susceptible to powdery mildew.

A. alpinus ♔ flowers in late spring and early summer on few-leaved stems up to 30cm (12in) tall. These bear the solitary flowerheads, up to 5cm (2in) across, above a mat of foliage. In the species, the ray florets surrounding the yellow disc are usually violet, but are white in **var. albus**. They are deep purple blue in **'Dunkle Schöne'** ('Dark Beauty'). **'Trimix'**, a seed-raised strain, is a mixture of white, shades of blue, and pink. A native of the Alps and Pyrenees, this species tends to be short-lived.

A. tongolensis is in many respects like a larger version of *A. alpinus*. A native of western China, it flowers in early summer, at a height of up to about 40cm (16in), and has flowerheads up to 6cm (2½in) across, with orange discs. Very free-flowering and quite undemanding, it is a good front-of-border plant, and a fine cut flower. **'Berggarten'** is lilac-blue. **'Wartburgstern'** is blue-violet, and comes true from seed.

A. thomsonii is known in cultivation only for its cultivar **'Nanus'**, which attains a height of up to 40cm (16in). A native of the Himalayas, it flowers freely over a long period. The flowerheads, solitary on well-branched stems, are up to 5cm (2in) across. The narrow lavender-blue ray florets are relatively few, giving the individual flowerheads an airy quality.

'Veilchenkönigin' ('Violet Queen') ♔ is a cultivar of the large-flowered European native, *Aster amellus*.

A. amellus (Italian aster, Italian starwort) is native to a large area of central and southern Europe, and to south-western Asia. Flowering starts in late summer or early autumn and continues into mid-autumn. The flowerheads, borne in loose, more or less flat-topped corymbs, are up to 7cm (3in) across and last well when cut.

Of the many cultivars, the dwarfest (40cm/16in) is **'Veilchenkönigin'** ('Violet Queen') ♔. Relatively late flowering, its flowerheads have deep violet ray florets. **'Blue King'** (60cm/24in), violet-blue, and **'King George'** ♔ (60cm/24in), purple-blue, are both particularly large flowered. **'Rudolph Goethe'** (75cm/30in) has lavender flowerheads.

Four good purple-pink cultivars are **'Brilliant'** (60cm/24in), **'Jacqueline Genebrier'** ♔ (75cm/30in) late, **'Rosa Erfüllung'** ('Pink Zenith'; 50cm/20in) late and rather paler in colour, and **'Sonia'** (45cm/18in) large-flowered and late.

A. × ***frikartii*** is a Swiss hybrid of garden origin between *A. amellus* and *A. thomsonii*. It is the most popular of all *Aster* species, other than the Michaelmas daisies. More robust and less susceptible to winter loss than either of its

PLATE V
China Asters and Other Annuals

Callistephus chinensis
'Pompon Mixed'

Callistephus chinensis
'Giant Princess'

Callistephus chinensis
'Tiger Paw Sea Star Mixed'

Callistephus chinensis
'Compliment White' and
'Compliment Light Blue'

All plants shown at approximately half lifesize

Centaurea cyanus
Florence Series

Callistephus chinensis
'Matsumoto'

Callistephus chinensis
'Single Mixed'

Ageratum houstonianum
'Florist Blue'

Unusually for its genus, *Aster sedifolius* flowerheads are fragrant. This is the relatively short cultivar 'Nanus'.

parents, it has a very long flowering period, from mid-summer to mid-autumn.

'Mönch' ♔ is the most widely grown cultivar. Named after the sister peak of the Eiger, it has flowerheads up to 8cm (3in) across, with pale lavender ray florets, and is up to 1m (3ft) tall. It has been rated by Graham Stuart Thomas, that doyen of garden writers, as the 'finest perennial aster'. 'Wunder von Stäfa' ♔ is closely similar while 'Flora's Delight' is just 50cm (20in) tall, and has smaller flowerheads with lilac rays.

A. pyrenaeus is akin to a small-flowered version of *A. × frikartii*, but is much later flowering, beginning in early autumn. Its pale lilac-blue flowerheads are about 4cm (1½in) across, but very freely produced on plants around 60cm (24in) tall. The cultivar 'Lutetia' is the sole representative of the species in commerce.

Other European species

Two species, which belong to none of the preceding groups, remain. Both European natives, the first is interesting rather than outstandingly garden-worthy, but *A. sedifolius*, the second, is one of the finest species in the entire genus.

A. linosyris (Goldilocks) is sometimes described as the only yellow-flowered member of the genus, but the claim is rather spurious, as it achieves this by having no ray florets. The erect, unbranched leafy stems attain a height of 60cm (24in). The deep yellow flowerheads, 2cm (¾in) across, are borne in dense corymbs in early autumn. It is found in the wild in dry soil conditions, and is naturalized in Britain.

A. sedifolius (syn. *A. acris*) is for me among the special joys of the genus. The erect stems, clothed with narrow leaves, branch repeatedly with the approach of the flowering period – late summer and early autumn. A prodigious floral display is produced across the broad top of the plant. The individual flowerheads are up to 3.5cm (1½in) across and are fragrant. The blue to lilac-pink ray florets are widely spaced round the small, yellow disc as there are no more than a dozen per flowerhead.

A. sedifolius is vigorous, long-lived and easy to grow. Division every third or fourth year is sufficiently frequent. It is not susceptible to powdery mildew. The species grows up to 1.25m (4ft) tall, and needs support just as most New York Michaelmas daisies do because of the weight of the inflorescences. The cultivar 'Nanus', with lavender-blue rays, is more widely grown, its height not exceeding 50cm (20in).

BOLTONIA

This North American genus of five species is distinct from the 250 or so in *Aster* for details of serious botanical importance, but horticulturally it can be regarded simply as an extension of it. Just one species is cultivated, *B. asteroides*.

B. asteroides is a fully hardy herbaceous perennial that is easy to cultivate and propagate (as for Michaelmas daisies). The species is a plant for owners of large gardens, owing to its height, 2–2.5m (6½–8ft), but there is one much shorter cultivar – 'Nana'. The flowerheads are very freely produced in large panicles from late summer to mid-autumn. Similar to Michaelmas daisies, they are either white or lilac to purple, are individually small, only 2cm (¾in) across, and have narrow rays around a small, yellow disc. They are good cut flowers.

'Snowbank', white-flowered of course, is 1.5–2m (5–6½ft) tall. **var. latisquama** has slightly larger flowerheads, which are white or bluish-violet. Its white-flowered cultivar 'Nana' is only about 75cm (30in) tall.

Boltonia will thrive in full sun or partial shade. All but 'Nana' need support. Plants are best divided every other year to remain vigorous. Like *Aster novi-belgii*, they are susceptible to powdery mildew.

KALIMERIS

The species of this small, Asian genus, closely related to *Aster*, were once placed in the even smaller genus, *Boltonia*, which is if anything more closely related still. Partly because of the similarity of the starry flowerheads to those of the smaller-flowered *Aster* species, until recently *Kalimeris* has had scant attention from gardeners. In the 1990s, however, *K. yomena* 'Shogun' emerged from Japan.

Kalimeris does best in full sun, but is fully hardy and easy to grow. Tolerance of particularly moist soils is a feature. Propagate by division in spring.

K. yomena 'Shogun' is a fine cultivar. The small, white-variegated leaves on a compact, bushy plant have a pronounced pink tinge when young and this is retained to some extent as they mature. The foliage alone makes it a valuable addition to the herbaceous flora. About 60cm (24in) tall, it produces an abundance of small, pale lilac flowerheads in large panicles through late summer and well into the autumn.

K. incisa, much less widely available, is similar but with green foliage and dark stems. It begins flowering in early summer and continues until early autumn. The florets are light purple. **'Alba'** is a white-flowered cultivar.

HETEROPAPPUS

Like *Kalimeris*, this is a small Asian genus, closely related to *Aster*. Only two species are currently available and both are easily cultivated, hardy plants. The perennial *H. altaicus* is grown as for the small-flowered species of *Aster*, and *H. meyendorffii*, a biennial, may be raised from seed sown outdoors in early summer. Alternative practices are to sow in a greenhouse either in early autumn, over-wintering the young plants very cool, or in heat in midwinter, in both cases planting out in spring.

H. altaicus grows to about 40cm (16in), and produces flowerheads to 5cm (2cm) across in autumn. The ray florets are purple, the disc yellow.

H. meyendorffii makes spreading bush-like plants 30cm (12in) tall, similar in character and size to the modern garden chrysanthemums. The blue-rayed flowerheads cover the plants in autumn. Up to 4cm (1½in) across, they also have yellow discs.

CALLISTEPHUS China aster

The plant breeders have been hard at work for many decades on the single species in the genus *Callistephus*, and it has proved a rewarding exercise. Nicholson's *Illustrated Dictionary of Gardening*, published in 1884, listed eleven classes of China aster cultivars, defined by form and size of flower, and by height. There is today a still wider range of flower forms and sizes on plants between just 25cm (10in) and around 75cm (30in) tall.

A distinctive feature of the China aster is the clarity of its colours – pinks, reds, blues, violet and white. The dwarf cultivars are suitable for containers and as bedding plants, while relatively tall ones are among the most attractive annual cut flowers in any plant family. As a bedding plant, it is quite slow to come into flower, not making its floral mark until late summer and early autumn. This is not to be taken entirely as a negative feature, though: there is definitely something to be said for the freshness of a later addition to the summer display.

Whatever its place in the garden, cultivation is straightforward enough. Although it is just about hardy enough to be sown outdoors in mid-spring in climates such as that of southern Britain, it is generally better treated as a half hardy annual. Any reasonably fertile soil in a situation that gets some sun will suffice, but this is not a plant for naturally dry soils. The taller cultivars need support.

One pest is of particular remark: aphids commonly establish themselves on young plants, often before planting out. They can check development quite severely, and control by spraying is very advisable. Aster wilt (see p.65) is soil borne, and once it occurs no attempt should be made to grow susceptible cultivars – the great majority – for at least seven years in the same soil. Cutting through the stems of a suspected victim just above soil level will reveal a brown ring of diseased tissue if wilting is caused by the fungal pathogen responsible for this disease.

C. chinensis is a branched, erect plant with dark green, coarsely toothed leaves. In its wild state, the flowerheads, to 13cm (5in) across, are white, mauve or violet with a yellow disc. The height of the cultivars below, where not otherwise mentioned, is 60–75cm (24–30in) and likewise flowerheads are double and up to 10–13cm (4–5in) in diameter.

Chrysanthemum-flowered cultivars have broad and slightly incurving ray florets. Of these, the dwarf **Milady Series** ♔ (25–30cm/10–12in) is very popular as a bedding plant.

Ray florets are quilled in a number of cultivars, such as **'Nova'**, **'Quadrille'** and the dwarf **'Teisa Stars'** (25cm/10in). They are incurving as well in the **'Tiger Paw Sea Star'** varieties.

The well-known **Ostrich Plume Series** has characteristically narrow and reflexing ray florets and is resistant to aster wilt. Among other variations in form of flowerhead are the pompons, about 5cm (2in) across. Cultivars of this type include **'Lilliput'** (30–40cm/12–16in). Those with conventional single flowers, such as **'Madeleine'**, are closest to the wild form. As cut flowers, their simplicity is their particular charm.

Much smaller-flowered are the modern semi-double **'Matsumoto'**, **'Serenade'** and **'Fan'** series. These have repeatedly branched stems and are very free-flowering indeed, with flowerheads about 5cm (2in) across. Most of the China asters currently grown commercially for cut flowers are of this type.

The flowerheads of the near prostrate *Erigeron karvinskianus* ♔ are like lawn daisies but even prettier.

ERIGERON

This is a large genus – over 150 species – comprising mostly herbaceous perennials, although a few species are annual or biennial. Many of the perennials are available from nurseries, but as most are low-growing natives of mountainous terrain, the great majority are almost exclusively the preserve of alpine-gardening enthusiasts. Two of these species are commonly seen though, *E. glaucus* and the pretty *E. karvinskianus*, an outstanding near-prostrate plant for dry stone walls, rock gardens and crevices in paving. There is also a group of fine garden hybrids mainly derived from *E. speciosus*. These – mostly 50–60cm (20–24in) tall – are widely grown as border plants, flowering mainly in early to midsummer. Their flowerheads, like those of the other *Erigeron* species described, are among the daintiest of the daisies on account of the large number of very slender ray florets in two or more rows. They are excellent cut flowers, though they should be allowed first to open fully on the plant.

All species described are easy to grow, given well-drained soil. They all do best in full sun. Propagation is usually carried out by division in spring (not autumn). The garden hybrids benefit from this every second or third year. While the species can also be propagated by seed, the garden hybrids do not generally come true, though seed of a few is available commercially.

The species and garden hybrids described below are all hardy herbaceous perennials.

Species and cultivars

E. glaucus is known as the beach aster in its native area, the Pacific seaboard of the USA. It has a tufted habit, with stout, sprawling stems, sparsely branched, but densely furnished with grey-green leaves up to 15cm (6in) long. Flowerheads, at a height of about 30cm (12in), are freely produced from late spring to midsummer. They are solitary or in few-flowered inflorescences, and are up to 6cm (2½in) in diameter, with lilac to violet ray florets and a yellow disc. Very much at home in rock gardens and dry stone walls, this is also a good front-of-border plant. Left undisturbed, individual plants can spread very widely. It is very salt-tolerant and is popular among coastal gardeners.

'Albus' is a white-flowered cultivar. **'Elstead Pink'** is deep pink. **'Roseus'** (syn. 'Seabreeze') is lilac-pink.

E. karvinskianus ♔, sometimes sold under the cultivar name **'Profusion'**, has slender, much-branched stems

Erigeron glaucus 'Elstead Pink' looks particularly well tumbling over the edge of a retaining wall.

that are prostrate except near their growing points. The plant spreads vigorously. Freely produced from late spring to early autumn, the flowerheads are about the size of a common lawn daisy, but the ray florets are slenderer and more numerous. These are white as the flowerheads open, and change colour prettily as they age, first to pink and then to purple.

This is much the most widely seen species suitable for rock gardens. Although native to Central America, it overwinters successfully in Britain. However, it can become invasive in mild areas and self sows in many gardens.

Of other dwarf species, all flowering in summer, **E. aurantiacus** has semi-double, orange flowerheads, up to 5cm (2in) across. Growing to 30cm (12in), it is too big for smaller rock gardens. It is usually short-lived.

E. chrysopsidis 'Grand Ridge' ♔ has rather smaller, deep yellow flowerheads and is only 5cm (2in) tall.

E. compositus and **E. leiomerus**, from the Rocky Mountains, are 15cm (6in) tall, and have small flowerheads, around 2cm (¾in) across. The rays are white or pale blue in *E. compositus* and lavender-violet in *E. leiomerus*.

Garden hybrids

A number of species have been involved in the parentage of these popular plants, the most significant being *E. speciosus*, now rarely seen in cultivation. This is a native of mountain areas in the north-west of the USA. Other species include *E. glaucus* and *E. aurantiacus* (see above). The hybrids form compact leafy clumps, and the numerous branched stems, leafy and slender, bear flowerheads that are solitary or in few-flowered corymbs, according to cultivar. There is a large number of these, some of the best and more widely available being tabulated below in approximate order of height. 'Dimity', 'Dignity' and 'Charity' were raised by the famous Norfolk nurseryman and writer Alan Bloom.

Cultivar	Colour	Height	Comments
'Dimity'	Bright pink	25cm (10in)	Short-lived
'Azurfee' ('Azure Fairy')	Lavender-blue	45cm (18in)	
'Dignity'	Violet-mauve	50cm (20in)	Early
'Charity'	Light lilac-pink	60cm (24in)	Early
'Dunkelste Aller' ('Darkest of All') ♔	Dark violet	60cm (24in)	Late
'Foerster's Liebling' ('Foerster's Darling') ♔	Deep reddish-pink	60cm (24in)	
'Quakeress'	White, flushed pink	60cm (24in)	Needs support
'Rosa Juwel' ('Pink Jewel')	Pale, bright pink	60cm (24in)	
'Schwarzes Meer' ('Black Sea')	Deep violet	60cm (24in)	
'White Quakeress'	White	60cm (24in)	Needs support

TOWNSENDIA

T. formosa, the best-known species of this American genus, has a good deal of similarity with the garden hybrids of *Erigeron*, producing flowerheads, 5cm (2in) across, in early summer, each with numerous narrow ray florets. These are violet, surrounding a yellow disc. The two genera are indeed quite closely related.

T. formosa is an erect plant about 40cm (16in) tall when in flower, and is suitable for front-of-border positions as well as larger rock gardens. The flowerheads are solitary. A rhizomatous perennial, it is fully hardy, but needs good drainage.

There are a number of attractive dwarfer species of particular interest to alpine plant enthusiasts. Although perennial, they are often short-lived. They too need good drainage, and some are also best sheltered from winter rain. They are sometimes grown in alpine houses. *T. rothrockii* is the most widely available. No more than 10cm (4in) high, and with leaves in rosettes, its flowerheads are about 4cm (1½in) across, with violet-blue rays and a wide yellow disc.

PLATE VI
Herbaceous Perennials 1

Aster eatonii

Erigeron
'Quakeress'

Echinacea
purpurea

Echinacea purpurea 'White Swan'

All plants shown at approximately
half lifesize

Erigeron glaucus
'Roseus'

Erigeron glaucus 'Elstead Pink'

Leucanthemum × superbum 'Aglaia'

Anthemis 'Sauce Hollandaise'

Leucanthemum × superbum 'Mount Everest'

Leucanthemum × superbum 'Droitwich Beauty'

Aster schreberi

9 Chrysanthemums and their Allies

The members of all the nine genera grouped here with *Chrysanthemum* are not only closely related in botanical terms, but in bygone years were actually placed within that genus. In the second half of the twentieth century, a great deal of reorganization of species into their current genera was carried out, necessarily but sadly at the price of confusing gardeners and nurserymen. The path of re-classification has not been smooth, and there have been several further renamings.

Gardeners whose interest in the genus *Chrysanthemum* extends back to the 1970s or 1980s – or even the earlier 1990s – are likely to have suffered a good deal of confu-

sion concerning what now correctly counts as a chrysanthemum and what does not. The following short digest of changes in classification may prove helpful.

In the 1950s, as a horticultural student, I learnt that in *Chrysanthemum* belonged the plants known to gardeners as marguerites, or Paris daisies (then *C. frutescens*), pyrethrum (then *C. coccineum*), feverfew (then *C. parthenium*) and the ox-eye and shasta daisies (then *C. leucathemum* and *C. maximum* respectively). All these, and a great many more besides, have since been moved to other genera at various times. For example, *C. frutescens* has been moved to *Argyranthemum*, *C. coccineum* and *C. parthenium* are now in *Tanacetum*, and the ox-eye and shasta daisies, so ubiquitous in early and midsummer, are now in *Leucanthemum*. The botanical arguments that have led to

Chrysanthemum Rubellum hybrid 'Clara Curtis' makes a pretty show at the Pershore garden of the Hardy Plant Society.

these changes are too complex to explain here.

Unfortunately, some species have been re-named more than once. (In the introduction to *Rhodanthemum*, which is now the correct genus for the former *C. hosmariense*, you may read a horror story of its kind.) More unfortunately still, in 1961, the parental species of the numerous varieties that constitute florists' chrysanthemums as garden and greenhouse varieties are collectively termed, were grouped into *Dendranthema* by a Russian botanist. His proposed changes became internationally adopted, but in 1997, following widespread protest, an authoritative decision was taken to return them to *Chrysanthemum*. Their restoration is being followed by the removal of the annual chrysanthemum species to the genus *Ismelia*.

The marguerites – genus *Argyranthemum* – have been much boosted in popularity by the ever-wider enthusiasm for container gardening. A large number of new cultivars were introduced in the 1980s and 1990s, and, lack of hardiness notwithstanding, this continues to be a genus well regarded by almost every garden lover. As already mentioned, *Leucanthemum* and *Tanacetum coccineum* give us the shasta and ox-eye daisies and the garden pyrethrums respectively, fine border plants all. *Leucanthemella* and *Nipponanthemum* provide distinctive white daisies in the autumn. In *Tanacetum* again and in the too often re-named *Rhodanthemum*, there is a number of fine rock garden plants. *Ajania* and – yet again – *Tanacetum* provide notable foliage plants.

Species formerly classified in *Chrysanthemum*

Old name	New genus
C. carinatum	*Ismelia*
C. coccineum	*Tanacetum*
C. coronarium	*Ismelia*
C. frutescens	*Argyranthemum*
C. catananche	*Rhodanthemum*
C. foeniculaceum	*Argyranthemum*
C. hosmariense	*Rhodanthemum*
C. leucanthemum	*Leucanthemum*
C. maximum	*Leucanthemum*
C. multicaule	*Coleostephus*
C. nipponicum	*Nipponanthemum*
C. pacificum	*Ajania*
C. paludosum	*Leucanthemum*
C. parthenium	*Tanacetum*
C. segetum	*Ismelia*
C. serotinum	*Leucanthemella*
C. uliginosum	*Leucanthemella*

CHRYSANTHEMUM

Worldwide, the chrysanthemum is quite the best-known and best-loved genus in the entire daisy family. Records of its cultivation in China go back at least to 500BC. In our times, it is one of the world's top three cut flowers, sharing the distinction with the rose and the carnation, neither of which begin to match its lasting qualities.

Many of the name changes described above have simplified this genus for our purposes. As a horticulturist, I am glad about what botanists have done, despite the inconvenience of learning new names. In *Chrysanthemum*, there remain the many varieties of florists' chrysanthemums, the Rubellum and Korean hybrids, and the garden chrysanthemums ('garden mums'). Additionally, there is a number of species, of which only two concern us here. Of all these, only the florists' chrysanthemums are insufficiently cold-resistant to be treated as ordinary hardy border perennials.

Hardy herbaceous perennials

Apart from the hardy hybrids mentioned above, there is a small number of old spray-flowered varieties of uncertain origin, characterized by a hardiness that sets them aside from the wide range of florist varieties.

All of these hardy chrysanthemums can be regarded as straightforward herbaceous perennials, usually multiplied (or rejuvenated) by division in early spring every second or third year. All are valuable for their autumn floral display, and the Korean and Rubellum hybrids also for their excellence as cut flowers. The modern 'garden' chrysanthemums are not more than 40cm (16in) tall, and densely branched. This makes them candidates for the front of borders and for containers.

All can be planted out in spring, as divisions of older plants or as rooted cuttings. Once individual stems reach a height of about 20cm (8in), branching is usefully encouraged by pinching out the top centimetre or two. For garden chrysanthemums, the same treatment can be given to any of the resulting side shoots that reach about 10cm (4in) in length at any time until two weeks after the longest day of the year. Once this date has been reached, they should be left in peace.

Korean and Rubellum hybrids that are expected to attain 75cm (30in) or more are usually best given support. The stems of most shorter varieties will stay upright without assistance in reasonably sheltered gardens, especially if flanking plants can be counted on to prevent collapse in autumn winds.

After the first hard frosts have killed any remaining flowers, plants are best cut down to about 10cm (4in) above the soil surface. The garden mums are an exception to this: they are more safely left as they are until new shoot growth is visible round the base of the plant in spring. In cold areas a dry mulch to protect the bases of the plants from damage by severe frost is worthwhile. If the soil lies wet in winter, particularly in colder areas, lifting and transfer to a coldframe or a greenhouse may prove a worthwhile insurance. Garden mums in containers can be overwintered in them, but they should be plunged into soil or chipped bark to protect the root system from being frozen. For all the herbaceous perennial chrysanthemums, in addition to division, propagation may be by cuttings, easily rooted in spring, or, for the species, seed.

C. weyrichii is very dwarf, 15–20cm (6–8in) in height, and when established develops into a loose-growing mat. Spreading by rhizomes, it is most often grown in rock gardens. It flowers freely in late summer and early autumn, producing pink or white flowerheads up to 5cm (2in) across. They have a distinctive appearance because the ray florets are not close enough together to overlap and create a continuous circle round the yellow disc. It is native to the far east of the former Soviet Union, and to the Sakhalin Islands.

C. yezoense (syn. *C. arcticum* hort) ♛ is a fairly similar Japanese species, but grows rather taller, usually to about 30cm (12in). It produces a mass of white flowers up to 5cm (2in) across in early autumn, and is a very fine front-of-border plant at that time. As with most chrysanthemums, its foliage is rather dull, and it is best among neighbours that direct attention away from it in the summer. There is a pink-flowered form **'Roseum'**.

The **Rubellum hybrids** are derived from another species of similarly unquestionable hardiness, native to Japan, Korea, China and Manchuria. Called *C. zawadskii*, it is much taller and larger flowered than *C. weyrichii* and *C. yezoense*.

The hybrids flower in early to mid-autumn, and the terms 'early' and 'late' in the descriptions refer to this period. They have attractively pinnatisect foliage. Flower size is up to 7cm (3in) across.

Cultivars include: **'Clara Curtis'**, which is pink, single and 70cm (28in) high; **'Duchess of Edinburgh'**, a wine-red, semi-double of 60cm (24in) high; **'Emperor of China'**, which has silvery old rose, double flowers, with quilled ray florets. Growing to 1.25m (4ft), it is late to flower and its foliage colours very attractively at the same time. **'Paul Boissier'** is a late, bronze double of 75cm (30in) high. Also late is **'Innocence'**, which is very pale pink, single and 60cm (24in) high. **'Mary Stoker'** is a rose-tinted, apricot-yellow – a lovely colour. Its flowerheads are single and early. It reaches 75cm (30in) in height.

The **Korean hybrids** arose in the USA during the 1930s as a result of hybridization between *C. coreanum* and a florists' chrysanthemum. They branch freely, and many of the varieties are dwarfer than the Rubellum hybrids. Only one is now still much seen. This is **'Wedding Day'** with its white ray florets and green disc. It is single, 75cm (30in) high and late. Another is **'Ruby Mound'** – a ruby-red double, which flowers mid-season and attains 45cm (18in).

The **garden mums** have been developed by selection and breeding from the Korean hybrids. They are characterized by hardiness, dwarfness – 25–40cm (10–16in) tall – and repeated branching. A large number of varieties had been introduced by the year 2000, first by the American breeders, Yoder Brothers, and then by a British company, Cleangro. Many more are expected to follow. They all flower in early and mid-autumn, when the densely bushy plants are covered with numerous flowerheads up to 6cm (2½in) across. Those listed below are among the plethora of good varieties. They are all double-flowered, except where stated.

Early autumn-flowering selection: **'Action'** copper-bronze; **'Braque'** small, pink and white; **'Bravo'** ♛ red; **'Debonair'** ♛ lavender; **'Harvest Emily'** orange; **'Hockney'** small, pink and white, single; **'Holly'** ♛ yellow, pompon; **'Pitstop'** small, white, anemone-centred; **'Popcorn'** small, yellow, single; **'Wizard'** creamy-white.

Mid-autumn-flowering selection: **'Fiery Barbara'** small, red-bronze, pompon; **'Firecracker'** yellow; **'Glamour'** dark pink, pompon; **'Linda'** white; **'Matisse'** small, pink, quilled and anemone-centred; **'Picasso'** small, peach; **'Raquel'** deep maroon-red; **'Sarah'** bronze, quilled; **'Sunny Linda'** yellow; **'Tripoli' family** small, purple, red, white and yellow, single.

In addition to the garden chrysanthemums and the Rubellum and Korean hybrids, there are other varieties of comparable hardiness, that behave satisfactorily when treated as hardy herbaceous perennials. In particular, there are a few older pompon types. These include: **'Anastasia'**, introduced in 1915, which is soft heather-pink, 60cm (24in) high and flowers mid-autumn; **'Mei-Kyo'**, which is darker with smaller, later flowers and is 75cm (30in), and its sport **'Bronze Elegance'**; and **'Nantyderry Sunshine'** ♛, which is yellow, 60cm (24in) high and early.

There are also a few other hardy cultivars. Among these are: **'Anne, Lady Brockett'** a single, pink, reaching 75cm (30in); **'Cottage Apricot'**, which is 60cm (24in) tall but may need support; and the orange-red **'Rumpelstilzchen'**, 75cm (30in).

Florists' chrysanthemums

Several thousand varieties of florists' chrysanthemums are in current cultivation. Botanically, they are grouped as *C. × grandiflorum*, but in their parentage *C. indicum* and a number of other Far Eastern species have been involved. They have been developed – initially in China and Japan – over many centuries, with the first varieties recorded as arriving in Europe in the seventeenth century. All are herbaceous perennials with woody-based stems and flower naturally from late summer to early winter, according to variety. Many are suitable only for greenhouse culture, mainly because outdoors their flowering time would result in the spoiling of the flowerheads by frost and autumnal rain and wind. The smaller-flowered varieties are outstanding as cut flowers. Their cultivation is outside the scope of this book, but Appendix VI lists publications which cover it comprehensively.

The cultivars flowering before the risk of flower damage by frost still cannot be confidently regarded as hardy in most gardens, though on freely drained soils in areas with relatively mild winters many will usually survive. Even so, the best results with these are only to be had by annual propagation from cuttings taken in spring from parent plants overwintered in a greenhouse or frame.

ISMELIA Annual chrysanthemums

Although now correctly under a different generic name, this small group of good-natured free-flowering plants will surely continue to be known as annual chrysanthemums for the forseeable future. The three species described give a long-lasting garden display, stretching from early summer to early autumn if deadheading is maintained. They are also good cut flowers. All three are very easy to grow, and all are hardy. They do best in a light soil and in a situation where they receive full sun, but usually do well in less favourable environments, too – though *I. segetum* prefers acid soils.

They are most commonly sown where they are to grow, but if you choose to raise plants in greenhouse or frame for subsequent planting out, minimize root disturbance by growing the seedlings in pots or cell trays. Sowing *in situ* should be in early or mid-spring, and the seedlings thinned to (or planted out at) about 15cm (6in) apart. In areas with mild winters and if the soil is well-drained, particularly large and early-flowering plants result from sowing very early in the autumn.

These plants only require weed control and – ideally – regular deadheading. Aphids quite commonly infest them, and powdery mildew may also trouble them.

I. carinata, the painted daisy, is the most widely grown of the species. A Moroccan native, in cultivation it makes a bushy plant usually 50–60cm (20–24in) in height, bearing flowerheads up to 7cm (3in) across on stiff stems. The leaves are bright green, almost succulent, and finely lobed. In the wild plant, the ray florets are white or yellow, with the bases of the rays often of another colour, so that a contrasting circular zone surrounds the purple disc. Selection in cultivars has resulted in a colour range from white and yellow to pink, orange, bronze, scarlet and maroon. Immediately round the central disc, all the flowerheads have a narrow, yellow zone, and many a broader zone of another colour around this. Seed is usually sold in a colour mixture, such as **Court Jesters**. The cultivar **'German Flag'** is a striking deep red with a yellow zone around the disc. If *I. carinata* were difficult to grow, it would be given a great deal more attention by gardening enthusiasts!

I. coronaria is a Mediterranean native of broadly similar description, somewhat later in coming into flower, and with rather smaller flowerheads, 4–5cm (1½–2in) across. They are yellow. **'Primrose Gem'** is semi-double, with pale yellow ray florets and a deep yellow disc. The foliage of **var. *spatiosa*** is widely used in oriental cuisine, as chop suey greens.

I. segetum is the corn marigold, and is also native to the Mediterranean area. It has become naturalized all over

Europe, including the British Isles. In the past it was a common weed of cornfields. Again, broadly similar in habit to *I. carinata,* its flowerheads are golden-yellow, and about 6cm (2½in) across. **'Prado'** differs in having slightly larger flowers with a dark reddish-brown disc.

ARGYRANTHEMUM Marguerite, Paris daisy

The popularity of container gardening has done great things for the profile of *Argyranthemum.* These slightly tender evergreen shrubs, native to the Canary Islands and Madeira, have enjoyed public regard as summer bedding since late Victorian times. However, for general gardeners, the relatively high cost of the plants, coupled with the need for a greenhouse to maintain them from one summer to the next, went against their becoming a garden favourite. Furthermore, the size that plants often attained within three months of planting did not always commend them where lack of space was a consideration. In containers, growth is still vigorous but lacks the sometimes unwanted exuberance that may occur in plants that have a free root run in beds or borders. Perhaps more importantly, a different psychology applies to the willingness to spend money on plants for container gardening.

A number of fine introductions have also helped further gardening interest in the genus. In 1981 *A. gracile* 'Chelsea Girl' was collected in Tenerife by Dr James Compton, then head gardener of the Chelsea Physic Garden. In 1987 Roy Cheek of Cannington College collected *A. foeniculaceum* 'Royal Haze', also in Tenerife. The popular cultivar 'Mary Cheek' was raised by him and is named after his wife. All three plants received an AGM ♔ at the Wisley trial of the genus in 1993.

The flowers of *Argyranthemum* – white, yellow or pink – are freely produced throughout summer and continue until the first frosts. The delightful froth of finely cut foliage, in and just above which these are borne, is a very important part of the appeal. Over a hundred cultivars are currently available, but unfortunately mis-naming is common: over 20 per cent of those submitted for trials at Wisley were mis-identified by the senders.

In the great majority of gardens, the marguerites are grown as half hardy bedding plants, just like fuchsias or zonal pelargoniums (geraniums). Plants for setting out in late spring, after frost risk has passed, are raised from cuttings taken late in the previous summer or early autumn, or from parent plants in greenhouses in late winter.

The plants do best in sunny positions, and although accommodating in the matter of soil, thrive most on naturally drier types. They are undamaged by salt carried in the wind close to coasts. In areas with mild winters, they will often overwinter successfully in favoured situations close to a wall: if serious frost damage does occur, they may well re-grow from the base, which should be protected with a wide, deep collar of a dry mulch material – chipped bark for example – put in position in autumn.

Young plants should be encouraged to branch by pinching out the growing points. Deadheading is, as ever, beneficial and rewards the time spent on it. When a flush of flowers has occurred, as it comes to an end, shears can be put to effective use for this purpose. If container-grown plants are to be overwintered in a greenhouse, frost exclusion alone will suffice. They will flower through autumn and winter if kept sufficiently warm: probably 7°C (45°F) at night and 12°C (54°F) by day would be the minimum requirement for continuity.

Propagation by tip cuttings is easily achieved. Make cuttings about 6 or 7cm (2½–3in) long from base to growing point. Once well rooted, the young plants are usually grown on in individual pots. A little artificial heat is very advantageous: 5°C (41°F) is enough. Aphids, leaf miners and capsid bugs may all feed on marguerites. In

'Summer Stars Pink' is one of the many *Argyranthemum* varieties introduced late in the twentieth century.

The number of flowerheads compensates for their small size in *Argyranthemum* 'Sugar Baby'.

Plant	Flowerheads	Foliage and habit
A. foeniculaceum 'Royal Haze' ♔	Small	Blue-grey, very fine
A. gracile 'Chelsea Girl' ♔	Small	Grey-green, very fine
A. maderense	Pale primrose, small	Blue-green, compact
'Butterfly' ♔	Creamy yellow	Grey-green
'Cornish Gold' ♔	Pale yellow, large	Grey-green
'Dana'	Very small	Grey-green, compact
'Double White'	Anemone-centred	Blue-green, vigorous
'Jamaica Primrose' ♔	Pale yellow, large	Vigorous
'Mary Cheek' ♔	Pink, double, small	Grey-green, compact
'Petite Pink' ♔	Pink, small	Grey-green
'Sugar Baby'	Small, copious	Compact
'Sugar Buttons'	Anemone-centred	Compact
'Summer Stars Pink'	Pink, anemone-centred	Blue-green, compact
'Vancouver' ♔	Pink, anemone-centred, large	Greyish-green

late spring and summer, red spider mites may be troublesome to plants under glass: if possible, move them outside where, in the cooler conditions, this pest problem does not usually persist.

Species and cultivars

There are over twenty species, of which only a few are widely cultivated. In conditions corresponding to their native environment, mature plants achieve heights between one and two metres (3–6½ft), with a spread at least equal to the height. Grown as half hardy plants, propagated afresh each year, heights usually range from 30 to 75cm (12–30in), and spreads from 50–100cm (20–40in) according to cultivar and growing conditions. Flowerheads are 2.5–7.5cm (1–3in) across, and are sometimes solitary but more often several together in loose corymbs. In all cultivated species and in cultivars the leaves are pinnatisect, with the segments varying from comparatively broad, as in *A. maderense*, to fine, as in *A. foeniculaceum* (the name means fennel-like), to almost thread-like in *A. gracile*.

In the selection below, unless otherwise indicated, flowerheads are single, ray florets are white, discs are yellow, leaves are straightforwardly green and plants in beds grow to 50–75cm (20–30in) tall (less in containers). Discs of all species and single-flowered cultivars are yellow. My own preference lies very much with the singles, for the greater grace of their flowers, complementing the unquestionably graceful foliage.

LEUCANTHEMUM Ox-eye daisy, Shasta daisy

This particular genus is without peer as the gardener's white daisy. The generic name translates quite simply from Greek as 'white flower', and all of its two dozen or so species fit the description, deviating only as far as a tinge of pink in some and of pale yellow in others. In the daisy family, only *Celmisia* is a serious challenger for whiteness, but it is in quite another league in popularity.

Species and cultivars

Just two species and one hybrid are generally cultivated. *L.* × *superbum* (formerly *Chrysanthemum maximum*) is one of the most widely grown of all herbaceous perennials and *L. vulgare* (formerly *C. leucanthemum*) is extensively used for naturalizing. Both are hardy, and both are good cut flowers. *L. paludosum* (syn. *Chrysanthemum paludosum*), is a very much smaller plant, usually grown as a half hardy annual. All three are easy to cultivate.

L. × **superbum**, the shasta daisy, is a hybrid between *L. lacustre*, native to Portugal, and *L. maximum*, from the Pyrenees. Both are similar to *L. vulgare*. The hybrid is a stiff-stemmed, hairless herbaceous perennial, with thick, dark green, lanceolate leaves, up to 20cm (8in) long. The flowerheads, up to 10cm (4in) across, are borne singly on stems up to 1m (3ft) in height. The long-lasting display starts in early summer, and is usually followed by a good second flush in early autumn.

The 2000–2001 edition of the *RHS Plant Finder* lists around 40 cultivars available in Britain. The following selection embraces the main variations in height and flower form: the flowers are single with white rays and yellow discs unless otherwise stated; 'fringed' means that the outer ends of the ray florets are divided lengthways into very narrow pointed strips.

Cultivar	Height	Flowerheads
'Aglaia' ♀	75cm (30in)	Semi-double, fringed
'Beauté Nivelloise'	1m (3ft)	Double, narrow rays
'Bishopstone'	75cm (30in)	Fringed
'Cobham Gold'	60cm (24in)	Fully double, central florets yellow
'Droitwich Beauty'	40cm (16in)	Fringed, anemone-centred
'Esther Read'	50–60cm (20–24in)	Semi-double
'Horace Read'	60cm (24in)	Double
'Mount Everest'	75cm (30in)	Large, classic single
'Phyllis Smith'	75cm (30in)	Ray florets twisted and recurved
'Silberprinzesschen' ('Silver Princess')	40cm (16in)	Comes true from seed
'Snow Lady'	30–40cm (12–16in)	Comes true from seed
'Sonnenschein' ('Sunshine')	80cm (32in)	Creamy-yellow ray florets
'Wirral Supreme' ♀	1m (3ft)	Double

Very straightforward to cultivate as hardy perennials, shasta daisies thrive in almost all situations and on most soils, but do particularly well on those that are moisture-retentive and alkaline. The taller cultivars are best given some support. Dividing and replanting immediately after flowering in alternate years will maintain vigorous growth and flowering. A second-best time for division is early spring; dividing in autumn may result in losses.

Propagation by cuttings in spring is easy if multiplication is wanted. Raising from seed is also easy: plants started by sowing in heated greenhouse conditions in early spring will flower the same year. Outdoor sowing for flowering the following year should be in late spring.

L. vulgare is the first of the three species into flower, in late spring, and shares the distinction, with *Anthemis punctata* var. *cupaniana*, of ushering in anew each year's succession of white daisy flowers. It is native to much of temperate Europe and western Asia. As a common wild species, it unsurprisingly enjoys a number of common names – ox-eye daisy, moon daisy, marguerite and dog daisy (why dog, I wonder?).

In flower, it is a graceful plant with slender stems. Sometimes branched, these may reach a height of up to 1m (3ft), though less is usual – 50–60cm (20–24in) – if the plants are competing with grass. The solitary flowerheads are usually 5–6cm (2–2½in) across. The floral display – about a month or so in length – is shorter-lived than for *C. × superbum*. The leaves, up to 10cm (4in) long, are spoon-shaped. It is almost always the species itself that is grown, but there are a few selections available. **'Maikönigin'** ('May Queen') is particularly early flowering and **'Maistern'** ('May Star') has larger flowers than the type. 'Maikönigin' comes true from seed.

Easy to cultivate, this species thrives on most soils and in most reasonably open situations. Support is unnecessary. Propagation is most commonly by seed, best sown in early summer. From a greenhouse sowing early in the year, flowering will occur in the first season, but unfortunately only at the expense of a reduced show of flowers in the following spring. If vegetative propagation is wanted, proceed just as for *L. × superbum* (see p.87).

L. paludosum (Mini-marguerite) is quite a charming little plant, less widely seen than it deserves. A half hardy herbaceous perennial, ordinarily grown as an annual, it makes a compact bushy plant up to 30cm (12in) tall. The white flowerheads are about 3cm (1¼in) across and have a relatively large, yellow disc. The narrow, toothed leaves are up to 5cm (2in) long. From an early spring sowing, flowering can be expected from midsummer onwards. **'Snowland'** has large flowerheads, to 5cm (2in) across.

COLEOSTEPHUS

The only cultivated species of this small genus can be looked on and grown as the yellow-flowered version of *Leucanthemum paludosum*, the mini-marguerite. Botanically very closely related, among differences other than the flower colour is the fact that it is a true annual.

A native of southern Europe, **C. myconis** (syn. *Chrysanthemum multicaule*) is a bushy, spreading plant about 20cm (8in) tall. Most of the foliage is at or near ground level. The flowerheads, on stiff stems with few leaves, are up to 4cm (1½in) across. They are entirely golden-yellow in **'Gold Plate'** but **'Moonlight'** has lemon-yellow rays around a deeper-coloured disc. The flowering period is long – from early summer to early autumn.

The plant can be treated as a hardy annual, or started by sowing indoors in early or mid-spring. It is useful planted out in edge positions, or grown in containers.

A sea of white daisies in early summer, created by a small drift of *Tanacetum niveum*.

TANACETUM

This genus, closely related to *Chrysanthemum*, is horticulturally noteworthy for a number of species grown principally for their fine foliage, and for *T. coccineum*, the garden pyrethrum, well known for its brightly coloured, long-stemmed, large daisy flowers in early summer. *T. parthenium*, feverfew, is very different in appearance, producing masses of very small flowerheads over a protracted period. These resemble pyrethrum in lasting well in water when cut, but they are cast for a supporting role in a vase of mixed flowers. In the garden, the plant is likewise grown primarily as a foil for flowers of more assertive appeal, largely because of the long-lasting attractiveness of its foliage.

Of similar appeal is *T. ptarmiciflorum*, which is used in summer bedding and in containers. *T. vulgare* var. *crispum* is a striking, tall, hardy perennial, again justifying a garden place for its finely divided foliage.

Species and cultivars

T. coccineum (syn. *Chrysanthemum coccineum, Pyrethrum roseum*) (Pyrethrum) is a well-known hardy herbaceous perennial, native to the Caucasus and south-west Asia. Its flowerheads were used in the preparation of the traditional garden insecticide of the same name.

Pyrethrum has long been a popular border plant, for its rather short-lived profusion of pink and red flowers in early summer. Up to 8cm (3in) across and borne singly on stems 60–80cm (24–32in) tall, they are excellent for cutting. The dark green leaves grow mostly in a basal clump, each one long and narrowly bipinnatisect.

Despite its good qualities, pyrethrum has lost much popularity during the last 20 years. The few cultivars still widely available include **'Eileen May Robinson'** ♔, a pretty, soft pink to 75cm (30in) high, and **'James Kelway'** ♔, which has deep scarlet rays and reaches 60cm (24in). **'Robinson's Pink'** and **'Robinson's Red'** are taller and come true from seed. All have yellow discs.

Cultivation is easy, though plants do best in full sun and have a longer life on light soils. Some support is needed to ensure that the rather slender stems do not keel over. After flowering, cut these back hard. If division and replanting is wanted, it is best carried out then: the alternative time is spring, but the resultant first flowering season is unlikely to be very satisfactory. It is susceptible to powdery mildew.

T. niveum is a hardy perennial, notable for its great profusion of small, white-rayed flowerheads in mid- and late summer. About 2.5cm (1in) across, with yellow discs, these almost completely conceal the attractive divided, grey-green leaves. In flower, the bushy plants are about 75cm (30in) tall and of equal spread. **'Jackpot'**, the cultivar by which the plant is known, is easily raised from seed.

T. parthenium (syn. *Chrysanthemum parthenium, Matricaria eximia*) (Feverfew, Matricaria) is a hardy perennial found in the wild in the Caucasus, and now widely naturalized throughout Europe and the Americas. The common name refers to its traditional use for relieving the symptoms of fever; it is currently used for treating migraine.

The plant attains a height of 60cm (24in), has much-branched, stiff, leafy stems and strongly aromatic and pinnatisect leaves, up to 8cm (3in) long, with deeply toothed margins. The flowerheads, borne in dense, many-flowered corymbs, are up to 2cm (¾in) across, with broad off-white ray florets and a yellow disc. The double-flowered cultivars **'Golden Ball'** (30cm/12in), **'Selma Tetra'** (white, 60cm/24in) and **'Snow Ball'** (30cm/12in) are most widely grown. The single-flowered **'Aureum'** has yellow-tinted ray florets, but its claim to garden distinction is its yellow-green foliage, which has earned it the name 'golden moss'.

T. parthenium is most often grown as an annual. Although it is hardy, for an early start, seed is commonly sown in heat in a greenhouse in early spring; a better result still is obtained by sowing outside where it is to grow in early autumn. It is easy to cultivate and is used as a border plant and, the dwarf cultivars, as edging for beds.

T. ptarmiciflorum (Silver feather) is found in the wild only on one of the Canary Islands: Gran Canaria. It is a shrubby, half hardy perennial, grown for its silvery-grey 2–3-pinnatisect leaves, with very narrow segments. It is usually treated as an annual, raised from seed sown in early spring. It finds particular use in summer bedding and in containers, as an elegant alternative to the better-known silver-leaved bedding plant, *Senecio cineraria*.

T. argenteum, *T. densum*, *T. densum* subsp. *amani* and *T. haradjani*, all dwarf subshrubs, are also all cultivated for their leaves – grey-green in the case of *T. densum*, more silver in the other three. All are plants for situations in full sun and with excellent drainage, in rock gardens, or better still on dry stone walls, where the stems and hairy foliage lie directly on rock rather than on soil. Where these conditions cannot be met, they are candidates for alpine house culture. Propagation is by division or seed.

T. balsamita (Costmary, Alecost) is primarily of historic interest for inclusion in herb collections. An easily grown hardy perennial, it may attain a height of up to 1.5m (5ft), and has loose clusters of small, yellow flowerheads in late summer and early autumn. It was used for a variety of flavouring purposes, and as an alternative to hops in the brewing of beer – hence the name alecost.

T. vulgare (Tansy) is broadly similar in height and in the size and colour of the flowers, though these are borne in distinctive flat clusters. Like alecost, it has been much used in the past both as a culinary and a medicinal herb. Native to Britain, with attractive foliage, it is not merely easily grown, but invasive in character.

The species itself is for larger gardens only, but **var. crispum** deserves wider consideration. Its finely divided leaves are its chief attraction: it commonly does not flower in cooler summers, but this is arguably not a deterrent, as it obviates the nuisance of self-seeding.

LEUCANTHEMELLA

The annual autumnal show of fine large white daisies on these tall herbaceous perennials does not so much justify their popularity, as make one wonder why they are not more popular still.

L. serotinum (syn. *Chrysanthemum serotinum*, and *C. uliginosa*) is a native of south-east Europe, where it is found mostly growing along stream banks. Anything up to 2m (6½ft) tall, the stiffly erect stems branch in their upper third. The flowerheads, to 7cm (3in) across, have greenish, hemispherical discs and are borne in loose corymbs of up to eight. The display, in early to mid-autumn, lasts for four or five weeks and the flowers are good for cutting.

Fully hardy, the plants tolerate partial shade, and have no special soil requirements beyond at least reasonably good moisture-retaining properties: they are among those in the daisy family that are happy in clay. Owing to their height and their top-heaviness when in flower, they need support. Again because they are tall, they need thoughtful placement, either in a large herbaceous border or bed, or among shrubs. Bear in mind that the flowerheads will turn to face the sun. They are easily propagated by either division or cuttings in spring. Young shoots are susceptible to slugs.

NIPPONANTHEMUM

The one species of this small, autumn-flowering shrub provides a climactic contribution to the seasonal galaxy of white-rayed daisies, which starts in earnest with *Anthemis punctata* subsp. *cupaniana* about six months earlier. Its particular distinction lies in its lateness, after even *Leucanthemella serotina* and the Korean chrysanthemum 'Wedding Day'. It is in any event very different in form from these, with dark green glossy foliage to serve as a foil against which the purity of the flowerheads can be appreciated to the full.

N. nipponicum (syn. *Chrysanthemum nipponicum, Leucanthemum nipponicum*) grows to a height of about 60cm (24in), the stems upright and slightly branched, with the spoon-shaped leaves mostly near their bases. The flowerheads are up to 7cm (3in) across, with a disc at first greenish, changing to yellow.

A native of coastal areas in Japan, the plant is unfortunately not fully hardy. Except in very mild areas it needs placement close to a wall of southerly or westerly aspect to minimize the risk of early frost spoiling the display. Well-drained soil and a protective mulch over the winter period are also advisable. Propagation is by division in late spring, or by seed.

RHODANTHEMUM

This small genus from north-west Africa might well be looked on as the chrysanthemum of the rock-garden enthusiast. All the cultivated species are appropriately dwarf, free-flowering, stoloniferous plants that develop a mat of growth over time. They were all once in *Chrysanthemum*, but few plants can have suffered so much re-naming. (Perhaps mercifully, some nurseries have been slow to move with the times, and still offer them under *Chrysanthemum*.) From *Chrysanthemum*, they were moved to *Leucanthemum*, along with the shasta and ox-eye daisies, and then to *Pyrethropsis*. This is but part of the tale, because for some periods in the recent past, *R. hosmariense* has also been *Chrysanthemopsis hosmariense* and *Leucanthemopsis hosmariense*. Having arrived, with its much re-named fellows, in its present genus, all gardeners trust it will be allowed to stay in peace. Of the three species described below, two have also been graced with more than one specific name during my lifetime.

They are all of less than totally reliable hardiness, but as with so many such plants, winter survival prospects are greatly enhanced by fast, free drainage. On a suitable soil, *R. hosmariense* is a very good plant for the front of a sunny border, because of its long flowering season. In such favourable environments as sunny situations in a rock garden or a raised bed, plants of all three species can survive frost exposure down to −10°C (14°F). Even then they are prone to failure in winters of high rainfall. They are excellent alpine house plants. Propagation is by cuttings, which root easily.

Species and cultivars
R. hosmariense ♔ (syn. *Chrysanthemum maresii* var. *hosmariense*) is the best-known and most easily grown species. Established plants are low-growing mats of lax, woody stems with attractive silvery-green foliage year round, bearing solitary flowerheads in spring and early summer, and again later in the year. On relatively long stems (20–25cm/8–10in), these are up to 5cm (2in) across, and have white, square-ended ray florets and golden-yellow discs.

R. catananche is a tufted plant with all the leaves at the stem bases. The flowerheads, to 5cm (2in) across, have cream to yellow ray florets, red towards the base. The flowering season, in summer, is shorter than for *R. hosmariense*.

R. gayanum (syn. *Leucanthemum mawii*) makes a small shrubby plant, 30–40cm (12–16in) tall. Again with a shorter flowering period than *R. hosmariense*, its flowerheads are also rather smaller, to 4cm (1½in) across, and have brown discs. The ray florets are a pretty pink, fading to near-white or white suffused pink, and in either case have a rose-coloured reverse. The cultivar **'Tizi-n-Tichka'** is white-flowered, with a red central ring.

AJANIA

A. pacifica has an arsenal of synonyms, including the descriptive *Chrysanthemum marginatum* and *Pyrethrum marginatum*. Otherwise it has been *Dendranthema pacifica* as well as *Chrysanthemum pacificum*. A wonderful evocation of frost is created by its silvery-green foliage, each lobed leaf very narrowly but sharply margined in white. The dense spreading mounds formed by this plant are enjoyed primarily for their foliage, but there are yellow flowerheads as well, very late in autumn, as a bonus. Individually small, they are clustered together in corymbs up to 10cm (4in) across. The inflorescences are similar to those of tansy, *Tanacetum vulgare*.

Plants are usually no more than 30cm (12in) tall, and spread to two or three times as great a diameter. The lobed leaves are unmistakably similar to those of the florist's chrysanthemum, and have upper surfaces just sufficiently hairy to give them their hint of silver.

The plant does best in a sunny spot on poor soil, and is a fine front-of-border plant to serve as a foil for more colourful neighbours. It is fully hardy, and plants propagated in early summer are sometimes used in patio containers, to provide ornamental foliage through the autumn months. Propagation is by cuttings taken in spring or summer.

10 Cornflowers

The four genera in this section share close kinship with the thistles, as all belong to the same tribe, the Cardueae. However, the cornflowers are in a sub-tribe of their own, differing from other genera in botanically significant respects. In the flowerheads of most of the cultivated species in the principal genus, *Centaurea*, the outermost of the tubular florets are enlarged, and radiate more or less horizontally away from the rest. They have much elongated lobes that are often divided, and at their outer ends have fine-pointed tips. These create the fringe-like effect typical of the cornflowers, giving us perhaps the most characterful and certainly the prettiest of all flowerheads in the daisy family. The small, related genus *Amberboa* has similar flowerheads.

Some important cultivated *Centaurea* species, together with species in *Leuzea* and *Serratula*, have conventional thistle-type inflorescences. In these the outer and inner florets are more or less undifferentiated, and together form a tuft, which as the flowerhead opens is on top of the involucre in the shape of an inverted cone.

CENTAUREA Cornflower, knapweed

Light-touched charm is the hallmark of the cornflowers, annual and – still more so – perennial. These share with other species of this 450-strong genus a tuft of tubular florets crowning an involucre that is often dark-coloured. However, in most of the cultivated species, the outermost florets are enlarged and spread horizontally, as described in the introduction. The best-known examples include *C. cyanus*, the annual cornflower, and the perennials *C. dealbata* and *C. hypoleuca*. Contributory attractions are the show of stamens protruding from the central mass of shorter florets, and in some species leaves that are grey or silver, or finely divided, or both.

The genus mainly comprises herbaceous perennials, though there are also some subshrubs, annuals and biennials. Most of the more widely cultivated species come from areas in and to the south of the Caucasus (the area between the Black and Caspian Seas). All the cultivated species are hardy except in areas with very severe winters.

Generally easy to cultviate, just as long as the soil drainage is good, most of the members of the genus do best in sunny positions and are tolerant of prolonged dry soil conditions. Most do well in alkaline soil, and in soils that are naturally hungry, like sands and gravels. *C. montana* is an exception in doing well in very moist soil. *C. dealbata* and *C. montana* are better for some support. Otherwise, deadheading is the only attention ordinarily needed.

Propagation of perennial species may be by seed, or more commonly by division every second or third year. On moisture-retentive soils, all species except *C. montana* are more safely divided in spring than in autumn. Several of the cultivated species can be increased readily by root cuttings – *C. dealbata*, *C. hypoleuca*, *C. montana* and *C. ruthenica* most notably. The only annual species ordinarily cultivated, *C. cyanus*, is hardy enough to sow outdoors very early in autumn, except in cold areas or on soils tending to lie wet in winter. Later-flowering and smaller plants result from spring sowing. The species described are generally free of serious problems, with the exception sometimes of powdery mildew.

Species and cultivars

The 16 species described below have been divided into four groups. The first of these contains three annual species. The other groups are all of herbaceous perennials. They are: perennials native to Europe and mainly of interest for wild gardens and naturalizing; yellow-flowered species; and finally the blue- and pink-flowered species, which constitute the largest and most significant group. Of these, the last two described are very dwarf, and make fine rock-garden plants.

Three notable species are no longer correctly classified in the genus: *C. cineraria* (Dusty miller) – see *Senecio cineraria* (p.130); *C. moschata* (Sweet sultan) – see *Amberboa moschata* (p.96); *C.* 'Pulchra Major' – see also *Leuzea centauroides* (p.96).

Annuals

C. cyanus (Cornflower) is widespread in the wild in northern temperate areas, including Britain Isles. Once a common weed of cereal fields, it has long been a popular garden flower. By common consent, it is one of the best of all blue cut flowers, for the depth and brilliance of the colour. The plants are erect in habit, up to 1m (3ft) tall, and come into flower from early summer onwards, according to time of sowing. Basal leaves are usually lanceolate, while the stem leaves are narrower.

The solitary flowerheads are up to 5cm (2in) across and in the species have violet-blue inner and dark blue outer florets. Colours available in cultivars, all of which have more outer florets than the species, include pinks, reds and white as well as blues. Among those available are **'Blue Diadem'** ♈, which is deep blue, 75cm (30in) tall and outstanding as a cut flower. Of dwarfer cultivars, the **Florence Series**, around 35cm (14in) tall, is outstanding for freely branching at the base of the plants, creating a bushy shape. **'Florence Pink'** and **'Florence White'** have both been awarded Fleuroselect Gold Medals.

C. americana (Basket flower) is seldom grown in Britain, but is much more familiar in gardens in the USA, where it is native. It does best in drier soil types, and is good as a cut flower. Similar in general character to *C. cyanus*, but at 1–1.5m (3–5ft) generally taller, the species has large solitary flowerheads with purple florets. These more closely resemble sweet sultan (*Amberboa moschata*) than *C. cyanus*, with long, narrow pointed ends to the lobes of the elongated outer florets, giving the flowerheads an almost fluffy appearance when viewed from a distance.

'Jolly Joker' has pale, rosy-lilac florets on flowerheads up to 10cm (4in) across. **'Aloha Blanca'** has white flowerheads which are larger still.

C. rothrockii, native to Mexico and the southern USA, is best treated as a biennial. About 1.25m (4ft) tall, its erect stems are sparingly branched. The solitary flowerheads, up to 5cm (2in) across, have creamy-yellow inner florets surrounded by a widespreading fringe of much elongated and finely divided outer florets, purple-pink in colour. They are good as cut flowers.

Species for naturalizing or wild gardens

These species, both native to Europe, including the British Isles, are of erect, branching habit, and flower from midsummer to early autumn.

C. nigra (Lesser knapweed, hardheads) has pretty tufted, purple flowerheads, up to 3cm (1¼in) across, on plants usually about 50cm (20in) tall. The outer florets are not noticeably different from the inner.

C. scabiosa (Greater knapweed) is up to 1.5m (5ft) tall with purple flowerheads about 5cm (2in) across, the outermost florets elongated and reflexing. It is found in the wild in dry grassland in England and across Europe into the Caucasus.

Yellow-flowered perennial species

The four species in this group all have thistle-like flowerheads, with upright tufts of more or less identical tubular florets.

C. macrocephala is much the most widely grown of the group. The stout, very leafy stems, usually rather over 1m (3ft) tall, bear large solitary flowerheads, up to 8cm (3in)

The flowerheads of *Centaurea argentea* add interest to its fine silvery foliage.

across, in midsummer. With their massive brown involucres, these resemble a small, yellow-flowered version of a globe artichoke. The large basal leaves are oblong-lanceolate, the stalkless stem leaves shorter and narrower. This is a plant that creates a dramatic impact when in flower, although some gardeners find it rather coarse in effect. Unlike most members of the genus, it needs moist, fertile soil to do itself justice. It is native to the Caucasus.

C. orientalis has stiff, branched but quite thin stems usually about 1m (3ft) tall. The straw-yellow flowerheads are about 4cm (1½in) across, with the outer florets longer than the inner ones. Its flowering season is mid- to late summer. This is an attractive plant in a very much more restrained fashion than *C. macrocephala*, and one that my wife and I like very much. Whether we can continue to keep it successfully on our clay soil I am uncertain, as it is reputed to need fast-draining soil, as well as full sun. It is a native of south-east Europe.

C. ruthenica grows up to 1.5m (5ft) tall and has pale lemon-yellow flowerheads, up to 5cm (2in) across, on slender stems. Narrowly pinnatifid, dark green foliage contributes to its garden value. It is not widely sold (the 2000–2001 edition of the *RHS Plant Finder* lists only one supplier), yet this Caucasian species must be worth consideration, for it has earned special praise in print from a positive pantheon of the most discerning gardening writers of the late nineteenth and twentieth centuries – William Robinson, Edward Bowles, Alan Bloom and Graham Stuart Thomas among them.

C. argentea has handsome pinnatifid, silvery foliage as its primary claim for attention. A mat-forming plant with ascending stems, it does not generally exceed 50cm (20in) in height. The solitary pale yellow flowerheads, up to 5cm (2in) across, are borne in early and midsummer. It is a native of Crete, and does best in dry soil, fully exposed to sun.

Perennial species with blue or pink flowerheads

C. montana (Perennial cornflower) is native to mountains in southern Europe, and has become widely naturalized in Britain. It spreads by creeping rhizomes, and is the most commonly grown perennial species. It is useful among herbaceous perennials generally in commencing to flower early – in late spring. The rather weak stems can reach up to 50cm (20in), but only if given some support. The flowerheads are up to 5cm (2in) across, the central florets violet-blue, and the rather widely spread and very elongated outer florets deep blue. Individual flowerheads are elegant, but would have greater visual impact if there were more of the long outer florets. A good cut flower.

subsp. *alba* has white flowerheads, and **subsp. *carnea*** (syn. *rosea*) pink. The cultivar '**Parham**' is purple-lavender and '**Violetta**' is dark violet.

C. triumfettii is closely related to *C. montana*, with flowerheads of very similar colour, but it is taller at around 75cm (30in). In gardens, however, the dwarfer **subsp. *stricta***, up to 50cm (20in), is more widely grown. The woolly leaves are grey-green, and well clothe the stems. As with *C. montana*, a second flush of flowers in late summer or early autumn is usual.

C. dealbata is a very widely and easily grown species, native to Corsica. It is similar in height to *C. triumfettii* and the flowerheads are comparable in size to those of *C. montana*, but open rather later, in midsummer, and the outer florets are bright pink and more numerous. The inner florets are white. Pinnatisect leaves, up to 20cm (8in) long, clothe the stems and are an attractive feature.

'**Steenbergii**', a popular cultivar, is a more strongly coloured carmine-purple. Both this and the species are good cut flowers and free-flowering border plants but are even more in need of support than *C. montana*. A second flush of flowers is common.

C. hypoleuca is similar to *C. dealbata* and also a Corsican native, but has the advantage of needing no support. It is shorter, at about 50cm (20in), with slender, branched stems and fragrant flowerheads that are rather larger. The species is known in cultivation only by one very popular cultivar, '**John Coutts**', which has deep rose-pink flowerheads produced over a long period, from midsummer to early autumn.

C. pulcherrima a Caucasian native, is a little shorter than *C. montana* at 30–40cm (12–16in) high, and has stiff though slender stems. The solitary pink flowerheads, about 5cm (2in) across, open in midsummer. The ray florets are quite densely displayed, and with the ends of the lobes elongated and pointed, the effect is very pretty. The silver-green pinnatifid foliage also looks good.

C. cuneifolia **subsp.** *pallida* is alone among the species in this group in having thistle-type flowerheads, as for the four yellow-flowered species described above. It may be offered by some nurseries as *C.* 'Pulchra Major'. Also offered under this name is the similar species *Leuzea centauroides* (see p.96). The main differences are that in *C. cuneifolia* subs. *pallida* the foliage is much greyer, the florets are pale pink, and the bracts of the large, silvery involucre are straw-like to the touch.

C. bella is a short, cushion-forming plant, suitable for rock gardens. The pink to pale purple flowerheads, about 4cm (1½in) across, are produced in midsummer on stiff white-woolly stems up to 30cm (12in) high. As in a number of other species, the pinnatifid foliage is attractive in its own right. It is another Caucasian native.

C. simplicicaulis is the shortest of all the species described, at about 20cm (8in). It too is a good and popular rock-garden plant, forming a dense cushion and bearing pink-lilac flowerheads, to 5cm (2in) across, which open from late spring. The leaves are another reason for choosing the plant – twice pinnatifid, and hairy enough on the upper surface to look silvery. Again native to the Caucasus.

The easily grown British native *Centaurea montana* flowers early and thrives in very moist soils.

AMBERBOA Sweet sultan

This small genus, of just six species, is closely related to *Centaurea*. *A. moschata*, the only one in cultivation, is widely known as *Centaurea moschata*. It is, in any event, a lovely hardy annual with scented, prettily fringed flower-heads produced on long, slender stems over a protracted period. They differ from annual cornflowers – *Centaurea cyanus* – in the length and narrowness of the lobes of the outer florets, giving the characteristic and very pretty fringed effect for which the flowerheads are admired. They are very good for cutting. A cottage-garden flower of very long standing – introduced in the seventeenth century – the current disfavour cast on taller annuals, and on plants that need some support, must account for the unmerited neglect of this one.

Apart from requiring support, it is otherwise very straightforward to cultivate as a hardy annual. It thrives on most well-drained soils, but particularly on lighter, alkaline ones, including those that are nutritionally poor, and otherwise merely needs reasonable exposure to sun. Sowing outdoors where it is to grow is usual, as for annual cornflower, *Centaurea cyanus*, (see p.93). It resents root disturbance, so if you elect to sow in a frame or greenhouse in early spring, raise the plants in individual pots or in cell trays so that no root breakage occurs in planting. It is susceptible to powdery mildew.

A. moschata (syn. *Centaurea moschata*) is a much-branched though slender, erect plant, growing to about 60cm (24in) in height. Its solitary flowerheads are borne over a long period, commencing in early summer. These are up to 6cm (2½in) across, and are in shades of pink and purple, and in white and yellow. The stem leaves are deeply lobed or cut. The species is native to Turkey and elsewhere in south-west Asia. Seed is usually sold in mixed colours, but **'Dairy Maid'** is yellow.

LEUZEA

The three species of this genus are native mainly to south-west Europe and North Africa. All have been at one time or another placed in the closely related *Centaurea*. One, *L. centauroides*, is a handsome plant, quite widely available and often known in the nursery trade as *Centaurea* 'Pulchra Major'. Unfortunately, there has been past confusion here, and it may be that some plants offered under this name are another species, either the larger *L. rhaponticum* or *Centaurea cuneifolia* subsp. *pallida* (see p.95). There is a very strong case for a national collection of the important genus *Centaurea* and its near relative, *Leuzea*, in which at least some of such doubts might be resolved. The genus is named in honour of a Frenchman, Deleuze, making the appropriate pronunciation ler-zee-a.

Both the species described are easy to grow in well-drained soil in full sun. In areas with cold, wet soils in winter, losses may occur, however. Propagation is by seed, division in spring, or root cuttings.

L. centauroides (syn. *Centaurea cynaroides*) is a Pyrenean native with stiff, simple or little-branched grey-hairy stems up to 75cm (30in) tall. In summer these bear large solitary flowerheads, with pointed bracts forming a green involucre up to 5cm (2in) across. Each of these is surmounted by a large tuft of tubular florets, which are deep lilac-pink to purple. The foliage is fine – the large basal leaves, silver-grey below, deeply cut into pointed lobes.

L. rhapontica (syn. *Centaurea rhapontica*) is listed by just one supplier in the 2000–2001 edition of the *RHS Plant Finder*, though, as already noted, it may be offered by

A pleasingly characterful plant, the autumn-flowering *Serratula seoanei* looks good in a rock garden.

some nurseries as *Centaurea* 'Pulchra Major'. A native of the southern Alps, its similarity to *L. centauroides* is close enough for it to have been considered a subspecies in the past. It is a larger plant, up to 1.75m (6ft) tall, with flowerheads up to twice the size.

SERRATULA Saw wort

From its 70 species, the genus *Serratula* currently offers to garden lovers but one confirmed winner, ***S. seoanei*** (syn. *S. shawii*). This is a compact, dwarf hardy perennial, notable for its profusion of pretty purple flowerheads that come usefully late, in the first two months of the autumn. It is an easy-going plant, though needing to be left undisturbed in a sunny position to do itself justice. Most widely seen in rock gardens, it has a wider merit for edge-of-border situations. It is native to northern Spain and Portugal, and to south-west France.

Each flowerhead of *S. seoanei* is an upright tuft of florets about 2cm (¾in) across, crowning a rather elongated tight cluster of dark-coloured bracts. They are borne on thin, branching stems in loose corymbs. In flower the plants are about 25–30cm (10–12in) high. Before flowering time, the dense mass of dark green, narrow, pinnately-cut foliage is quite attractive in its own right.

S. tinctoria is a taller though otherwise similar plant, suitable for a wild garden. It grows to about 1m (3ft) in height, and is widely native in Europe and North Africa. The leaves yield a yellow dye.

11 Ornamental Thistles

The ornamental thistles belong to the Cardueae, the same tribe as the cornflowers. All are more or less spiny, and all but *Echinops* (Globe thistle) have the typical thistle inflorescence: an erect tuft of florets, in the shape of an inverted cone, crowning the involucre.

Echinops is the most generally esteemed and valued member of this group. *Cynara* and *Onopordum* are grown for the dramatic effect of their foliage, extended particularly in the case of the former by the impressive flowerheads. These are both genera of truly architectural value in plantings, but neither are for small gardens. Arresting foliage is also the forte of the biennials *Galactites* and *Silybum*, while the appeal of *Cirsium* and the annual *Carthamus* is in their pleasing flowerheads.

Most genera in this group resent root disturbance: if raising them from seed, do so in pots so that transplanting is not a traumatic experience.

ECHINOPS Globe thistle

Of the small number of genera which can fairly be described as ornamental thistles, *Echinops* is the most widely grown, and deservedly so. As a hardy herbaceous perennial, it is without rival for its characteristic form – handsome, divided foliage, and stiffly erect stems surmounted, drumstick fashion, by spherical flowerheads of blue or white. They are very attractive to bees, and as cut flowers not only last long when used fresh, but also dry very well. Each inflorescence comprises a large number of single tubular florets, from which the stigma and the blue-grey anthers protrude.

The genus is quite large, with around 120 species dispersed over central and western Asia, eastern Europe, the Mediterranean area and mountainous parts of tropical Africa. *Echinops* is typically a plant of dry environments, flourishing on stony, sun-exposed hillsides and dry grassland. The small number of cultivated species do well in comparable garden environments, but will thrive on almost any soil, and in any situation other than one that is heavily shaded. They are easy to cultivate, but if grown on moist, fertile soil, the taller species may need support.

The earlier flowerheads should be removed as the peak of their attractiveness passes, in order to encourage the production of more. If any are wanted for use as dried flowers, they should be cut before the first florets open. Treated in this manner, they retain their colour in their dried state for many months. Propagation may be by division in spring, but these plants are very readily and productively increased by cutting the thick fleshy roots into pieces 5–7cm (2–3in) long in the dormant season, and inserting them upright in pots placed in a coldframe or greenhouse. The species can also be raised from seed.

Aphids are very commonly seen on *Echinops*, and if insecticidal spraying against the pest is being carried out, the globe thistles should be included.

Species and cultivars

All the species listed are European natives. The flowering period is mid- to late summer. The leaves of all are pinnately lobed or cut, and more or less spiny. The cultivars 'Veitch's Blue' and 'Blue Globe' are the most reliably repeat-flowering.

E. ritro ♔ is the dwarfest of the species described, at 60cm (24in), and has branched stems and a compact habit. Its bright metallic-blue flowerheads are up to 4.5cm (1¾in) in diameter.

Otherwise similar, **'Veitch's Blue'** is taller, approaching 1m (3ft). **subsp. *ruthenicus*** ♔ is taller again, up to 1.25m (4ft) and has little-branched or unbranched stems, densely covered in white hairs. Its dark green, glossy leaves, much more finely divided than in the type of the species, are a particularly attractive feature. 'Undoubtedly the gem of the genus,' according to the discerning Graham Stuart Thomas. The flowerheads are bright blue.

E. bannaticus differs principally from *E. ritro* in its greater height and spread, and in having hairy upper leaf

The intriguing structure of a globe thistle inflorescence is seen here in *Echinops ritro* ♛.

surfaces. The species is little grown but two vigorous cultivars are widely available, **'Blue Globe'** to 1.5m (5ft), and the light blue **'Taplow Blue'** ♛ which is 1.5–1.75m (5–6ft).

E. sphaerocephalus is also a very vigorous plant, up to 2m (6½ft) tall. The greyish-white flowerheads, up to 6cm (2½in) across, are borne on stout grey hairy stems. **'Arctic Glow'**, an introduction of the 1990s, is outstanding for its contrasting dark reddish-brown stems. It is also much dwarfer than the species, at about 1m (3ft). Propagation by seed is possible.

E. 'Nivalis' ('Niveus') is white-flowered and of slender habit, grows to 1.5–2m (5–6½ft) tall and has silvery foliage, deeply cut. A beautiful plant for foliage effect, it is of garden origin, possibly with a very spiny species, *E. tournefortii*, as a parent.

CYNARA Cardoon, Globe artichoke

The one species in widespread cultivation is a monarch among thistles, outstanding both for its great silver-grey leaves and its huge purple thistle flowerheads. These are characteristics shared with *Onopordum*, as is its stature.

C. cardunculus embraces both the plant called the cardoon, and its very close relative the globe artichoke. The latter is now regarded by most botanists as the result of selection over centuries for flowerheads of particularly large size, with fleshy bracts that lack spines. It is, of course, just these bracts and the disc-shaped receptacle from which they arise that are the parts of the plant usually eaten.

The treatment of globe artichokes as dual-purpose occupants of beds and borders is sometimes advised, as both beautiful and at the same time productive for the table. I cannot agree with this: I feel that you must choose between enjoying the immature flowerheads on the plate, or the crowning glory of the plants, their great tufts of violet-blue florets, in the garden.

The cardoon, *C. cardunculus* ♛, produces more flowerheads than the selected forms and cultivars which comprise the globe artichoke group. They are also smaller, up

Cardoons (*Cynara cardunculus*) and the little-grown white-flowered *Echinops microcephala* at Oxford Botanic Garden.

Cynara cardunculus flowerheads are a colourful mass of central florets cradled by the large, pointed bracts.

to 10cm (4in) across, and markedly spiky, each involucral bract coming to a long, sharp point.

Cardoon plants are usually taller than globe artichokes – up to 2m (6½ft). The silver-grey leaves are up to 50cm (20in) long, and deeply cut, the lobes often ending in long spines. The best foliage effect is claimed to be produced by removing the flowering stems. If this is the case, I think it is gained at too great a price, except where the height of the flowering stems is unwelcome. The flowering period is from midsummer into the autumn.

A native of parts of the Mediterranean area, *C. cardunculus* does best in sunny positions. It does itself full justice only on more fertile soils, but nevertheless has wide tolerance, including heavy clays. Propagation is best by cuttings taken in mid-spring, using the quite large young shoots. These must be removed from the crown of the plant at their point of origin, shortly below soil level. It is best to wait until the first rootlets can be seen pushing out from their bases.

On the one occasion on which I raised cardoon plants from seed I found considerable variation in both foliage and flowerhead characteristics, including spininess. It is probably this variation that accounts for conflicting descriptions of leaf colour and plant height.

ONOPORDUM Cotton thistle, Scotch thistle

These spectacular silver-leaved biennials are commonly seen in large gardens open to the public, and are among the plants most often cited by garden designers as of architectural value. The elegant, branching stems, furnished with large handsome leaves, bear magnificent purple thistle heads, commonly well above eye level, which are notably attractive to bees. Owing to their size, these are not plants for small gardens, but are a commanding choice for sufficiently wide beds or borders, or for sunny positions in semi-wild gardens. They are seen to best advantage when grown against a background of dark foliage.

Generally regarded as biennials, though sometimes behaving as short-lived perennials, they are ordinarily sown in early summer to flower the following year. If practicable, they are best sown where they are to grow, as they resent root disturbance. The alternative is to raise plants in pots for planting out early in the spring following sowing. They need a sunny situation to thrive, and prefer alkaline soil but will do well in most soils. These spiny plants should be handled with gloves. They are attractive to slugs and snails.

Species and cultivars

O. acanthium is reputedly the plant chosen by James V as the Scotch thistle, and the flowerheads are those represented on some British coins. Plants grow up to 3m (10ft) tall, and have freely branching spiny stems, hairy and winged, which bear pale purple or white flowerheads, up to 5cm (2in) across, in summer. Sometimes solitary, these are more often borne a few together in a tight terminal cluster. A bold tuft of tubular florets opens up on the top of each formidable sphere of involucral bracts. The long spiny tips of these protrude from a tight mass of cobwebby white hairs. The silvery-grey hairy leaves are pinnatifid and spiny-toothed.

This species, the most commonly grown in Britain, is native to much of Europe and Asia, and is fully hardy.

O. nervosum ♆ (syn. *O. arabicum*) is native to Spain and Portugal. It may not be reliably hardy in the colder areas of the British Isles. Of similar height to *O. acanthium*, it has slightly smaller flowerheads, with purple-red to purple-pink florets. The leaves are larger, hairless above, silvery-green rather than silvery-grey, and have very noticeable pale venation.

PLATE VII
Ornamental Thistles and Cornflowers

Onopordum acanthium

Echinops sphaerocephalus

Echinops ritro

All plants shown at approximately three-quarters lifesize

Cirsium rivulare 'Atropurpureum'

*Cynara
cardunculus*

*Centaurea
dealbata*

*Centaurea
argentea*

*Centaurea
orientalis*

Onopordum magnificum, here growing in the Hiller Garden in Warwickshire, is a visually dramatic plant.

O. bracteatum is native to south-east Europe and again generally similar to *O. acanthium*. Although little seen in gardens, it deserves special mention because it is named as the most striking species of the genus in the classic German book by Jelitto and Schacht – *Hardy Herbaceous Perennials* (1990).

GALACTITES

Its striking foliage is the claim of **G. tomentosa** to a place in the garden. The only cultivated species in its small genus, it is a biennial, native to the Mediterranean area. Up to 1m (3ft) tall, it has deeply pinnatisect leaves, with narrow spiny-tipped segments projecting almost at right-angles to the midrib. The sharp tips are elegantly elongated. Both the midrib and the central vein of each segment are conspicuously white, so giving the entire plant a silver-grey cast. The stems and undersides of leaves are white-hairy. The purple, cornflower-like flowerheads are pleasing in their own right.

It is a plant that is easy to grow in a sunny spot, and readily self-seeds. Best sown where it is to grow, the most impressive specimens result from treating plants as conventional biennials, sowing in early summer. It can also be sown very early in the autumn, and will flower in the same year from a sowing in spring, although on plants of lesser stature.

SILYBUM Blessed thistle, Our Lady's milk thistle

Dark green, glossy, white-marbled and white-veined, the spiny-margined foliage of **S. marianum** is produced in a large basal rosette. Individual leaves grow up to 50 × 25cm (20 × 10in), are deeply lobed into triangular segments and have spectacularly banded veins. The flowering stems of this handsome biennial reach 1.25–1.5m (4–5ft), and bear slightly scented, purple flowerheads. Their removal often enhances the foliar effect and may add a further season to the life of the plant.

Native to much of the Mediterranean area, and eastwards to Afghanistan, this is a sun-loving plant, doing best on well-drained soils that are not particularly fertile. It will often self seed. Where the mature size of the plant is unwelcome, it is sometimes grown just for the impact of its foliage in spring, and subsequently pulled out. Thick gloves should be worn for handling it. Sowing is best done where the plants are to grow, in late spring or early summer. *Silybum* is attractive to slugs and snails.

CARTHAMUS Safflower, Saffron thistle

C. tinctoria is the only species commonly cultivated in gardens that is undoubtedly both an annual and a thistle. It has a long history in agriculture in warmer countries, for the dye from its orange or yellow flowerheads and for the low-cholesterol oil yielded by its seeds, which are, incidentally, much liked by parrots. In recent times, it has attracted interest among commercial growers of cut flowers, for the orange-flowered forms in particular, and it enjoys a certain esteem for inclusion in mixed bouquets.

A native of South Africa, it is hardy enough to be sown where it is to grow in mid- or late spring. If sown in a frame or greenhouse, avoid high temperatures during germination, and root disturbance at planting: plants should be raised in pots or cell trays. It needs reasonable exposure to sun, but is otherwise an undemanding plant.

It will do well in dry soils. The fresh flowers last reasonably well in water, and also dry well. It is usually free from pest and disease problems, other than birds and mice between sowing and germination.

C. tinctoria is a plant of erect habit, 60–100cm (24–40in) tall, with a stiff stem branching near the top. The flowerheads – upright tufts of florets each at the top of a conspicuous sphere of green involucral bracts – are up to 4cm (1½in) across, and are vivid light orange-yellow, yellow or cream. Flowering is from midsummer to early autumn. The leaves are tipped and toothed with small spines, though plant breeders have largely suppressed this characteristic in some cultivars. Seed is sold both in mixed and in separate colours.

CIRSIUM Plume thistle

This large genus is best known to most gardeners for its decidedly unwelcome contributions to the perennial weed flora – *C. arvense,* creeping thistle, for example. Many species do, nevertheless, have distinctive flowerheads of attractive colour and form. Several are in cultivation, and two in particular deserve consideration for a place in a wild garden, or perhaps a larger herbaceous or mixed bed or border. Though they, too, spread by underground rhizomes, they do so only in acceptable moderation, and indeed *C. japonicum* is often short-lived.

Be warned, however, that both species spread also by self-seeding. They have spiny leaves, and are best handled with gloves. Culture is undemanding; both species are fully hardy and will thrive in any situation that gets some sun. They are also unfussy about soils and are among the limited range of plants which do well in ones that tend to lie wet. Propagation is by seed, of course, and, for *C. rivulare,* division.

C. rivulare is a native of central and eastern Europe, often found in wet situations (*rivulare* means by the waterside). Height may be up to 1.5m (5ft), and flowering takes place over a prolonged period in mid- and late summer on thin, wiry stems, more or less leafless in their upper halves. The flowerheads are solitary or in clusters of up to five, the dense tuft of the tubular florets, up to 3cm (1¼in) across, well exceeding the diameter of the involucre below. The only cultivar – perhaps just a selection from the species – is **'Atropurpureum'**, with florets of crimson-purple. The dark green, shiny, deeply toothed leaves, up to 45cm (18in) long, are handsome enough.

C. japonicum is as short-lived as a perennial, often behaving as a biennial. It has somewhat larger flowerheads than *C. rivulare.* In cultivation, it is represented by two cultivars, **'Pink Beauty'** and **'Rose Beauty'**, both about 75cm (30in) in height.

CARLINA Carline thistle

The two species of this genus in relatively common cultivation are best known for their large, stemless flowerheads, produced immediately above the basal rosette of attractive spiny leaves. The botanical feature that distinguishes all members of this genus is the striking ring of much elongated inner bracts of the involucre, which radiate around the wide central disc of tubular florets. These numerous narrow bracts, rather like thick, stiff paper in texture, are shiny with pointed ends. They fold up in the evening and on rainy days, just like the ray florets of many South African daisy genera, and a descriptive common name sometimes used is Weather thistle.

The two species described, both fully hardy, are plants for the larger rock garden or scree bed. They are best in sunny positions, and on fast-draining, hungry soils. For me personally, both species seem more interestingly curious than they are attractive. They are easily propagated by seed, which should be sown either where the plants are to remain, or in pots if they are to be transplanted, as they do not tolerate much root disturbance.

C. acaulis is a native of southern and eastern Europe, mainly in mountain terrain. Plants are short-lived, often to the point of dying after flowering for the first time. The solitary flowerheads, usually stemless, are produced from midsummer onwards and are up to 10cm (4in) across. The long inner bracts are silvery-white or pale pink and the tubular florets of the disc are brown. The spiny toothed leaves, to 30cm (12in) long, are pinnately toothed or cut.

subsp. *simplex* (syn. var. *caulescens*) produces branching stems up to 60cm (24in) tall, bearing between two and six rather smaller flowerheads. These dry well and are used as characterful dried flowers.

C. acanthifolia is closely similar to *C. acaulis*, but has slightly larger flowerheads with straw-yellow bracts. The leaves are often white-hairy above, and always so beneath. Plants die after flowering, which occurs two or more years after sowing.

12 Everlasting Flowers

This section contains nearly all the genera of everlasting flowers in the daisy family that belong to the tribe Gnaphalieae. The best-known is golden everlasting or strawflower, *Bracteantha bracteata*. Most of the tribe is Australian. The characteristic feature of the plants in this chapter is that they have enlarged, papery and outwardly radiating inner involucral bracts surrounding the small, tubular disc florets. Unlike ray florets, absent in this tribe, these bracts survive drying, changing little during the process; they last long in the garden and very long indeed indoors.

Through renaming, the genus *Helichrysum*, much the largest in the tribe, now has no commonly cultivated species that are used as everlasting flowers. It does, however, still number among its species some fine and valuable garden plants.

I have put some members of the Gnaphalieae in other chapters, simply because no one thinks of them as everlastings. For example, the shrubby *Cassinia* and *Ozothamnus* are in chapter 18 with other shrubby species, such as *Brachyglottis* and *Olearia*. Likewise five members of the tribe which are very dwarf plants suitable for rock gardens have been given their own section in chapter 16. The most famous of these is edelweiss, *Leontopodium*. Among daisy genera that do not belong to this tribe but that have flowerheads which dry well are *Echinops* (chapter 11) and *Xeranthemum* (chapter 17).

HELICHRYSUM

With around 600 species, largely from southern Africa, *Helichrysum* is another of the considerable number of very large genera found in the daisy family. Like all of these, it contributes relatively few species of notable horticultural worth to our gardens, but among these there are jewels. The genus was best known for *H. bracteatum*, which has now been moved to *Bracteantha* (see p.106).

The species described are herbaceous perennials or small shrubs, all characterized by more or less hairy foliage, which is grey-green to silver-grey. All have small, yellow flowerheads in flat-topped corymbs, with the outer florets female and the inner ones hermaphrodite.

The attractiveness of the colour and texture of the foliage alone looms large in the appeal of the genus. For example, the trailing species *H. petiolare*, which features in the summer planting of more hanging baskets than not, has insignificant flowers, and foliage is all. Another well-known species, the aromatic *H. italicum*, the curry plant, is also favoured primarily for its silver-grey leaves, though its flowerheads do add to its summer interest. The genus is also notable for a number of very dwarf species, almost universally grown on rock gardens or scree beds.

The name – *Helichrysum* – translates directly from the Greek as 'golden sun'. Not only is this apt enough for the characteristically yellow flowerheads, but the name happens to make a cultural point. This is in general a sun-loving genus, which also does best in relatively dry, fast-draining soils. Cultivation of the more popular species is otherwise easy, though some of them may prove short-lived without protection from winter wet. Propagation of the herbaceous perennials is by division in spring, or by seed. Shrubby species are easily multiplied by taking semi-ripe cuttings with a heel, in early to midsummer. As with many members of the daisy family, powdery mildew may be troublesome on some species.

The entries below are divided into shrubs, herbaceous perennials, rock garden plants and annuals. A number of shrubby species formerly included in this genus are now in *Ozothamnus*.

Shrubs

H. italicum ♀ (syn. *H. angustifolium*) (Curry plant) is an evergreen shrub, native to southern Europe. It is grown for its linear, silver-grey leaves, about 3cm (1¼in) long and closely spaced on slender, short-haired white stems which attain a height of up to 60cm (24in). The leaves have a curry aroma, and are used in flavouring.

A fine front of border plant, Helichrysum 'Schwefellicht' provides a long lasting floral display.

The growth habit is quite spreading, particularly once the yellow flowerheads develop, from midsummer onwards. These are individually very small, up to 4mm (⅛in) in diameter, but there are many in each loose corymb, which may be up to 8cm (3in) across. This plant is hardy in areas with mild winters, and may survive elsewhere in sheltered positions.

subsp. *microphyllum* has shorter-jointed stems with smaller leaves. As it has less tendency to sprawl than the type of the species, it is a useful choice for container growing. **subsp. *serotinum*** is also more compact than the species, not usually exceeding 40cm (16in) in height, but has rather longer leaves.

H. splendidum ♔ is a silver-grey-leaved shrub that is broadly similar to *H. italicum*. It differs in attaining a greater size, up to 1.25m (4ft) tall, having stiffer stems, and coming into flower later, in late summer. It is also rather hardier. The leaves, though narrow, are somewhat broader than in *H. italicum*. The species is native to east and south Africa.

H. ambiguum is again similar to *H. italicum*, but it has hairy leaves that are longer, broader and whiter. The fine cultivar **'Korma'** is narrower-leaved.

H. petiolare ♔ (syn. *H. petiolatum*) is also native to south Africa and is not winter-hardy. A shrub in natural conditions, it is widely grown as an annual foliage plant in containers for its long trailing stems furnished with attractive hairy leaves. These are grey in the species, more or less round, and up to 3.5cm (1½in) across. A vigorous plant, the species itself is appropriate for relatively large containers. For smaller ones, the less rampant cultivars are better choices and less likely to overwhelm the other occupants: **'Limelight'** ♔ has lime-green foliage; **'Variegatum'** ('Aureum') ♔ has grey-green leaves, variegated cream; **'Roundabout'** is a smaller-leaved and shorter-jointed version of 'Variegatum', and probably arose as a sport from it; **'Goring Silver'** is in turn a sport of 'Roundabout', and shares its characteristics, but the foliage is not variegated.

Herbaceous perennials

H. thianschanicum (syn. *H. lanatum*) is a woolly-hairy, clump-forming herbaceous perennial with erect or ascending stems that attain up to 40cm (16in) in height. Flowering occurs in early and midsummer. The dense corymb-like inflorescences, comprising yellow flowerheads, are similar to those for the other species described above. **'Goldkind'** ('Golden Baby') is dwarfer, to 30cm (12in), and has deeper-coloured flowerheads.

This Asian species is fully hardy, but may need protection from prolonged wet conditions.

H. 'Schwefellicht' ('Sulphur Light') is a fully hardy herbaceous perennial that forms clumps of erect stems 30–40cm (12–16in) tall. The corymbs of long-lasting, small, pale-yellow flowerheads deepen in colour almost to orange as they age, and are produced all summer long. The silvery-grey, felted leaves are an attraction – up to 4cm (1½in) long and lance-shaped.

This is an excellent front-of-border plant.

Rock garden plants

These species are all very dwarf, and all flower in late spring or summer. They need excellent drainage, and although some are more or less fully hardy, most need at least partial protection from winter rain. They all have densely hairy foliage and stems.

H. bellidioides (15cm/6in) from New Zealand, and *H. milfordiae* ♛ (to 10cm/4in) from South Africa, both have solitary flowerheads. For the genus, these are large (about 3cm/1¼in across), because the small, yellow disc is surrounded by expanded white, papery involucral bracts in the same way as is found in the golden everlasting flower. In *H. milfordiae* these have crimson reverses, making the buds very striking. **H. frigidum** also has flowerheads like those of *H. bellidioides*.

H. sibthorpii (to 10cm/4in), from Greece, has smaller flowerheads in clusters. The bracts are pink at first, but then turn white. The white-woolly leaves are relatively large. **H. orientale** resembles *H. sibthorpii* in flower.

Annuals
H. bracteata. See *Bracteantha bracteata* (p.107).
H. cassinianum. See *Schoenia cassinianum* (p.107).

H. subulifolium is an Australian annual about 50cm (20in) tall. Its yellow flowerheads are unmistakably akin to those of other annual everlastings. Up to 4cm (1½in) across, they are solitary on stiff, unbranched, leafless stems. Freely produced in mid- and late summer, they dry well.

A single circle of shiny yellow involucral bracts surrounds the disc, yellow also, in **'Golden Sun'**, while **'Valentine'** approximates to being semi-double.

Cultivation is easy in a sunny spot, preferably on a light, hungry soil.

BRACTEANTHA Golden everlasting, Strawflower

Best-known of the everlasting flowers in the daisy family, the single species cultivated is native to much of Australia, where it grows in rocky terrain and among scrub. Formerly placed in the genus *Helichrysum*, *Bracteantha bracteata* is a perennial, though it is treated as an annual in Britain and elsewhere to produce flowers for drying.

There is more to the species than dried flowers, though. There are at least three cultivars on the British market which are, in gardening terms, small shrubs. In the USA and their Australian homeland a wider choice is available and some reach 1m (3ft) in both height and width.

The traditional erect, long-stemmed cultivars are grown annually from seed and favoured for dried flowers. There are also two very dwarf and bushy versions. These are characterful plants, only about 40cm (16in) tall

In a warm, sheltered position *Bracteantha* 'Coco' may be grown as an outdoor shrub.

at most, for use in beds and borders, or in containers. They provide a long-lasting display of flowerheads, some of them of pleasingly subtle coloration.

All *Bracteantha* do best in sunny positions and on light soils. Those grown as perennials are only likely to overwinter outdoors in areas with mild winters, and even then need a sheltered spot. They are otherwise best grown as container plants, and moved to a frost-free greenhouse from autumn to spring. They like to root deeply so avoid shallow containers.

The cultivars grown as shrubs may be propagated by cuttings taken in mid-spring. In warm, humid conditions downy mildew may cause serious damage to foliage. Others are normally treated as half hardy annuals, sown in early spring. In very favourable conditions, plants simply intended to provide flowerheads for cutting and drying can be grown by sowing *in situ* in mid-spring. If drying is the intention, they are best in the vegetable garden, as the floral display has to be removed prematurely.

B. bracteata is an erect, slightly bristly perennial, up to 1.5m (5ft) tall in the wild, with stiff, leafy, branching stems. The flowerheads are solitary and up to 8cm (3in) across. Yellow tubular florets form the central disc, but it is the numerous enlarged inner bracts of the involucre for which the species is grown. These are outwardly spreading and blunt-ended and are yellow in the species, but there is a range of colours among cultivars. In those that are double-flowered, the innermost bracts remain incurving to a greater or lesser extent, and may sometimes permanently conceal the disc. The flowerheads look more interesting if the disc is exposed, giving a pleasing contrast with all bract colours other than yellow.

'**Monstrosum**' is the inelegant name given by the seed trade to the large-flowered, fully double type most often chosen for drying. About 1m (3ft) tall, its colour range is white, yellow, orange, rose-pink and red. The **Bright Bikinis Series** and the **Chico Series** are characterized by a dwarf (30cm/12in) bushy habit. Both have double flowerheads in the same colour range. Both are pleasing container plants.

Better container subjects, however, are to be found among the cultivars usually grown as perennials and propagated by cuttings. The **Florabella Series** and **Sundaze Series** are both compact, much-branched, bushy plants, growing to about 60cm (24in) tall. They are excellent in beds as well as in large containers. The flowerheads, up to 5cm (2in) across, are abundant throughout the summer. Florabella comes in gold, white and pink, Sundaze in bronze, gold, lemon and pink. '**Matilda Yellow**' is a spreading plant, up to 30cm (12in) tall. It is successful as a subject for containers and hanging baskets.

Two erect cultivars are '**Coco**' (60cm/24in), with cream bracts, named after Coco Chanel, and '**Dargan Hill Monarch**' (1m/3ft), single-flowered, with golden-yellow pointed bracts. The last comes true from seed and will flower freely the first year from an early sowing.

SCHOENIA

This small Australian genus yields us a pleasing, easy-to-grow annual, *S. cassinianum*. Previously called *Helichrysum cassinianum*, its renaming is less disruptive than many in this group of plants, simply because it is known to relatively few. However, it deserves a wider acquaintance among gardeners for its profuse display of pretty flowerheads over a long summer period. As with the other Australian genera closely related to *Helichrysum*, it thrives to the full in a sunny position on drier soil types. Again as with the others, it is usually best treated as a half hardy annual.

The characterful flowerheads of *Bracteantha* 'Dargan Hill Monarch' are best appreciated on container-grown plants.

S. cassinianum is a bushy, branching plant to about 50cm (20in) tall, with mostly basal foliage. The pink or white flowerheads, 2–3cm (¾–1¼in) across, are in flat-topped clusters of up to ten. They are single, and the involucral bracts are few in number, giving a starry appearance to the individual flowerheads. A small tuft of tiny, yellow tubular florets constitutes the disc. Production of more flowers is stimulated by continual cutting: they last well in water as fresh flowers, or may be dried.

'**Gabriele**' and '**Rose Beauty**' are pink-flowered, and '**Tanner's Pride**' is white.

CHRYSOCEPHALUM

Prior to the 1990s, this genus was little-known outside its native Australia. '**Nullarbor Golden Buttons**' has now become available and is a spreading herbaceous perennial with a suckering habit. Growing to about 30cm (12in) tall, it produces clusters of flowerheads, each about 1.5cm (½in) across, over a long period. They have a relatively large central boss of numerous orange tubular florets, encircled by many pointed, golden-yellow bracts, horizontal or slightly reflexed.

In Australian conditions, the flowering period extends over at least nine months each year, plants being sheared down to ground level in early spring as new basal growth is seen emerging. This cultivar has been used successfully both as a perennial dwarf groundcover plant, and for containers, including hanging baskets.

Its hardiness is likely to prove similar to that of *Bracteantha* cultivars grown as perennials, such as 'Dargan

PLATE VIII
Everlasting Flowers

Bracteantha bracteata
'King Size New Rose'

Bracteantha bracteata
'King Size New Red'

Rhodanthe chlorocephala
subsp. *rosea*

Bracteantha bracteata
'King Size Silvery White'

Bracteantha bracteata
'King Size New Golden'

Bracteantha bracteata
'King Size Salmon'

Xeranthemum
annuum

Ammobium
alatum 'Bikini'

All plants shown at approximately half lifesize

Hill Monarch', i.e. winter hardy in milder areas if grown in a sheltered position.

AMMOBIUM Winged everlasting

A. alatum is one of only two or three species of this Australian genus. It is a very attractive summer-flowering plant with graceful, loose clusters of small, silvery-white flowerheads, brought to life by bright yellow central discs. This species stands comparison with any white-flowered annual of similar height and season.

Like some cultivars of the much better-known *Bracteantha bracteata*, it is a perennial species but is almost

The Australian native *Rhodanthe manglesii* has flowerheads that are the prettiest of the everlastings.

invariably grown as an annual. The common name derives from the narrow, protruding wings of leaf-like tissue that run down the lengths of the flattened stems.

Cultivation as such is straightforward: grow it as a half hardy plant. A sunny situation is desirable, and performance is best on drier, relatively poor soils. On well-drained soils in areas with mild winters, it can be grown as a herbaceous perennial. As already indicated, it is an attractive plant for a bed or border. It is also very free-flowering, and a proportion of the flowering stems could be cut for drying without spoiling the overall effect.

A. alatum is erect, with a dense growth of sparsely-leaved stems, usually branched, growing from a basal rosette of white-woolly foliage. The stems attain a height of around 75cm (30in) in garden conditions. Flowerheads are about 2.5cm (1in) across. As in *Helichrysum* and *Bracteantha*, the petal-like organs are involucral bracts, which at first incurve quite markedly around the relatively wide yellow disc, but later open out to roughly horizontal positions. **'Bikini'** is a compact version of the species, not more than 40cm (16in) tall. It is in the small élite of seed-raised plants treated as annuals that have been awarded a Fleuroselect Gold Medal.

RHODANTHE

The flowerheads of *R. manglesii* (Swan River everlasting) are among the prettiest in the entire daisy family. It is one of two cultivated species in an Australian genus of considerable size, about 45 species, all of which are annuals. *R. manglesii* and *R. chlorocephala* subsp. *rosea* are very suitable for drying, and are widely used for the purpose.

The first of these stands entirely on its own merit as a most attractive annual, irrespective of any intention to use it for drying. The second is to my mind more like the *Bracteantha* cultivars grown from seed as annuals, perhaps not quite good enough to justify a garden place other than as a plant to give flowers intended for drying. Both species have suffered from renaming, having formerly been assigned to one or both of the obsolete genera *Acrolinium* and *Helipterum*.

They are easy to grow as half hardy annuals. Like *Bracteantha* and *Ammobium*, both also Australian natives, both species of *Rhodanthe* will do best on light soil rather poor in nitrogen. They appreciate full sun, and a further reason for giving them priority for an appropriate spot is that the flowerheads close in shadow, just as they do in dull weather.

Species and cultivars

R. chlorocephala* subsp. *rosea (syn. *Acroclinum roseum, Helipterum roseum*) is an erect plant, usually around 50cm (20in) tall, with solitary semi-double flowerheads up to 7cm (3in) across on stiff, slender, sparsely-leaved stems. The involucral bracts surrounding the yellow discs are white or pink and spread more or less horizontally outwards as they open. The leaves are short, narrow and pointed. **'Pierrot'** has white bracts and a black disc. **'Tetred'** has deep rose bracts.

R. manglesii (syn. *Helipterum manglesii*) (Swan River everlasting) is a thin-stemmed, delicate-looking plant, not usually exceeding 40cm (16in). The nodding flowerheads are borne singly on the short final branches of the repeatedly divided stems. They are just 3cm (1¼in) across, with white or pink bracts, and the open flowerheads are typically shaped like broad, upside-down cones. The stalkless leaves are broad, and one is borne at each stem joint.

'Paper Star' has white bracts; those of **'Paper Cascade'** are also white, but purple reverses to the outermost ones add to the attractiveness of the flowerheads before opening. **'Timeless Rose'** has rose-pink bracts, with the innermost ring darker than the rest.

PTEROPOGON

Formerly *Helipterum humboldtianum* (syn. *H. sandfordii*), **Pteropogon humboldtianum** is a distinctive low-growing annual, attractive for someone looking for a different plant to try at the front of a bed or border. The small, yellow flowerheads, borne in more or less flat-topped clusters, to 8cm (3in) across, dry well, but change colour to a metallic green.

The plant, a South Australian annual, does best in the same conditions as other everlasting flowers from the same continent – in full sun, on fast-draining, dry, poor soil. It is usually treated as a half hardy annual, but given suitable site and soil can be sown *in situ*.

Height reached is usually 30–40cm (12–16in). The stems are freely branched, shortly below flowering level. The flower display is from midsummer to early autumn.

CRASPEDIA Drumsticks

One species of this small, Antipodean genus is occasionally found in gardens, and in dried flower arrangements. Other species are rarities. *C. globosa* is unlikely to be confused with any other cultivated plant, with its almost perfectly spherical mustard-coloured inflorescences topping long, stiff, un-branched and near-leafless stems. Few common names of plants are more apposite than drumsticks is to this plant (see photograph p.181).

C. globosa is an Australian native, and is a herbaceous perennial. Though almost invariably grown as a half hardy annual, it has been known to survive milder British winters. A white-hairy plant, it forms a basal rosette of light green, rather silvery, narrow leaves, which are up to 30cm (12in) long and taper to a point. The compound inflorescences are produced on the erect stems at a height of 60–100cm (24–40in). They are up to 3cm (1¼in) across, each comprising many very small, closely crowded flowerheads of 4–6 tiny discoid florets.

The inflorescences dry well, and in arrangements of dried flowers are matched only by *Echinops* for their shape. For owners of clay soils, it is noteworthy that ones favoured by this species in the wild are moist and heavy. The soil preferences of all other genera in this group of everlastings are quite different, with the one exception of *Anaphalis* (below).

The foliage is attractive to slugs and snails.

ANAPHALIS Pearl everlasting

Three hardy herbaceous perennial species of this large genus are all equally valued for their grey foliage, particularly by gardeners on moisture-retentive soils, on which most grey-leaved plants do not thrive. They are natives of cooler environments, mostly in eastern Asia, and need at least reasonably good soil moisture levels to thrive. In this they are quite unlike grey-leaved genera such as *Artemisia* and *Santolina*, rich in species adapted in the wild for sun-exposed habitats on fast-draining soils.

Attractive, easy to please, shade-tolerant garden plants in their own right, *A. margaritacea* and *A. triplinervis* are also fine dried flowers. Roughly 50cm (20in) tall, they are good for front or near-to-front of border positions, where they are useful in providing an attractive foil for more flamboyant occupants. They make up for the small size of the individual flowerheads by the numbers that are grouped together in more or less flat-topped corymb-like inflorescences. Each tiny cluster of yellow tubular disc florets is encircled by pearly-white involucral bracts. A characteristic feature of the genus is that the disc florets are unisexual, though florets of both sexes are present in each flowerhead.

A. nepalensis var. *monocephala* is a dwarf, long-lived plant for rock gardens. The white-woolly leaves may dictate a need for protection from winter rainfall.

Propagation is by division in autumn or spring, or by seed. Plants spread quite rapidly, and frequency of division may be determined by the need to curtail them.

Species and cultivars

A. triplinervis ♟ has rather lax stems, with numerous pale grey-green leaves, up to 10cm (4in) long, and about a third as wide: they have 3-5 conspicuous parallel veins. The inflorescences develop in mid- to late summer, each comprising up to a dozen flowerheads about 1cm (½in) across, with pointed, shiny white bracts radiating outwards from the tiny disc. If required for drying, it is important to wait until the disc florets can be seen before harvesting.

'**Sommerschnee**' ('Summer Snow') ♟ is dwarfer than the species and has whiter bracts.

A. margaritacea, a rhizomatous plant, is broadly similar to *A. triplinervis* except in the size and appearance of the flowerheads. The stems are more upright, however, and the leaves, although variable, are usually narrower, with rolled-back margins. Individual flowerheads are very small, and the encircling bracts are blunt-ended and comparatively erect at flowering, forming a cup-shaped surround to the disc florets. They are produced from midsummer to early autumn, and are crowded close together in large numbers in terminal corymbs up to 15cm (6in) across.

'**Neuschnee**' ('New Snow') is more compact and has long, grey-green leaves. It can be raised from seed. **var. cinnamomea** has brown-felted reverses to its broader leaves. **var. yedoensis** ♟ is 20cm (8in) or less tall, and, by comparison with the type of the species, has shorter, linear leaves, woolly on both surfaces, and whiter bracts in the flowerheads.

A. nepalensis **var. monocephala** (syn. *A. triplinervis* var. *monocephala*, *A. nubigena*) grows to a height of about 15cm (6in). It is otherwise similar to *A. triplinervis*, but densely bushy and rather spreading, with larger flowerheads, up to 1.5cm (½in) across. These are borne either singly on the stems, or in twos or threes. In full flower an established clump is a spectacle in miniature.

The pearl everlasting, *Anaphalis margaritacea*, likes moisture-retentive soils, and tolerates shade.

13 Dahlias

ahlia is the only genus with a chapter to itself: there are no genera, closely related or more distant, with which it could reasonably constitute a horticulturally credible group and it stands on its own on the grounds of cultivation methods and garden use. For its diversity of flower form, size and colour, it is scarcely to be wondered at that many gardeners would wish it to stand not merely on its own, but on a pedestal into the bargain.

For the record, it is a member of the sunflower tribe, Heliantheae, and its particular sub-tribe contains a number of other good garden genera, including *Coreopsis* and *Cosmos*. But no one other than a botanist would regard these as particularly appropriate partners for the dahlia. Oddly enough, however, the least grown of the three important *Cosmos* species, *C. atrosanguineus*, does provide a cultural match, being a tuberous-rooted half hardy herbaceous perennial. In gardening terms, though, it is as much on its own in its genus as *Dahlia* is in the daisy family.

Of all the scores of genera in the family cultivated in gardens, none has so great a range of colours and flower forms as the dahlia. With *Aster* and *Chrysanthemum*, it dominates the autumn floral display in innumerable gardens. It has a lengthy flowering period, especially in years when the first autumnal frosts arrive late. And the show of bloom usually goes from strength to strength as the weeks of autumn succeed one another. Although the largest flowers come early, the greatest abundance and the best colours – especially of reds – do not arrive until mid-autumn. The excellence of the dahlia as a cut flower, and in some cultivars the enhancing effect of the bronze-red or purple foliage, make further contributions to its formidable garden value.

The genus *Dahlia* is native to Mexico and adjacent countries, and has 28 species. The parents of the vast range of modern cultivars are believed to be two Mexican species, *D. coccinea* and *D. pinnata*. Seed of these, the first of the genus to reach Europe, was received at the botanic garden in Madrid in 1789, and by early in the following century dahlias were being cultivated in a number of European countries.

Their capacity for variability was realized at a very early stage, and indeed was probably well in evidence in Aztec gardens long previously. For the rapidly burgeoning numbers of varieties of garden origin, the name *D. × variabilis* was adopted, to mark this characteristic, and to indicate their hybrid origin. British plant breeders seized upon this recently arrived genus, and the Victorian passion for competitive flower shows found the growing wealth of dahlia cultivars a highly suitable subject. The British National Dahlia Society was formed in 1891, and equivalent organizations have also long existed in France, the USA, Australia and India.

Dahlias are herbaceous frost-tender perennials almost universally treated in gardens in the same general way as half hardy bedding plants like *Pelargonium*. Food reserves, in the form of a starch-like compound called inulin, are accumulated in summer and early autumn in the tuberous roots, which are usually dug up when the top growth dies down after the first frosts, and overwintered in a frost-free environment. They can be simply replanted in spring, but can also be used for propagation (see p.114).

The stiff, upright, rough-hairy stems of dahlias are hollow, and branch freely only in the upper, flowering part. Plant height varies very widely. Leaves, borne in pairs, are usually pinnately or bipinnately divided, and their margins are toothed. The number of leaflets in each leaf, and the degree of dentation, varies with cultivar and with the stage of development of the plant, with leaves on lateral shoots larger and more divided than those first produced by the plant. A small number of cultivars have bronze, red or purple foliage, the best-known being the bronze-leaved, red-flowered 'Bishop of Llandaff', introduced in 1928. They are of particular value, and are being increasingly used in mixed plantings as well as for conventional bedding.

The single flowerheads of *Dahlia* species usually have eight broad ray florets, which are effectively sterile. The short tubular florets of the central disc are yellow. Double-flowered cultivars have up to 300 ray florets of various shapes. Examples are blunt and tubular, with incurving margins, as in ball-flowered cultivars, or long and pointed, with their margins rolled outward to form a narrow tube, as in cactus dahlias. Ray florets may be of almost any colour except blue, and of any length up to

12cm (5in). The flowering period is from midsummer (some cultivars late summer) until the first frosts.

Cultivation and propagation

Many books dealing exclusively with dahlias have been published (see Appendix VI). These appeal most strongly to collectors and exhibitors, and are especially relevant to the cultivation of the larger-flowered cultivars, for which the challenge of achieving perfection on a given show date is sharpest. I shall deal only with the smaller-flowered dahlia cultivars, grown as half hardy garden plants and often also valuable as cut flowers.

In terms of cultivation, the dahlia is quite closely comparable with *Pelargonium zonale*, the bedding geranium, and in the daisy family with most *Osteospermum* species. None of these can overwinter successfully outside where frosts of any severity occur. However, the dahlia is very conveniently taken from one growing season to the next in the form of a dormant cluster of tuberous roots, whereas *Pelargonium* and *Osteospermum* can only survive from one growing season to the next as green plants, for which at the very least a good frost-excluding garden frame is needed.

Dahlias will thrive on most soils provided they are in a reasonably sunny spot. Unlike so many members of the daisy family, they deliver their full potential only when their large demands for nutrients and moisture are met. Therefore, on light, fast-draining soils it is beneficial to incorporate liberal amounts of bulky organic matter during preparation. Shortly before planting, a general-purpose fertilizer should be forked into the top 15cm (6in) or so, too.

Planting of rooted cuttings or of young plants raised from seed should be done as soon as possible after the risk of late spring frost has passed. Alternatively, tubers may be planted, either as a complete cluster, or as a single tuberous root. If the latter, it is important that a shoot bud is attached, otherwise it will be incapable of growth. Shoot buds are found at the junction between the swollen root and the stem base. These buds should be covered with soil to a depth of around 5cm (2in), so planting of tubers can safely be done a fortnight or so before the anticipated last date on which late frost might occur.

The multiple shoots developing from tuber clusters are not usually stopped, but otherwise plants benefit from removal of the stem tip just above the fifth pair of leaves. In windy conditions, dahlia stems are very prone to breakage at the point where they arise from older stem growth, so all but the dwarfest cultivars should be provided with support. Plants respond well to watering and feeding in mid- and late summer.

After the first autumnal frosts have blackened the foliage, plants should be cut down to about 15cm (6in) above soil level. The tuber clusters should then be lifted carefully, cleaned of loosely adhering soil, and placed upside down in a dry, frostproof place to allow the rest of the soil to dry out. After its subsequent removal, the tubers should be dipped in a solution of the fungicide benomyl, allowed to dry again, and then stored in containers of very slightly damp peat, sand or perlite in a cool but frost-free place.

In early spring, they can be restarted into growth in shallow trays of compost in greenhouse conditions in order to produce cuttings. These, about 4cm (1½in) long, should be taken with a sharp knife. Standard practice is to cut just below the bottom pair of leaves, leaving a very short basal stub behind to resprout. Some authorities, however, believe that subsequent tuber production is improved if each cutting includes a tiny sliver of the tuber. In either case, they are very easily rooted if bottom heat can be provided, to maintain a temperature in the rooting medium of about 20°C (68°F). Once rooted, grow them on individually in 10–11cm (4–4½in) pots.

Tuber clusters can also be divided and used directly to produce pot-grown plants for setting out in the garden when frost risk has passed. For this, tubers should be restarted in the same way, about a month later than for production of cuttings. When shoot bud growth is clearly visible, use a very sharp knife to help split the woody stem base of the old plant so that each tuber has one or more shoot buds attached. Pot these up as above.

Seed

Dahlia cultivars do not come true from seed, but some dwarf bedding strains are reasonably consistent in general characteristics of height, habit, flower size and type, and plants of these are normally raised afresh as half hardy annuals each year. Sowing should be in early to mid-spring. Growth is rapid, and young seedlings should either be transferred individually to pots or to large cells in cell trays or be widely spaced in ordinary seed trays.

Problems

Slugs can be troublesome for a short while after planting out. Subsequently, aphids and capsid bugs may infest young stems and foliage, and earwigs can be notoriously damaging to the flowerheads. Virus diseases are carried by aphids: dahlia mosaic causes stunted growth and cucumber mosaic makes the foliage yellow-mottled. Infected plants should be destroyed.

Species

The species are all single-flowered. Just one, *D. merckii* , is fairly widely grown, while *D. coccinea* and *D. sherffii* are occasionally seen.

D. merckii grows up to 2m (6½ft) tall, if its thin flexing stems are supported in an upright position. The plant looks generally better given partial artificial support and otherwise allowed to flow into and over the growth of adjacent plants. Flowerheads are up to 8cm (3in) across, and the broad but pointed ray florets are pale lavender to purple. There is also a white form.

D. sherffii is similar to *D. merckii* but has somewhat larger flowers.

D. coccinea grows up to 3m (10ft) tall, though usually much less, and the flowerheads are up to 9cm (3½in) across. It is a very variable species. The ray florets are usually orange to red, or lemon-yellow. They are broader and blunter-ended than those of *D. merckii*.

Cultivars

About 20,000 cultivars were known to exist worldwide at the end of the twentieth century. The millennial edition of the *RHS Plant Finder* lists nearly six hundred available in the UK. A further large range is imported from Dutch wholesale producers. Many of these are not listed in the *Plant Finder* but account for most dahlias offered for sale in British garden centres and by mail order.

In the early twentieth century, the Royal Horticultural Society and the National Dahlia Society established a classification system for the multitudinous assortment of flower forms and sizes. The classification was eventually agreed internationally. It defines ten groups on the basis of the form of the flowerhead. The best-known examples are the decorative, pompon, cactus, and semi-cactus groups.

Dwarf bedding

Dwarf bedding varieties are divided between the single-flowered and decorative groups. They have expected attributes such as dwarfness, bushy compact habit, and small flowers abundantly produced over a long period.

Charming flowerheads on flexing stems give *Dahlia merckii* a distinctive character.

Seed-raised strains, of mixed colours, have flowerheads up to 8cm (3in) across. They include the single-flowered **'Coltness Gem Hybrids'**, which are up to 60cm (24in) tall, the semi-double **'Diabolo'** and **'Redskin'**, both dark-leaved and about 40cm (16in) tall, and the dwarfer **'Figaro'** at 30cm (12in).

Vegetatively propagated cultivars, up to 40cm (16in) tall, include the double-flowered **'Ellen Harston'** ♔, which has scarlet flowerheads with purple foliage, and **'Longwood Dainty'**, which is apricot. **'Bednall Beauty'** resembles the famous 'Bishop of Llandaff', with its semi-double, crimson flowerheads and its dark foliage, but is only 50cm (20in) tall. Notable single cultivars, all also dark-leaved, are **'Yellow Hammer'** ♔, **'Moonfire'**, which is red-tinted gold, **'Roxy'**, which is cerise-pink and dwarf, and the taller **'Tally-Ho'**, which is bright red and about 75cm (30in).

The Lilliput (or Baby) dahlias, about 40cm (16in) tall, also have single flowerheads, but these are only about 3cm (1¼in) across: examples are **'Omo'**, which is white, and **'Harvest Inflammation'** ♔, orange – the name surely being an infelicitous translation from the original Dutch!

Patio

Pot-grown plants of patio dahlias, grown from cuttings and usually well in flower at the time of sale, are widely available from late spring onwards. These dwarf, small-flowered cultivars have been bred for their precocity of flowering, compact habit and suitability for culture in

PLATE IX
Dahlias and their Relatives

Dahlia 'Redskin'

Dahlia
'David Howard'

Dahlia 'Fascination

Dahlia 'Redskin'

Dahlia
'Redskin'

*All plants shown at
approximately half lifesize*

Cosmos sulphureus
'Cosmic Orange'

Zinnia 'Profusion Orange'

Tithonia rotundifolia
'Fiesta del Sol'

Cosmos bipinnatus
'Sonata Pink Blush'

Cosmos sulphureus
'Cosmic Yellow'

containers throughout their life. Grown accordingly – as distinct from planted out in beds – they do not usually exceed 40cm (16in) in height, and many cultivars are a good deal dwarfer. Mainly of Dutch and German origin, they made their appearance in the 1990s and continued development and improvement can be expected. They do not come true from seed.

The **Dahlinova Series**, **Dalina Series** and **Gallery Series** have flowerheads up to 8cm (3in) across and are all more or less double. The **Bambi Series**, semi-double or double according to colour, and the **Dahlstar Series**, single or semi-double, are both smaller-flowered. The **Bambini Series** and **Micronetta Series** are smaller still, with flowerheads of comparable size to those of the Lilliput dahlias, but on plants growing to only about half their height. **'Amazon'** is a very attractive semi-double

Introduced in 1965, the dark-foliaged *Dahlia* 'David Howard' ♔ still enjoys wide popularity.

with rose-pink rays deepening to rose red around the yellow disc.

Collerette

Collerette dahlias are a variant of the single-flowered form, characterized by an inner ring of much shorter ray florets surrounding the disc. Flower diameter is 10–15cm (4–6in). They are particularly good for cutting. **'Claire de Lune'** ♔ has large yellow ray florets forming the outer ring, and cream florets the inner, while the colours of **'La Cierva'** and **'Harlequin'** are purple and white.

Waterlily

Waterlily dahlias have fully double flowerheads, 10–15cm (4–6in) across, of very formal appearance with relatively few, broad, almost flat ray florets. Long, stiff stems contribute to the popularity of the group as cut flowers. **'Gerrie Hoek'** (pink) and **'Glorie van Heemsteede'** ♔ (yellow) are long-established favourites; **'John Street'** ♔ (red) and **'Kyoto'** (red and white) are less well known.

Decorative

Decorative dahlias are the most widely grown group. The fully double flowerheads have more ray florets than waterlily dahlias, giving them greater depth. They are also less formal in appearance, often because the florets, although flat, are slightly twisted. In the small-flowered category (flowerhead diameter 10–15cm/4–6in) are **'Abridge Bertie'**, which is red, **'Edinburgh'**, purple, tipped with white, **'Hamari Fiesta'**, yellow, tipped with red, and **'Pearl of Heemsteede'** ♔, pink.

Miniature-flowered cultivars (under 10cm/4in) include the outstanding **'David Howard'** ♔, which is orange-yellow, with dark foliage, **'Jeanette Carter'** ♔, yellow, and **'Karenglen'** ♔, red.

Cactus and semi-cactus

Cactus dahlias have pointed ray florets with the margins rolled under for more than half their length. This gives the flowerheads a spiky appearance. Small-flowered cactus dahlias include the pink-flowered **'Kathleen's Alliance'** ♔, and **'Pink Paul Chester'** ♔, **'Doris Day'**, which is red and **'Superfine'**, which is yellow.

Semi-cactus dahlias are intermediate between decorative and cactus flowerheads – the margins of their pointed ray floret are rolled under for less than half their length. Small-flowered cultivars include **'Dana Iris'**, red, **'Hillcrest Albino'** ♔, white, and **'Scottish Relation'** ♔, purple. Among miniature-flowered cultivars in this group are **'Andries Orange',** the orange-bronze **'Andries Amber'** and **'Kenora Petite'**, which is pink.

Miscellaneous

The bronze-leaved, red-flowered **'Bishop of Llandaff'**, already mentioned, falls into the catch-all miscellaneous group in the classification. Although its yellow central disc is fully exposed, it has two rings of ray florets, not one, and for that reason cannot be placed in the single-flowered group. A complementary series of bronze-leaved cultivars was introduced in 2000, all of similar flower form and height (just over 1m/3ft): **'Masquerade'** and **'Poème'** are orange, **'Rosamunde'** is rose-pink and **'Swan Lake'** cream.

Among the oldest *Dahlia* cultivars available is the fine bronze-foliaged 'Bishop of Llandaff'.

14 African Daisies

The eight genera in this group are an assorted bunch botanically, belonging to four different tribes. What they all share is a native habitat in the African continent. Accordingly, they are predominantly half hardy. Included among them are some distinguished annuals, notably in the genera *Arctotis*, *Dimorphotheca* and *Felicia*. Added to these are some perennials usually treated as annuals, particularly species and cultivars of *Gazania* and, again, *Arctotis* and *Felicia*. The genus currently attracting most attention is undoubtedly *Osteospermum*, and most would rate it outstanding for the clean-cut appeal of its flowerheads and the length of the flowering period. Unlike other genera, some of its species and cultivars are hardy in much of Britain and most parts of the coastal USA.

An unfortunate feature of all the African daisies is the closure of the flowerheads in dull weather and in shade. All need positioning where they are as fully exposed to the sun as possible. They are most appreciated where prolonged summer sunshine can be relied upon.

GAZANIA Treasure flower

The gazania in sunshine is among the showiest of plants, yet it was called 'a plant for the optimist', by James Evison, a distinguished former director of Brighton parks in his classic book *Gardening for Display*. It is, of course, the fact that the flowerheads do not open in cool, dull weather that holds the gazania back from even wider popularity. Native to southern and tropical Africa, it is deservedly grown very widely nonetheless.

The species and hybrids grown are half hardy herbaceous perennials, easily propagated and cultivated in any reasonably drained soil. They are most often treated as half hardy annuals, raised from greenhouse sowings in early spring.

The neat plants seldom exceed 30cm (12in) in height, and produce flowerheads up to 8cm (3in) across in a very long succession from midsummer until early autumn. Each of the sterile ray florets is broad and more or less pointed. Colours range from white, through cream and yellow to intense orange, bronze and red, to pink. The central discs are usually yellow, and often surrounded by a ring formed by a dark blotch at the base of each ray floret.

Gazanias are primarily plants for a sunny position at the edge of a bed or border, but will do well in a container (in which they tolerate rather casual attention to watering). By the same token, they are successful on a dry stone wall. They thrive in any soil that is at least reasonably well-drained, and are able to do very well on naturally dry soils, even in prolonged drought conditions. Avoid adding fertilizers containing nitrogen to the soil as this would have the effect of promoting vigorous leaf development at the expense of flowering. Tolerant of exposed sites, gazanias also resist damage by wind-borne salt in coastal areas. Wherever they are grown, once established, they seldom need any attention other than regular deadheading.

In warm positions and on well-drained soils in areas where little frost is usually experienced, the plants commonly survive the winter outdoors. Elsewhere, they can be lifted in early autumn and overwintered in a greenhouse or frame from which frost can be excluded. Numbers of plants are most easily cared for if planted in boxes about 15cm (6in) deep. Whether in pots or boxes, give minimal watering until early spring.

Propagation is easily achieved by sowing indoors in early spring. Seedlings in plugs are obtainable from garden centres and by mail order. Alternatively, cuttings taken in late summer or early autumn root easily. These are simply the outermost basal shoots detached from the parent plant. A cool greenhouse is needed to overwinter the young plants.

Gazania is little troubled by pests and diseases, though if plants are being overwintered, they may become infested with aphids. If they are kept in prolonged humid greenhouse conditions in winter, grey mould (botrytis) may cause losses.

G. rigens (syn. *G. splendens*), from South Africa, is the only species much grown. Its flowerheads are orange, with a dark circular ring around the disc. They are up to 7cm (3in) across, and borne on stems about 20cm (8in) tall. The narrow, oblong leaves, clustered around the bases of the flowering stems, are dark green above and silver beneath. **var. *uniflora*** ♕ differs from the species in having yellow flowers. **'Variegata'** ♕ has gold and cream variegated foliage.

G. rigens is one of the parents of a considerable number of garden hybrids. These include a number of seed-raised series, all of them precocious in flowering. Cultivars within each series are reasonably uniform with one another, and come true to flower colour and size, leaf form and height. The large-flowered **Kiss Series** is compact in habit, and attains a height around 20cm (8in), with dark green, deeply lobed leaves. The rather older **Daybreak Series** is taller, at 25–30cm (10–12in). Its varieties **'Bright Orange'**, **'Garden Sun'** (golden-orange) and **'Red Stripe'** (each yellow ray floret with a pronounced central red stripe along its length) have all received a Fleuroselect Gold Medal.

The **Mini-Star Series**, 20–25cm (8–10in) in height, is older again, and has silvery-green leaves, deeply toothed. The **Talent Series**, 20cm (8in), is distinguished by its silvery-white foliage. Flower size, at about 6cm (2½in) across is rather less than in the green-leaved varieties.

'Aztec' ♕ is among the best of the cultivars that do not come true from seed and must be propagated vegetatively. It is silver leaved, and has white ray florets, each with a maroon purple central stripe along its length, very dark towards the base. **'Christopher'** has dark pink flowerheads, while those of **'Cookei'** ♕ are deep orange, with a broad dark ring round the central disc.

OSTEOSPERMUM

Like *Gazania*, with which *Osteospermum* is often compared, this plant produces a summer-long display of flowers. Like *Gazania* again, it is a plant for a sunny spot. In hardiness, however, there is range found in this genus which is lacking in *Gazania*. At one extreme, *O. jocundum*

The characteristically glowing colours of gazanias are shown here by the Kiss Series, introduced in 2000.

and *O. ecklonis* are fully hardy where winters are mild, such as in southern England. At the other, many of the numerous garden hybrid varieties need greenhouse protection in winter.

There are about 70 *Osteospermum* species dispersed over much of Africa and Arabia, and annuals, herbaceous perennials and shrubby growth habits are all represented. The proliferation of garden hybrid varieties was a phenomenon of the last two decades of the twentieth century, with major introductions from Cannington College in Somerset, and from professional breeders in Denmark and Germany. The sharp rise in popularity of the genus has been assisted by the rise in interest in gardening in containers.

Any well-drained soil in any sunny garden position will suffice. If 'White Pim' or another of the more spreading garden hybrids is chosen, they give particularly pleasing results where they can be allowed to spill over the edge of a retaining wall.

The two species commonly grown and the garden hybrids behave as herbaceous perennials where winters allow their survival outdoors. Densely bushy as young

Modern *Osteospermum* cultivars from the Cape Daisy Series, bred in Denmark.

plants, they form loose mats of growth in their second and subsequent years. The foliage is unremarkable except for its distinctive and quite pleasing aroma. Heights attained are between 15 and 60cm (6–24in) according to species or cultivar. In areas with hard winters, plants are set out in the open in late spring each year. Once established, the only attention usually needed is deadheading.

The flowerheads are 5–10cm (2–4in) across, with characteristically small discs. The colour range of the ray florets is white, yellow, pink and purple. Flowering extends over a very long period, from late spring or early summer to the first serious frosts of the autumn. It does, however, tend to occur in flushes, and flower production is depressed by spells of hot weather. Plants do best in coastal areas because, in warm summer conditions, nights there are typically cooler than inland. In hot summers *Osteospermum* is at its best early and late in the flowering season. I am writing this in late October and the plants in my Worcestershire garden are still very much in flower, with numerous buds to maintain the succession until frost strikes.

Propagation is easily achieved by means of cuttings. Early (or even mid-) autumn is the ideal time for the purpose, as plants obtained from cuttings in late spring or early summer will take up too much greenhouse space

over the winter period. The resulting young plants may be used as a routine strategy for overwintering the less hardy cultivars or as an insurance against the loss of the parent plants during winter outdoors. Frost-proof greenhouse or frame conditions are required until the following spring. Control of pests and diseases is not often needed, but the genus is susceptible to aphid infestation and to downy mildew.

Species and cultivars

O. caulescens. See 'White Pim' (under **'White'**, opposite).

O. ecklonis (syn. *Dimorphotheca ecklonis*) is probably the most widely seen species in the genus. In its native South Africa, it is a shrubby plant reaching heights of up to 1m (3ft). In cultivation in cooler climates, it is dwarfer, seldom exceeding 50cm (20in). The usually solitary flowerheads, up to 8cm (3in) across, have dark blue discs surrounded by white ray florets with indigo-blue lower surfaces. Flowering, which starts by early summer, is at its most free during the first month or so but continues until early autumn. The growth habit varies from upright to more or less prostrate. The narrow, grey-green leaves are up to 10cm (4in) long, and have toothed margins.

O. ecklonis **var.** *prostratum.* See 'White Pim' (under **'White'**, opposite).

O. hyoseroides. See *Tripteris hyoseroides* (p.126).

O. jocundum ♔ (syn. *O. barberae, Dimorphotheca barberae*) is also South African and is the hardiest species grown in British gardens. It does not usually exceed 25cm (10in) in height, is of neat but spreading habit, and produces solitary mauve-pink to magenta-purple flowerheads, up to 5cm (2in) across, over the same long period as *O. ecklonis.* The reverse sides of the ray florets are bronze-purple and the central discs purple when the flowerheads open, changing later to gold.

This fine garden species has produced a number of varieties. **'Blackthorn Seedling'** ♔ is of more compact growth, with darker-coloured flowers. **'Langtrees'** ♔ has pink ray florets, bronze on their reverse sides.

Hybrids

There are currently around 100 cultivars available. All of them were introduced during the last quarter of the twentieth century, and in their parentages several species have been involved. It is likely that the flow of new introductions will continue, and good progress is being made in breeding cultivars with flowers that stay open longer in dull conditions.

Hardiness varies according to parentage, and with new introductions gardeners are likely to have to experiment for themselves to find out how well or otherwise they overwinter outdoors. In general, plants with variegated foliage need greenhouse shelter during the frosty months of the year, as do yellow-flowered cultivars. The more compact types and those with a spreading habit are likely to be found hardier than the taller-growing ones.

The following brief selection of cultivars is divided according to ray floret colour or form. An asterisk indicates that it is known to be at least fairly hardy, but absence of an asterisk may simply mean that its hardiness has so far not been thoroughly tested.

White: 'Arctur' (compact), 'Lady Leitrim' ♔, 'Nairobi'★ (dwarf, spreading), 'Silver Sparkler' ♔ and 'Uranus' (both with white-variegated foliage), 'Weetwood'★ ♔ (dwarf), 'White Pim'★ ♔ (syn. *O. ecklonis* var. *prostratum, O. caulescens*).

Yellow: 'Alex', 'Buttermilk' ♔, 'Zulu' (all three of erect habit, and not hardy).

Purple: 'Cannington Roy'★ (dwarf, prostrate), 'Denebola' and 'Mira' (both compact), 'Lusaka'.

Pink: 'Caroline' (compact), 'Chris Brickell' (tall), 'Gemini' (spreading), 'Orania Peach'.

Spoon-flowered: In these cultivars, the edges of the central portion of each ray floret are folded together, but the tip is fully expanded. The same phenomenon is found in some chrysanthemum cultivars. 'Nasinga White', 'Vega' and 'Whirligig' ♔ are whites. 'Antares' is pink, as are 'Nasinga Dark Pink' and 'Pink Whirls'. 'Sonja' is purple, as is 'Nasinga Purple'.

DIMORPHOTHECA Star of the veldt

For gardeners *Dimorphotheca* can be regarded as the annual equivalent of *Osteospermum*. The two genera are closely related and have, in fact, seen a considerable traffic of species between them, as botanical opinion has moved in this way or that: *Osteospermum ecklonis*, for example, is still widely catalogued, and spoken of, as *Dimorphotheca ecklonis*. The generic name means 'with seed cases (*thecae*) of two shapes', those formed from the fertile ray florets differing from those of the disc.

Just two of the seven species in the genus are generally cultivated. These are graceful in both the form of the

PLATE X
Herbaceous Perennials 2

Brachyscome 'Mini Yellow'

Gazania Kiss Series – mixed colours

Bidens ferulifolia

Osteospermum 'Volta'

Euryops pectinatus

Osteospermum 'Namaqua'

Osteospermum 'Zulu'

Osteospermum 'Kalanga'

Brachyscome
'Jumbo Mauve'

All plants shown at
approximately half lifesize

Arctotis
× *hybrida* 'Flame'

Argyranthemum
'Vancouver'

Argyranthemum
'Petite Pink'

Argyranthemum
'Chelsea Girl'

Argyranthemum
'Double White'

The *Osteospermum* hybrid 'Nasinga Dark Pink' is called spoon-flowered due to the variant form of the ray florets.

flowerheads and their display and poise on the wiry stems. They are both quite low annuals, spreading enough in habit to cover the ground effectively with foliage, above which the showy flowerheads develop profusely in a sunny spot. The ray florets have a characteristic sheen, which adds to their attractiveness.

Placement where there is maximum exposure to sun is important but given this, culture is easy. Plants flower best on well-drained, dryish soil, usually commencing within three months of sowing and continuing well into early autumn. They thrive on rockeries and dry stone walls with a southerly aspect. In the southern half of England and most of the USA, direct sowing in mid-spring where they are to grow can be perfectly satisfactory. For convenience, and an earlier start to flowering, they are more often raised as half hardy annuals. Properly hardened off, plants will tolerate slight frost.

D. pluvialis has white, scented flowerheads, up to 5cm (2in) across, with a small, dark brownish-purple disc. The undersides of the ray florets are tinged purple. Plant height is up to 40cm (16in). **'Glistening White'** differs in having ray florets with a dark blue base, thus forming a narrow ring of this colour round the disc.

D. sinuata (syn. *D. aurantiaca*) is very similar except that its flowerheads are usually orange-yellow, but sometimes of paler colours or white. In the garden hybrids, derived from crossing the species with *D. pluvialis*, the colour range is wider still, with rose and purple as well. Unfortunately, *D. sinuata* and its hybrids are without scent. Plant height is about 30cm (12in). Although seed of the garden hybrids is sold in mixed colours, some tastefully formulated colour blends are to be had. **'Pastel Silks'** range from white to yellow and orange, via shades of cream and buff, **'Salmon Queen'** comprises shades of salmon and apricot, while **'Passion Mixed'** is rose, purple and white.

TRIPTERIS

There are about 20 species of *Tripteris*, a genus closely related to *Osteospermum*, and regarded as a section of it by some botanists. Just one species, the annual *T. hyoseroides*, is occasionally cultivated. Its requirements are the same as for the much better-known annual species of *Dimorphotheca*. As a garden plant, it is an alternative to *D. sinuata* and *Ursinia*, visually distinct from both by the comparatively broad ray florets. Like them it is free flowering over a long period.

A native of South Africa, about 50cm (20in) tall, ***T. hyoseroides*** has flowerheads up to 5cm (2in) across with vivid orange-yellow ray florets, and a yellow disc darkening with age. These are borne well above the foliage in loose few-flowered corymbs on strong but slender stems.

URSINIA

This genus includes a number of free-flowering annuals of graceful character, bearing orange and yellow daisies.

A graceful annual, *Dimorphotheca pluvialis* has ray florets with a characteristic sheen.

Their thin, wiry stems rise from a froth of finely cut aromatic foliage to bear the narrow-rayed flowerheads. The consensus of opinion is that these show a lesser tendency to close up in dull weather conditions than those of other South African daisies.

Although undeniably attractive plants, ursinias have become less widely grown in recent years. This is a pity, and one with a personal resonance, since *U. speciosa* was the first annual flower I can remember growing, and very well it did in the sandy soil of my parents' Surrey garden.

Culture is very straightforward – as half hardy annuals. They do best on poor, light soil which is freely drained. They are useful for containers, both outdoors and in a cool greenhouse. Properly hardened off, plants may be set out in the open in late spring even though a risk of slight frost persists at the time.

The following three species are all true annuals and all attain a height of about 30cm (12in). They have flowerheads about 5cm (2in) across, very freely produced in summer and early autumn.

U. anthemoides has yellow or orange flowerheads, the ray florets each with a purple-brown base so that a narrow dark zone encircles the small golden-yellow disc.

U. calenduliflora has yellow flowers, again with a dark purple zone at the base of the ray florets.

U. speciosa has yellow or orange-yellow flowerheads with purple centres.

ARCTOTIS

This South African genus is quite well known for the showy, intensely orange flowerheads of the annual species *A. fastuosum*, not inappropriately also called 'the monarch of the veldt'. It is still better known for the perennial hybrids between this species and *A. venusta*, of which some, such as 'Flame', are undeniably classy plants for a container or bed in a sunny position. Botanically, *Arctotis* is closely related to *Gazania*. Horticulturally, the habit of the plants is more akin to the much less closely related *Dimorphotheca*. Some species used to be placed in the now obsolete genus *Venidium*. To a greater or lesser extent, as with other African daisies, the flowerheads close when the sun goes in, and the choice of growing situations must be made accordingly.

Apart from *A. fastuosum* and *A. venusta*, there are a very few other species, which are occasionally cultivated.

All are annuals of modest height with relatively long-stemmed solitary flowerheads very freely produced from midsummer to early autumn.

The leaves, stems and flowerheads of all cultivated *Arctotis* are more or less hairy, and their grey-green colour adds to the attractiveness of the plants. None of the species cultivated is frost-tolerant. Cultivation as a plant for summer beds or for containers is perfectly straightforward, just as for *Dimorphotheca*.

From late spring or early summer sowings, a good show of flowers may be had in a cool greenhouse during autumn, with more to follow the next spring. A special sowing may not always be necessary: I have been delighted with the results from plants of 'Harlequin New Hybrids' dug up from the garden in early autumn and transferred to large pots.

Plants of both the annual species and of the *A.* × *hybrida* mixtures should be raised in usual bedding-plant fashion, sowing in early spring. Occasionally germination is slow or unsatisfactory because of dormancy in fresh seed: year-old seed is more dependable, though as you cannot buy it as such, you will have to carry out the storage for yourself. Named cultivars are easily propagated by cuttings, just as for *Gerbera*.

Potential pest problems may be with aphids and, particularly just after planting out, slugs. Young plants being overwintered in greenhouses are susceptible to loss by fungal attack and should be kept as dry as possible.

Species and cultivars

A. fastuosum (syn. *Venidium fastuosum*), an annual, grows to a height of about 60cm (24in). Flowerheads are up to 8cm (3in) across, with many brilliant orange ray florets surrounding a very dark central disc. There is a white form, seeds of which are sold as **'Zulu Prince'**. A striking mixture of this with a selection of the orange-flowered type of the species is available under the name **'Jaffa Ice'**. In both forms a narrow zone immediately around the disc is contrastingly coloured – dark purple in the orange-flowered version, dark purple-red and orange in the white.

A. venusta is a short-lived perennial, sometimes behaving as an annual, growing to 75cm (30in) high. It has flowerheads about 5cm (2in) across with a very dark blue-red centre. Ray florets may be white, pinkish or reddish-purple. There are fewer in each flowerhead than in *A. fastuosum*, giving them an airiness lacking in the annual.

Arctotis venusta is a parent of the more popular *Arctotis* hybrids like 'Flame' (below).

The species is not often grown in gardens, but is important as a parent of **A. × hybrida** (syn. × *Venidioarctotis* hybrids), the plants by which the genus is best known. The other parent is *A. fastuosum*. The plants are of sprawling habit but have strong-stemmed flowerheads intermediate in size and character between those of the parents and in a colour range embracing shades of pink, purple, orange, red and white. Those of **'Harlequin New Hybrids'** (height 50cm/20in) have a characteristic dark zone immediately round the disc. Of the vegetatively propagated named cultivars, **'Apricot'**, the tangerine-orange **'Flame'** ♔, more upright in habit than most, and the pale reddish-purple **'Wine'** are among the best. These are about 40cm (16in) tall.

For gardeners with enough suitably sunny space and an experimental turn of mind, other *Arctotis* species are worth a trial. For example, **A. auriculata** has yellow flowerheads, and **A. hirsuta** white. Both are about 50cm (20in) tall.

FELICIA Blue marguerite, Kingfisher daisy

Pretty blue flowerheads – relatively small but correspondingly abundant – are the distinctive feature of the cultivated members of this genus of 85 species. None of the other well-known daisy-flowered plants native to South Africa have flowerheads of this colour. A sunny position is as much needed for *Felicia* as for the other genera in this chapter.

All the cultivated *Felicia* species have a long flowering period, commencing in midsummer and ending in early autumn. The long-stemmed flowerheads are solitary, with comparatively small, yellow discs. The ray florets are female.

Although they also make attractive greenhouse plants, the perennial species are most often used outdoors in summer, for containers such as patio tubs, window boxes and hanging baskets. Their blue flowers complement white or pink argyranthemums very well. The annual species are commonly used in the same way, though they are more often used as dwarf bedding plants. *Felicia* will perform well in relatively wind-exposed sites.

Propagation of the annual species is as half hardy plants by seed sown in early spring in greenhouse conditions. *F. rosulata* and *F. uliginosa* are divided in early spring, and *F. petiolata* is propagated by layering. For all other perennial

Arctotis hybrid 'Flame' ♔ is a fine, vegetatively propagated cultivar for a sunny position.

species cuttings are usually taken in early spring from plants overwintered in cool greenhouse conditions. The new plants will flower freely in the same season. For growing on to flower in a greenhouse or conservatory, cuttings taken in late summer give better value.

Annuals

F. bergeriana (Kingfisher daisy) is a mat-forming plant, only about 15cm (6in) high. Its flowerheads have rather widely spaced, narrow, bright blue ray florets and are about 3cm (1¼in) across.

F. heterophylla is a little taller, about 20cm (8in), and has broader ray florets. **'The Blues'** has an all-blue flowerhead, the disc similar in colour to the rays. **'The Rose'** has rose-pink ray florets and a yellow disc. Seed of the two is sometimes sold in mixture.

Perennials

F. amelloides (syn. *Aster coelestis* and *F. capensis*) (Blue marguerite) is the most popular species. A subshrub in the wild, the bushy plants have opposite leaves, and flowerheads up to 5cm (2in) across.

Its cultivars **'Read's Blue'** and **'Read's White'** make compact plants, up to 30cm (12in) tall. The more popular **'Santa Anita'** ♔ is rather taller, and has rich blue flowerheads. Also blue-flowered, the widely grown **'Variegata'** has foliage margined creamy-white. Height is again about 30cm (12in), but the flowerheads are smaller. It is a very attractive container plant.

F. amoena (syn. *Aster pappei*) is a good hanging-basket plant, with bright blue flowerheads to 3.5cm (1½in) across. As a bedding plant it may reach 30cm (12in) tall. **'Variegata'** is less vigorous, with cream and green leaves.

F. rosulata (syn. *Aster natalensis*) is rhizomatous and has a different habit: its leaves are in rosettes, and the 4cm (1½in) diameter flowerheads are produced on stems up to 20cm (8in) long.

F. uliginosa is a spreading, prostrate plant, which produces small, blue flowerheads about 2.5cm (1in) across. It is more or less hardy.

F. petiolata differs from all the other species described in being a shrub, hardy in sheltered positions where winters are mild. It is the hardiest of the species described here and is worth much wider recognition. The very lax stems give the plant a spreading habit and it eventually makes a dense mound of growth up to 75cm (30in) tall, and considerably greater in width. Small pink flowerheads, up to 2cm (¾in) across, open in abundance from late spring to midsummer. It flowers from its second year.

GERBERA Barberton daisy

Most well-stocked florists' shops offer these large, long-stemmed daisies, often in colours that seem almost fluorescent. They are particularly popular as cut flowers in some countries of continental Europe. Dwarf cultivars grown commercially as pot plants have recently become a garden centre commonplace and this may boost demand for the *Gerbera* as a cut flower elsewhere.

The parents of the hybrids by which gardeners know this genus are both herbaceous perennials, native to Africa. In countries with markedly cooler climates, the hybrids need to be grown in a greenhouse. From a sowing in mid- or late winter, in heated conditions, plants can be expected to flower from late summer on. For cut flowers, one plant in a 20cm (8in) pot or – easier to manage – three in a 35–40cm (14–16in) pot should be grown. A suitable pot size for the dwarf cultivars is 12cm (5in). Once flowering ceases in late autumn, plants should be overwintered cool and as dry as possible short of causing prolonged wilting.

Propagation from cuttings detached from the base of the plants in early spring is an alternative to seed. In any event plants are usually best replaced after their third year. They are susceptible to fungal attack at the crown. Watering from below, if possible, and keeping dry in winter, help to minimize the risk of loss.

G. jamesonii, one of the parents of the hybrids, has spreading basal rosettes of dark green, wavy-edged, pinnatifid leaves up to 50cm (20in) long. The leafless flower stems, up to 60cm (24in) long, carry solitary flowerheads up to 10cm (4in) across. The garden hybrids are similar in growth habit and flowering. Another species, **G. viridifolia**, has also been involved in the breeding of modern cultivars with flower colours that include shades of yellow, red, pink and orange. Seed is usually available only in colour mixtures. The **Pandora Series**, **Happipot Series**, **Festival Series** and **Masquerade Series** have been bred for use as pot plants, and on these smaller plants the flower stems do not exceed 30cm (12in).

15 Senecio, Lactuca and their Allies

The relationship between the two principal genera in this chapter, *Senecio* and *Lactuca*, is distant – they are placed together here purely for convenience. However, other genera within the tribes (Senecioneae and Lactuceae) that these two belong to do have a close botanical relationship with one another.

Senecio and some relatives

The four genera that are included within this section are all members of the tribe Senecioneae, which is the largest tribe in the entire daisy family. Four of the *Senecio* species included here are hardy herbaceous perennials, as are the members of the other three genera. However, as *Senecio* is a huge genus and also contains a wide array of horticulturally disparate annual, woody perennial, half hardy and tender plants, I have also described a number of these.

Other genera that belong to the Senecioneae, but for gardening purposes fit more properly in other chapters include *Brachyglottis*, *Othonna* and *Euryops*, which are with the shrubs, *Doronicum*, which is with the yellow daisies and *Emilia*, *Pericallis* and *Steirodiscus*, which are with the annuals.

SENECIO

With around 1,250 species, this is the largest genus in the daisy family and one of the largest genera in the entire plant kingdom. It is distributed worldwide, and among British natives are groundsel and that persistent hazard to grazing livestock, ragwort. Considering its size, its worldwide distribution and its range of habitat, remarkably few species are horticulturally worthwhile. Some gardenworthy members have been reclassified, however. The best-known example is that of the most widely grown of all grey-leaved shrubs, the *Brachyglottis* cultivar 'Sunshine', formerly known as both *Senecio greyi* and *S. laxifolius*.

Among its horticulturally valuable species, *Senecio* has two grown as silver-leaved bedding plants, one annual and two herbaceous perennials with striking purple daisy flowers, two further perennials for wild gardens in boggy or very moist conditions, and three tender climbers.

Full exposure to sun suits outdoor species best unless otherwise indicated. Other cultural requirements and methods of propagation differ quite widely, so are covered under each entry.

Annuals and shrubs grown as annuals

S. ciliocarpa (syn. *Jacobea elegans*, *S. elegans*, *S. purpurea*) is a true annual, best cultivated as a half hardy annual, and native to South Africa. Its erect, branched stems take the plant to about 60cm (24in). The flowerheads, purple or reddish-purple with yellow centres, are 2.5cm (1in) across and borne in corymbs from midsummer onwards.

S. cineraria (syn. *S. candicans*, *S. maritimus*, *Cineraria maritima*) is an evergreen – or should I say ever-silver? – shrub, native to Mediterranean areas. Grown as an annual, plants attain a height of about 30cm (12in) with the stout, freely branching stems bearing silver-grey leaves up to 15cm (6in) long. These vary from coarsely toothed to pinnate.

Three cultivars account for almost all the millions of plants of this species grown each year, and all come true from seed. The most widely grown of these is 'Silver Dust' ♔, with deeply divided leaves, nearly silver-white, and a compact habit. 'White Diamond' ♔ is similar, while 'Cirrus' has silvery-green, elliptic, deeply toothed foliage. They are usually grown from seed, and treated as half hardy annuals, but semi-ripe cuttings can also be taken in late summer and the young plants overwintered in a cool greenhouse.

Although not fully hardy, plants will overwinter outdoors in mild areas. In their second year they will grow to about 50cm (20in) tall, and produce small flowerheads of an intense yellow. These arguably do nothing for the attractiveness of the plant and are better removed.

S. viravira ♀ (syn. *S. leucostachys*) is a more elegant counterpart to the previous species. A native of Argentina, the plant has a more spreading habit than *S. cineraria*. It eventually grows to about 60cm (24in), or against a wall, taller – 1m (3ft) or more. Because of its finer foliage and the colour of the small flowerheads, a pleasing creamy yellow, I suggest you choose this species rather than *S. cineraria*, if you want to treat it as a small shrub rather than an annual bedding plant. It does, however, need a sheltered place where the hardest frosts are unlikely to exceed −5°C (23°F). Unfortunately, it is a very brittle plant, and the branches need tying to supports. The best foliage colour develops on plants in nutritionally poor soils. Propagation is by cuttings, best taken in early spring and rooted in greenhouse conditions.

Herbaceous perennials

S. doria (syn. *S. macrophyllus*) grows to 1m (3ft) or more in height, and in early to midsummer bears masses of small, yellow flowerheads, not more than 2.5cm (1in) across, in dense compound corymbs. Of erect habit and glossy-leaved, this very hardy but somewhat coarse plant is native over a wide area of Europe and in the wild grows in wet soils. In the garden, it is a species for the wild garden near the water's edge. Propagation is by division or seed.

S. smithii is another coarse species with a good deal in common with *S. doria* – similar in height and hardiness, and suitable for wet soils in particular. Its flowerheads are a good deal larger, up to 5cm (2in) across, and have white ray florets around a yellow disc. They are borne in fairly dense corymbs on stout, erect stems, up to 1.25m (4ft) tall, furnished with large, dark green leaves. A native of the southern tip of South America, including the Falkland Isles, this species has become naturalized in Scotland and the Shetlands: in both natural and adopted environments, it is a plant of wet places. Propagation is by division or seed.

S. polyodon is an African native, but fully hardy. Erect in habit, it has slender flowering stems, about 50cm (20in) high, which arise from rosettes of dark green, lance-shaped leaves. The lilac-purple or pink flowerheads, much like those of the florists' cineraria (*Pericallis hybridus*) but smaller, are up to 2.5cm (1in) across and are very freely produced from early summer onwards. Plants will flower into the autumn if deadheaded. Propagation is by division or seed.

A Mediterranean native, *Senecio cineraria* makes a fine shrub where mild winters allow it to survive.

Moist soil and semi-shade suit Chinese groundsel, *Sinacalia tangutica*, a striking but invasive plant.

S. pulcher is quite a choice autumn-flowering daisy, bearing flowerheads up to 8cm (3in) across, with brilliant purple ray florets surrounding a yellow disc. These are in loose, few-flowered corymbs on erect stems up to 60cm (24in) high. A South American native, it is hardy only in areas with mild winters, and needs a sheltered spot. Partial shade and good soil are preferred. Propagation is by division or seed.

S. tanguticus. See *Sinacalia tangutica*.

Tender perennial climbers

The following three daisy-flowered species, all evergreen twining climbers, are suitable for a cool greenhouse or conservatory, in which a minimum temperature of 7°C (45°F) is normally maintained. In most conditions in cultivation, stem lengths seldom exceed two-thirds of those given in the descriptions. If the roots are restricted by growing in containers, as is usually done, stems may be shorter still. All may be propagated by seed, layering or leaf-bud cuttings.

S. confusus (Mexican flame vine) in the wild may climb to 6m (20ft) or more. Its showy, fragrant flowerheads are orange-yellow, darkening to orange-red, and are 5cm (2in) across. They are freely produced in corymbs, mostly in summer.

The slender stems of **S. macroglossus** (Cape ivy) can extend up to 3m (10ft). The variegated form, **'Variegatus'** ♛ is almost always grown, its triangular, ivy-like, cream-variegated leaves being its principal attraction. These are thick and glossy and up to 6cm (2½in) long. The cream or pale yellow flowerheads, of about the same diameter, are mostly produced singly during winter.

S. scandens produces slender stems up to 5m (16ft) long, and is of particular value for its flowering period – autumn and winter. The yellow flowerheads are quite small, to 1.5cm (½in) in diameter, but are in corymbs up to 13cm (5in) across.

SINACALIA Chinese groundsel

Just one species of this small Chinese genus is cultivated: **S. tangutica**. Previously named both *Ligularia tangutica* and *Senecio tanguticus*, it is an erect and very hardy herbaceous perennial, 1–1.5m (3–5ft) tall, with very dark stems and handsome, pinnately cut foliage. The small, yellow flowerheads open from mid- to late summer, and the display continues into the early autumn. The large inflorescences, roughly broad-conical in shape, have an airy character, largely because each flowerhead has just 2 or 3 narrow ray florets. The floral display is succeeded by feathery seed clusters, giving the plant an attractiveness extending into the winter months.

The vigour of the plant and its creeping rootstock make it invasive, and despite its attractiveness, *S. tangutica* is a satisfactory choice only for larger gardens. It does best in moist soils and in semi-shade, and looks particularly fine in a poolside position. Propagation is by division.

LIGULARIA

Some of the most striking herbaceous perennials in any family are found in *Ligularia*. There are about 125 species, all herbaceous perennials native to temperate Asia and Siberia. The small number in cultivation are all hardy natives of the Far East, mainly China and Japan. The name derives from the Latin 'ligula', a little tongue, and refers to the shape of the ray florets.

Fine examples of garden species are *L. stenocephala* and *L. przewalskii* with their long, slender, yellow-flowered racemes rising from a basal cluster of handsome dark green foliage. An established group of either in a favourable environment presents a memorable garden spectacle in summer. Rivalry in form is posed by few other plants, with perhaps only *Eremurus*, the foxtail lily, springing to mind.

For *L. dentata* and its two cultivars 'Desdemona' and 'Othello', it is the coloured leaves which are the prime attraction: I find it difficult to enthuse about the flowers as such, presented to the eye as a cluster of no particular visual appeal. A distinguished American horticulturist, Dr Allan Armitage, even urges their removal as distracting attention from the plant's much better feature, its foliage.

These are not plants for all gardens, by any manner of means: moisture-retentive soil, preferably humus-rich, is needed, and at very least some shade during the hotter part of the day. Ideally, they should be grown by the edges of streams, large pools or lakes, or in semi-wild conditions in woodland. Unfortunately, these are not conditions that most gardeners can provide: it is not by chance that the three National Collections in Britain are situated near Sheffield, in Cumbria, and in the Glasgow area, all places where cool summers and high rainfall are expected climatic features. Nevertheless, it is well worth giving them a trial in the most favourable situation you can provide, so long as your soil is moisture retentive and you have both the space and some part-day shade for them. At one stage in my career, I was confronted with taking over the planting of a herbaceous border in spring, in very disadvantageous conditions. Without benefit of waterside or woodland, *L. przewalskii* became the star turn of the border during its first two years.

The plants in cultivation are summer-flowering, of medium or tall stature, with large, long-stalked broad leaves. The ray florets, few in number, are female, and yellow or orange. The individual flowerheads, although quite showy, are not specially attractive, partly because of the wide spacing of the ray florets. Nevertheless, the inflorescence as a whole is very handsome in the species in which they are an elongated raceme. The colours of leaves, leaf stalks and stems contribute to the attractiveness of many species and cultivars. The genus is botanically quite close to *Senecio*, but one distinguishing difference is that the lower ends of the leaf stalks completely ensheath the stem.

Given suitable basic conditions, cultivation is undemanding. They are gross feeders, however, as well as having high moisture needs. They are, therefore, particularly likely to repay a generous mulch of compost or well-rotted stable manure in late winter or very early spring, as well as a fertilizer top-dressing at the same time. They are plants in the priority league for watering in dry summer conditions. Propagation is usually by division in spring, though the species can easily enough be raised from seed. Slugs and snails may be troublesome in spring.

All featured species and cultivars flower from mid- to late summer and have yellow ray florets, unless otherwise described. I have divided them into two groups, according to the character of the inflorescence.

Elongated racemes or panicles

In my opinion, these are the most generally garden-worthy members of the genus.

L. przewalskii (pronounced 'pshavalskee-eye') grows up to 1.75m (6ft) tall and has deep purple stems bearing numerous small flowerheads in a slender inflorescence up to 1m (3ft) long. Individual flowerheads have very few ray florets – usually two only. The foliage is a garden glory in its own right: the dark green leaves are up to 30cm (12in) long and deeply palmately cut, with the narrow, pointed segments themselves deeply and sharply toothed.

L. stenocephala is a closely related species, differing in being rather shorter, to 1.5m (5ft) and in commencing to flower earlier, in early summer. Before this time, the most obvious difference is in its foliage. The large leaves, heart-shaped to triangular in outline, are up to 30cm (12in) across with emphatically toothed margins and a finely pointed tip.

'The Rocket' ♛ is thought to be a hybrid between

the two previous species. It grows rather taller than *L. stenocephala*, and the strikingly handsome leaves are very deeply toothed, almost jagged edged. The open flowerheads present a more definitely solid colour effect in the inflorescence than in the more airy racemes of the parental species. As in *L. przewalskii*, the flower stems are very dark.

L. tangutica. See *Sinacalia tangutica*.

L. veitchiana is much less commonly seen than 'The Rocket' or its parent species. Growing to a similar height, up to 1.75m (6ft), its long-stalked, bright yellow flowerheads are relatively large, to 6cm (2½in) across, with 8–12 ray florets, and the inflorescences are accordingly broader than those of *L. stenocephala*. The large, long-stalked leaves are rounded, to 60cm (24in) across, deeply sinuate and with distinctly toothed margins.

'**Zepter**' is a chance seedling of which *L. veitchiana* is one parent and *L. przewalskii* is thought to be the other. The slender racemes, up to 1m (3ft) long, may take the overall plant height to over 2m (6½ft). The rays are deep yellow and the flowering stems almost black.

L. wilsoniana (Giant groundsel) is similar to *L. veitchiana*, but has smaller flowerheads, only about 2.5cm (1in) across, with 6–8 ray florets. It is a later-flowering species, from late summer to early autumn.

L. fischeri is less seen than *L. veitchiana* and *L. wilsoniana*, but is similar in general characteristics. Its flowerheads are slightly smaller than those of the first species. The racemes are up to 75cm (30in) long.

Flat-topped or conical clusters of flowerheads

Grown primarily for its foliage, **L. dentata** forms a dense clump of large, long-stalked and quite handsome, mid-green leaves, up to 30cm (12in) long, and rather greater in width. They are kidney-shaped, or rounded with heart-shaped bases. The stalks of the basal leaves are red.

The flowering stems grow to a height of up to 1.25m (4ft) and carry lax, flat-topped corymbs of flowerheads, up to 12cm (5in) across, each with about 10 orange-yellow ray florets. It is a native of China and Japan.

Ligularia 'The Rocket' ♀ is a handsome and imposing plant valued for its striking leaves and stems, as well as for its dramatic yellow inflorescences.

Though the species itself is quite handsome, its two dark-leaved cultivars '**Desdemona**' ♀ and '**Othello**' are much more widely grown, though their leaves may be damaged by strong sunlight. 'Desdemona' has purple stems, leaf undersides, leaf stalks and veins. The upper leaf surfaces are very dark brownish-green. The rays of the flowerheads are deeper in colour than the species. 'Othello', an older cultivar, is quite similar, with the upper leaf surfaces purplish-green. Both cultivars come more or less true from seed.

L. hodgsonii is a similar species to *L. dentata*, but with smaller leaves and flowerheads. It can be a better proposition when space is limited. It reaches about 75cm (30in) in height. The rays are orange or bright yellow.

L. × palmatiloba has as parents *L. japonica* and *L. dentata*. It grows to about 1.75m (6ft), and has deeply lobed or jaggedly toothed foliage, giving it an attractiveness in leaf form which *L. dentata* lacks. The flowerheads, up to 10cm (4in) across, are borne in rather flat-topped inflorescences on sometimes long stalks. Although the two parents are handsome, I place the hybrid top.

'**Gregynog Gold**' ♀ is a hybrid between *L. wilsoniana* and *L. dentata*, and an imposing plant for a large garden. It grows to a height of about 1.75m (6ft) with orange-yellow flowerheads about 10cm (4in) across in large, conical inflorescences, intermediate in form between those of the parents. The cordate leaves are very large, and plants in flower are a commanding spectacle. It will thrive in full sun provided the soil is sufficiently moist to meet its needs.

L. × hessei, thought to be another hybrid between *L. dentata* and *L. wilsoniana*, is similar to 'Gregynog Gold' but comparatively little grown.

PETASITES Butterbur, Sweet coltsfoot

This is a genus primarily for large, wild gardens where there is room to accommodate their rampantly spreading nature. Some of the most striking plants in the daisy family, *Petasites* species earn their place in a suitable environment partly for their extraordinary inflorescences, in most cultivated species produced very early in the year, before the leaves emerge. The foliage itself is the longer-lasting feature of gardening remark, creating a ground-cover of such comprehensiveness that other herbaceous plants seldom succeed in maintaining their place in competition beyond a year or so. In most cultivated species the individual leaves are large and in *P. japonica* very large indeed: leaf blades up to 1.5m (5ft) wide may develop on petioles of commensurate length.

These rhizomatous plants are unisexual, producing flowerheads of both sexes in a panicle on an erect, unbranched stem. This is often furnished with small, often scale-like leaves. Though the stems are very short at flowering time, they later elongate greatly. (The British native, *Tussilago farfara*, coltsfoot, belongs to a closely related genus, but has solitary yellow flowerheads with numerous long rays.)

Petasites species are most at home in moist soils and in partial shade. Woodland and pool- or streamside positions show them to best advantage. All the species are fully hardy, except the Mediterranean native *P. fragrans*. Where temperatures fall below −10°C (14°F), it needs siting in warm, favoured spots. Once established, plants of this genus are both invasive and difficult to eradicate, as the rhizomes run deeply. Propagation is by division or seed.

Species

All species produce inflorescences before the foliage unless otherwise stated.

P. fragrans (Winter heliotrope) is the best-known species and the earliest to flower: from midwinter to early spring. It has become naturalized in places in Britain, and a weed in some gardens, and can do well in drier soils than other species of the genus. Only the male plant is cultivated: its pretty, fragrant flowerheads are purple-pink and white, and are produced on stems up to 50cm (20in) high at about the same time as the first leaves. These are kidney-shaped and up to 20cm (8in) across.

Although also the smallest species described here, it is at least as invasive as the others, which is why it is sometimes grown in a large container. It is valuable, nonetheless, for its earliness of flowering and its strong scent, variously likened to vanilla and heliotrope.

P. albus flowers in late winter and early spring, with broadly bullet-shaped inflorescences, each comprising many small flowerheads of tiny white florets. The stems, about 30cm (12in) high at flowering time, are closely furnished with wide, pale green bracts, appearing clustered together below the inflorescence as the flowerheads open. The lobed, rounded leaf blades are on stalks up to 30cm (12in) long, and may be up to 40cm (16in) across.

P. palmatus is similar to *P. albus* in flowering time, flower colour and leaf size, but the scented flowerheads are borne on a more rounded inflorescence, and the leaves are palmately lobed, rather like rhubarb.

P. paradoxus is also similar to *P. albus*, but flowers later. It has red-pink to white florets, and reddish-brown involucres and stem leaves.

P. japonicus has yellowish-white flowerheads, up to 1.5cm (½in) across, closely packed together in a conical inflorescence, which appears in late winter and early spring. The kidney-shaped leaves are very large in the species itself, and larger still in the **var. *giganteus***, which is the form usually grown. At the extreme, they exceed 1.5m (5ft) wide on petioles up to 2m (6½ft) long. Its cultivar **'Nishiki-buki'** (syn. 'Variegatus') has foliage streaked and blotched with yellow.

P. hybridus, a British native, is the latest species to flower in spring. The male flowerheads, borne 20cm (8in) above ground, are bright purple, and densely clustered in a bullet-shaped inflorescence. They are more attractive than the female: only male plants are cultivated. The leaves, lobed though rounded in outline, are up to 60cm (24in) across, forming a canopy up to 1m (3ft) high.

The lettuces

This section covers genera that belong to the lettuce tribe, Lactuceae, that are important for their perennial species. They are characterized by the double-flowered appearance of the flowerheads, and partly by their distinctive ray florets, square-ended and five-toothed. No members of the tribe are of front-rank importance as ornamental plants, but among them are some very pleasing contributions to the garden flora.

LACTUCA and CICERBITA

The lettuce genus, *Lactuca*, has about 75 species, of which only *L. perennis* is of any importance as an ornamental garden plant. Unless, that is, you think the fringed, red-tinted leaves of that prettiest of all culinary lettuce varieties 'Lolla Rossa' deserves a place in a flower bed!

L. perennis (Blue lettuce) is native to much of continental Europe, mainly in dry, sunny positions on limestone. It is a hardy perennial, growing to about 75cm (30in) with freely branched stems producing loose panicles of flowerheads in summer. These are up to 4cm (1½in) across, with quite narrow, blue to lilac ray florets tapering to a point, giving the flowerheads a dainty appearance.

Cicerbita alpina (syn. *Lactuca alpina*) belongs to a very closely related genus. Sometimes known as the mountain sow thistle, it is a native of mountainous areas in Europe, including – as a rare plant – Scotland. A very hardy perennial, it has an erect habit and may exceed 2m (6½ft) in height. The small, violet-blue flowerheads, up to 2cm (¾in) across, are produced in long, airy panicles in mid- and late summer.

Unlike *Lactuca perennis*, it does best in moist soil with some shade. Both species are usually propagated by seed.

CATANANCHE Cupid's dart

One hardy perennial species of this small genus is popular as a border plant and as a cut flower, both fresh and dried. At first glance its solitary flowerheads are quite cornflower-like in appearance, but they have the square-ended, five-toothed florets characteristic of the lettuce tribe. Of the few members grown as ornamentals, I think *Catananche* is the most valuable.

C. caerulea thrives in naturally dry, fast-draining soils and does best in full sun. It is short-lived, especially on heavy soils, and is sometimes deliberately treated as a biennial. It is most often grown from seed, but propagation from root cuttings is a productive alternative. If sown in winter in a greenhouse, flowering occurs in the first year. *Catananche* is susceptible to powdery mildew.

C. caerulea is native to dry places in much of southern Europe. The wiry stems, with few leaves, bear the flowerheads from midsummer to early autumn, 50–80cm (20–32in) above the grass-like, hairy, grey-green basal leaves. Lilac-blue to blue, with a darker eye, they are usually around 4cm (1½in) across.

There is a white-flowered cultivar, **'Alba'**, and one that is white with a dark centre, **'Bicolor'**. **'Major'** 🏆 has deep lavender flowerheads, to 5cm (2in) across. Seed of 'Bicolor' produces a proportion of entirely white-flowered plants. 'Major' does not come true from seed.

CICHORIUM Chicory

Like *Lactuca*, this is a genus better known for the table than for its floral attributes. *C. endivia* is endive, and *C. intybus* is chicory, and gives us the fat, cream-coloured leafy buds, forced in darkness and known in Belgium and Holland as Witloof (white leaf). This plant's root, dried and ground, has long been used as a coffee substitute.

C. intybus, a tap-rooted herbaceous perennial, also has flowerheads of the most lovely pale powder blue. It is in other respects a plant of no particular appeal, but for this colour it warrants consideration for a place in large gardens. As it is possibly a British native and is certainly found growing wild in Britain, it is perfectly hardy, and easy to please wherever it gets a reasonable amount of sun. It can be left largely to look after itself, and commonly self-seeds. The flowering period is mainly early to midsummer. The stout stems, around 75cm (30in) tall, bear spike-like inflorescences with flowerheads, similar in form to dandelions, usually about 3cm (1¼in) across. Their double-flowered appearance is typical of members of the lettuce tribe.

There are also white- and pink-flowered versions. All are usually propagated by seed.

HIERACIUM Hawkweed

The hawkweeds are better known as wild flowers than as ornamental garden plants, but a few species are grown for their attractive foliage. Members of a large and widely distributed genus of herbaceous perennials, they all have yellow dandelion-like flowerheads. Just like the dandelion, they also have milky sap and apparently double flowerheads.

They are easy plants to grow, showing their best qualities in full sun, on infertile soil. All fully hardy, they are most at home in rock gardens and on dry stone walls. Wherever they are grown, self-seeding is a potential menace. As the flowerheads are of unspecial nature, if anything detracting from the effect of the foliage, they are as well removed before they open. Propagation is, to borrow the wry words of Dr Jack Elliott in *The Smaller Perennials*, 'only too easy by seed'.

Species

H. lanatum (syn. *H. tomentosum*) is a shaggy-hairy, lime-loving plant with white-felted, wavy-edged leaves, up to 10cm (4in) long and 4cm (1½in) wide. The spread of established clumps can exceed 50cm (20in). In its native France and Northern Italy it is found on limestone.

H. maculatum is a clump-forming plant with leaves deep green or grey-green, and blotched or spotted blackish-purple. Their upper surfaces are usually only slightly hairy. Leaves are a little larger than *H. lanatum*.

H. villosum is also clump-forming, with long, white hairs covering the grey-green leaves. These are similar in length to those of *H. lanatum*, but narrower. This is much the largest flowered of these three species, with flowerheads up to 5cm (2in) across.

PILOSELLA Orange hawkweed, Fox and cubs

Closely related to *Hieracium*, this genus is known in gardening for one species, native to the British Isles. This is **P. aurantiacum** (syn. *Hieracium aurantiacum*), an easy-to-grow and somewhat invasive herbaceous perennial. Its distinctive feature is the dense clustering of small, orange-red flowerheads at the tops of stiff, almost leafless stems, which are usually 20–30cm (8–12in) long, and densely covered in long, very dark hairs. The flowerheads, dandelion-like in form, are up to 2cm (¾in) across, and a very pleasing colour. Up to ten, and occasionally more, are in each cluster, and the flowering period is summer-long.

The plant is very drought tolerant, and will do well in poor, dry soil, in rock gardens and on the tops of dry stone walls. It spreads strongly by leafy rhizomes, and is amply robust enough to place in a wild garden. It is attractive to bees and butterflies. Propagation is by seed or division.

CREPIS Hawk's beard

Several *Crepis* species are natives of the British Isles, and have yellow flowerheads very similar to those of their relative *Hieracium*, the hawkweeds. The only two species of any note for gardeners, however, are from southern Europe and are pink-flowered. One perennial and one annual, both are hardy and both have the apparently fully double flowerheads characteristic of their tribe. Their leaves are mainly in basal rosettes.

They are suitable for sunny positions at the front of a bed or border, or on a rock garden. Both need well-drained soil, but cultivation is straightforward. Propagation is by seed.

The perennial **C. incana** ♛, sometimes called the pink dandelion, produces corymbs of pink flowerheads that are about 3cm (1¼in) across and are carried on branched stems 20–30cm (8–12in) tall. The usually hairy leaves are dandelion-like in shape.

C. rubra is an annual or short-lived perennial of similar height. The flowerheads are also similar in size but are borne singly or in pairs. They are pinkish-red or white.

ANDRYALA

Closely related to the hawkweeds, **A. agardhii** is a dwarf, densely tufted plant, at home in a rock garden and giving a succession of solitary clear yellow, dandelion-like flowerheads, to 2.5cm (1in) across, through the summer. The greyish foliage is quite attractive for its covering of silky, white hairs. A native of southern Spain, it is hardy in areas with mild winters, such as southern Britain, but may succumb to prolonged very cool, wet conditions in winter. A dry stone wall suits it admirably, and it is also a good alpine-house plant. In any event, it does best in full sun and in poor soil. Propagation is usually by seed, or by cuttings taken with a heel in summer.

LEONTODON Hawkbit

L. rigens (syn. *Microseris rigens*) is a humble hardy perennial, notable primarily for foliage effect, easy to grow, and dwarf. It is useful enough in a bed-edge position for its dense clumps of stiffly upright, toothed leaves which are there year-round, ever fresh and green. They are up to 50cm (20in) long and 15cm (6in) wide. Throughout the summer they are complemented – though not to any great effect – by clusters of small, yellow flowerheads on leafless stems 30–40cm (12–16in) or so long. About 2cm (¾in) across, they resemble those of *Hieracium*, to which *Leontodon* is related. The cultivar **'Girandole'** ('Candelabra') is a selection of the species.

This plant is sometimes used in the mixed planting of a large container, for its foliage contribution. Cultivation is very easy and propagation is by seed or division.

UROSPERMUM

U. delachampii looks quite closely akin to the rather better-known *Leontodon rigens*; in fact, the two genera are closely related. The flowerheads of *U. delachampii* differ in being a good deal larger, up to 5cm (2in) across, and solitary. Borne on stems 40cm (16in) or so tall, they are lemon-yellow, with a red stripe often present on the lower surface of the florets. The grey-green hairy leaves are quite attractive, the more basal ones similar in shape to those of the dandelion. Though native to the Mediterranean area, the plant is quite hardy.

Cultivation is easy in any reasonable soil and in a position with some sun. Propagation is by seed or division.

16 A Selection of Perennials

This chapter contains a selection of genera which had no logical place in any other. It would be a serious error to think that this implies a second-class status: on the contrary, some of the finest plants in the daisy family are here.

Of the six genera of major horticultural importance included, five are united by the common feature of lacking typical daisy flowerheads. Many of their species are garden gems on any standards. *Achillea*, for example, offers the extraordinary sculpted inflorescences of *A. filipendulina*, while the dense, long-lasting spikes of *Liatris* are favourites with flower arrangers. *Eupatorium* and *Solidago* are again distinctive. *Artemisia* offers us little joy for its flowerheads, but is among the richest genera in any family for its true glory, its foliage. To turn to flowerheads more or less easily recognizable as daisies, those of *Echinacea purpurea* are unmistakably different, and generate widespread admiration and affection. Some members of the family might justify dismissal as just another daisy, but never this one. Less obviously daisy-like, but also outstanding is the lovely *Stokesia laevis*.

Also featured (pp.158–161) are some fine plants for the rock garden, including the white daisies of *Celmisia*, the distinctive *Raoulia* and, of course, *Leontopodium*, the famous edelweiss of the European Alps.

ACHILLEA Yarrow, Milfoil

Legend has it that Achilles, the great leader of the ancient Greeks, was the first to discover and utilise the medicinal qualities of *Achillea millefolium*, and the genus is named after him. Whether he did, indeed, use it to staunch the flow of blood from his soldiers' wounds, we shall never know, but it is certainly a plant with which he would have been acquainted. Along with most of the 115 species of its genus, it is distributed in the wild in Europe and western Asia.

All *Achillea* species are herbaceous perennials and all those described here are fully hardy. They are generally rhizomatous plants, some of them being aggressive spreaders. Almost all of them have very finely divided, aromatic foliage. In many species this is grey or silver, adding to their ornamental value. The comparatively few species used in gardens include some fine border plants for sunny positions, and a number of dwarf species of distinction as rock garden plants. All the taller species and hybrids described – notably *A. filipendulina* and *A. millefolium* – are excellent as cut flowers, both fresh and dried.

The flowerheads are small or very small, but in many species are massed tightly together in dense, flat-topped clusters. These inflorescences have a form unlike those of any other widely cultivated genus in the daisy family. In the popular yellow-flowered *A. filipendulina* they have an almost sculpted quality, providing a distinctive contrast to the flowers and inflorescences of neighbouring plants. Ray florets are in many species so small as to escape attention as individuals, but where they are larger, they will be noticed as characteristically broad and few in number in each flowerhead.

All the cultivated species are summer-flowering plants, generally with long flowering periods. Cultivation of the taller ones appropriate for use in beds and borders usually presents no great problems, as those described will thrive in any reasonably fertile garden soil that is well-drained. Heavy soils, however, do not suit most species, and the best results are to be had on relatively poor, dry soils in positions fully exposed to sun. This is particularly true for the dwarfer members of the genus, cultivated as rock-garden plants.

Propagation is usually by division in spring, or by cuttings taken at that time. The species and some cultivars

'Coronation Gold' ♛ is rated the 'best upright yellow yarrow' by American authority Allan Armitage.

come readily from seed, and will usually flower the year after sowing. Members of the genus are susceptible to attack by aphids and by powdery mildew. *A. ptarmica* can be particularly badly affected by the disease.

Tall species and cultivars

The more widely grown, taller species (40cm/16in or over), which are of value as border plants and as cut flowers, conveniently fall into two groups. In the first, flowerheads are borne separately from one another in loose inflorescences; the three species concerned here are *A. ptarmica*, very well known for its double-flowered cultivars, and the similar but smaller-flowered *A. cartilaginea*, and *A. ageratum*. In the second, larger group are the species in which the very small flowerheads are densely packed together to form characteristic flat-topped, umbel-like inflorescences. These are *A. filipendulina*, *A. grandifolia*, and *A. millefolium*.

Some species of *Achillea* hybridize quite readily, with the result that, in addition to the species themselves, there is also a large number of fine garden hybrids.

A. ptarmica (Sneezewort) is widespread in the wild in Europe and western Asia. It has freely branched stems growing up to 1m (3ft) in height. These terminate in loose corymbs of up to 15 off-white flowerheads, each up to 2cm (¾in) wide, on a slender stalk up to 8cm (3in) long. The flowering period is summer-long. The common name derives from the fact that the powdered dry foliage, taken as snuff, induces sneezing. The dark green leaves, unusually for the genus, are not finely divided, but are very narrow, finely toothed and up to 9cm (3½in) long. The plants spread aggressively by rhizomes.

The widely known **Pearl Group** is double-flowered and more or less pure white. Height is up to 75cm (30in) but the plants are generally self-supporting. It can be raised from seed, but a proportion of the plants will give single flowers only. The vegetatively multiplied selections within the group – **'Boule de Neige'** and **'The Pearl'** ♛ – are dependably double-flowered. **'Perry's White'** has larger flowerheads, which are also whiter, but the somewhat taller stems generally need some artificial support. **'Nana Compacta'** has semi-double flowers on plants up to 40cm (16in) tall.

A number of stocks of 'The Pearl' were sent for trial at the RHS gardens in Wisley in 1997–99, and were found to vary considerably in height and other features. The one given an AGM ♛ was the stock submitted by Wisley garden itself.

A. cartilaginea resembles a smaller-flowered version of *A. ptarmica*, with leaves about twice as wide. It attains a height of up to 60cm (24in).

A. ageratum ♛ (syn. *A. decolorans*) (Sweet Nancy, for its aroma) is native to the western Mediterranean and Portugal. It is not invasive. Very small, deep yellow flowerheads are produced throughout summer in dense corymb-like clusters on wiry, erect stems up to 80cm (32in) tall. The dark green leaves are small and narrow, the basal ones being pinnately cut or divided. **'Moonwalker'** is a selection, and thus yellow-flowered. **'W. B. Childs'** has fewer but much larger flowerheads, around 1cm (½in) across, with white ray florets and a darker disc.

A. filipendulina, one of the three best-known species, is a native of western and central Asia. Its stout stems, up to 1.5m (5ft) tall, bear flat-topped, umbel-like inflorescences, each up to 15cm (6in) across, and made up of a mass of very tightly packed, tiny, golden flowerheads. The flowering period is from midsummer to early autumn. The densely hairy leaves, grey-green to green, are pinnately divided. They are up to 20cm (8in) long, with as many as 15 pairs of oblong to lanceolate, lobed or toothed segments.

'**Gold Plate**' ♈, differs little from two other widely available cultivars, '**Parker's Variety**' ♈, and '**Cloth of Gold**' ♈, though the last-named is the tallest of the three. They come true from seed. '**Altgold**' ♈ and '**Neugold**', both probably of hybrid origin, are dwarfer – about 75cm (30in) – and slightly later flowering. They are very closely similar.

A. clypeolata is itself less grown than it deserves, but is important as a parent species for two much more widely grown hybrid varieties. In summer the unbranched stems, up to 70cm (28in) tall, bear small, deep golden, plate-like inflorescences. Just as in those of *A. filipendulina*, each is made up of tiny flowerheads very closely packed together. The basal tufts of pinnatifid, grey-green leaves are handsome, and provide enough justification on their own to grow this species in the garden.

A. '**Coronation Gold**' ♈ is a hybrid between the two preceding species. It is rather shorter – at 60–70cm (24–28in) – and better branched than *A. filipendulina*, and the grey foliage is more attractive.

A. '**Moonshine**' ♈ is a hybrid between 'Taygetea' (p.143) and *A. clypeolata*, introduced by Alan Bloom. It is of similar height to its parents, and produces pale yellow flowerheads in inflorescences up to 15cm (6in) across from early summer onwards. The grey-green leaves are finely divided.

A. grandifolia is a plant with a commanding presence, forming a bold clump of handsome grey-green leaves, up to 25cm (10in) long and deeply divided into about five pairs of lobed or toothed segments. The stout, branched and hairy stems, up to 1.5m (5ft) tall, bear flat inflorescences, up to 12cm (5in) across of small, creamy-white flowerheads. The species is native to the Balkans.

A. millefolium is the common yarrow, originally native to much of Europe and western Asia, and now widely naturalized in much of North America and Australia. It is a familiar roadside plant and lawn weed in Britain. The specific name means thousand-leaved, in tribute to the filigree-fine segments into which each deep green leaf is ultimately divided. The alternative common name,

The red flowerheads of *Achillea* 'Feuerland', one of the Galaxy Hybrids, fade attractively as they age.

milfoil, is an Anglicized version of the Latin. Apart from its use for treating wounds, already mentioned, many other claims for its medicinal value have been made. These include benefits to both the digestive system and the circulation of the blood.

A vigorously spreading, mat-forming plant, its white, many-flowered, flat-topped inflorescences are borne throughout summer and early autumn on erect, usually unbranched stems. In the wild, some flowerheads in various shades of pink are found, and in cultivation a wide range of colour has been developed. Among the most popular are **'Cerise Queen'** (75cm/30in), **'Lilac Beauty'** (60cm/24in), **'Paprika'**, which is orange-red (60cm/24in), and **'Sammetriese'**, which is dark red (60cm/24in). (The 'Galaxy Hybrids' form another group of cultivars of which *A. millefolium* is one of the parents, see below.)

Seed of some of the above and of other named cultivars is available, but results are likely to be variable in terms of colour. For raising from seed, a better proposition is to choose a colour mixture in the first place. The range **'Summer Pastels'** embraces pink, rose, orange-red and purple. In **'Colorado'**, apricot, yellow, beige and bronze are predominant.

Plants raised from seed come into flower in early summer from a sowing in late spring or early summer of the previous year. Alternatively, seed may be sown late in the previous summer, overwintering the young plants in a cool greenhouse or frame. A further option is to sow in warm greenhouse conditions in midwinter, which will result in first flowering from late summer onwards.

A. **'Taygetea'** is a hybrid of garden origin, producing creamy-yellow flowerheads in flat, dense inflorescences, that are up to 10cm (4in) across. The stems are about 60cm (24in) long, and the foliage greyish-green and pinnatifid.

A. **Galaxy Hybrids** are the results of crossing 'Taygetea' with *A. millefolium*. The foliage is similar to the parental species, but the flowerheads take after 'Taygetea' in being larger and borne on stiffer stems.

Among selections of the Galaxy Hybrids, all about 75cm (30in) tall unless otherwise indicated, are: **'Apfelblute'** ('Appleblossom'), peach-coloured and

Stiffer-stemmed and larger-flowered than the Achillea millefolium cultivars, the Galaxy Hybrids include 'Terracotta'.

taller; **'Credo'** ♛, creamy-yellow and also taller: it needs support; **'Fanal'** ('Beacon'), rich bright red, highlighted by yellow discs; **'Feuerland'** ('Land of Fire'), red, fading to orange and yellow, taller; **'Hoffnung'** ('Great Expectations'), deep cream; **'Lachschönheit'** ♛ ('Salmon Beauty'), taller; **'Martina'** ♛, light greenish-yellow; **'Summerwine'** ♛, red, fading to soft pink as the flowerheads age, needs support; **'Terracotta'**, orange-yellow, fading to cream, taller; and **'Wesersandstein'**, deep salmon-red, fading with age, dwarfer.

Dwarf species

A number of low-growing grey- or silver-leaved species are rock-garden plants of considerable distinction, as is evidenced by the AGM's ♛ given to three of the six following. All natives of southern Europe, they require excellent drainage – on dry stone walls, for example – if they are to survive winters with substantial rainfall, as in the British Isles. Given this, all the species are hardy, and *A. ageratifolia*, *A. clavennae* and *A. tomentosa* are very cold-resistant. Their flowering period is summer.

A. **ageratifolia** ♛ is a tufted plant, up to 20cm (8in) tall when in flower. The white flowerheads are usually solitary, and up to 3cm (1¼in) across.

A. **chrysocoma** is mat-forming and, unlike the other species described, has bright green foliage. The small, golden-yellow flowerheads are in broad, flat-topped inflorescences, rather like miniature and more graceful versions of *A. filipendulina*. **'Grandiflora'** is a larger-flowered version.

A. **clavennae** is also mat-forming and has pinnate or pinnatifid, silver-downy leaves. Its white flowerheads, up to 1.5cm (½in) across, are borne in loose clusters 15–20cm (6–8in) above ground level.

A. × **kolbiana** forms cushions of narrow, silver-grey leaves. Plants attain 25cm (10in) in height and a similar width, and bear white flowerheads up to 2cm (¾in) across in loose, few-flowered corymbs.

A. × **lewisii 'King Edward'** ♛ has buff-yellow flowerheads in corymbs up to 10cm (4in) across on stems about 20cm (8in) tall. A woody-based plant, with hairy, grey-green, pinnatifid leaves, it forms semi-evergreen mats only about 10cm (4in) high.

A. tomentosa ♔ produces erect, unbranched stems, up to 30cm (12in) or more tall, bearing small, lemon-yellow flowerheads in dense flat-topped corymbs up to 8cm (3in) across. The usually grey or silver, pinnate leaves are finely divided. **'Aurea'** is dwarfer, and has flowerheads of a brighter colour, but is less floriferous.

ANACYCLUS

Of the dozen species of *Anacyclus*, which is closely related to *Achillea*, only **A. pyrethrum** is known to horticulture. Native to the Atlas Mountains of North Africa, it is a mat-forming plant, 5cm (2in) or so tall, with abundant, short-stalked, solitary, white-rayed flowerheads, 5cm (2in) across, in summer. They are red in bud because of the characteristic stripe on the reverse of each ray floret. Numerous rosettes of finely divided, grey-green leaves, 2- or 3-pinnatisect are produced on the creeping stems. **var.** *depressus* is the form almost always grown.

Hardy to −5°C (23°F), it is suitable for a rock garden or scree bed, but as it has limited tolerance of prolonged wet weather, it is better as an alpine house subject for areas with wet winters. Propagation is by seed or by cuttings taken in late spring or early summer.

CHAMAEMELUM Roman chamomile

The one widely cultivated species of this genus, *C. nobile*, is grown for its finely divided foliage, which when trodden on or rubbed, has a pleasing apple-like scent. A native of southern England and Wales, as well as much of continental Europe, it has been cultivated for many centuries as a medicinal herb and was widely used for strewing.

A low-growing and very hardy perennial, it is sometimes used to make a lawn, which will usually be short-lived and will require frequent cutting; rolling or treading usefully fosters its natural mat-forming tendencies. The non-flowering cultivar 'Treneague' is usually chosen for this purpose and as a plant for informal paved areas. The species itself and its double-flowered form are popular in herb gardens.

Cultivation is undemanding, though *C. nobile* does best on light soil in full sun. Propagation is by seed, or in the case of 'Treneague', by division.

C. nobile (syn. *Anthemis nobile*) grows to 30cm (12in) and has a creeping habit; the lower parts of the stems root where they touch the ground. Solitary daisy-like flowerheads − white rays around a yellow disc − are up to 1.5cm (½in) across. The double-flowered **'Flore Pleno'** is dwarfer, to 15cm (6in) tall. **'Treneague'** is dwarfer still and does not flower.

ARTEMISIA Wormwood, Sage brush

It is likely to come as a mild surprise to many readers that this genus is a member of the daisy family. There is indeed nothing at all obviously daisy-like about its flowerheads, which are inconspicuous and frequently unattractive in almost all of the more widely grown species. Yet, in the daisy family, *Artemisia* has one of the largest numbers of AGMs − 13, as against, for example, eight for the showy *Gazania*, one each for *Anthemis* and *Solidago*, and three for *Tanacetum*.

Though future RHS trials will alter these scores, what has been long recognized is that *Artemisia* contains a large number of species and cultivars with outstandingly attractive foliage. Herbaceous perennials or small shrubs, leaves come in a range of silvers and greys, and of patterns of division and dissection, that can scarcely be found in any other genus. Some of the most widely seen and highly valued of all foliage plants are in *Artemisia*, such as *A. absinthium* 'Lambrook Silver', *A. ludoviciana* 'Silver Queen' and *A.* 'Powis Castle'.

In Greek mythology, the goddess Artemis, after whom the genus is named, was the deity both of the hunt and of women. There is a very long history, extending back to ancient Egypt, of claims for the efficacy of various species in bringing forward and regularising menstrual flow, and as an abortifacient. Assertions of many other medical properties have also been made over the centuries. These include the effectiveness of some species as vermifuges, from which it has become known as wormwood. The foliage of most species has a characteristic aroma and markedly bitter taste, which accounts for the use of various species as culinary herbs (*A. dracunculus* is tarragon), in the flavouring of alcoholic drinks, most notably vermouth, and as a constituent of perfumes.

Altogether there are 400 species, of which the majority are widely distributed through temperate regions of Europe, Asia and western North America. Almost all of the cultivated species are found in the wild in rather dry situations, and apart from *A. lactiflora* are very drought-tolerant. They do best in full sun, on well-drained soils which are neutral or alkaline. The herbaceous species described are all very hardy, as are nearly all the shrubby species, except *A. alba* and *A. arborescens* and its putative hybrid 'Powis Castle'.

Stems of herbaceous species, such as *A. lactiflora*, should be cut back to ground level in autumn. Those with woody or woody-based stems are best left until spring before cutting back hard. Examples are *A. abrotanum* and *A. arborescens*. Aphids are usually the only problem of note.

Propagation of the herbaceous perennials is most commonly by division, with spring rather than autumn the preferable time. Shrubby species and cultivars such as *A. 'Powis Castle'* are propagated from semi-ripe cuttings taken with a heel in mid- or late summer. Once rooted, they are best potted and overwintered in a frame or greenhouse. If available, seed is a further propagation method for species.

In the following descriptions, flowerheads are mentioned only for *A. lactiflora*. In other species they are of little or no aesthetic interest, and indeed they are sometimes deliberately removed as they appear.

Annuals

A. annua (Sweet wormwood) is one of the relatively few annual species in this large genus. A native of southeastern Europe and Iran, it is a much-branched plant, capable of rapid growth, and may attain a height of up to 1.5m (5ft). The hairless, sweetly aromatic foliage is pale green and finely divided. It is hardy enough on well-drained soils in a sheltered position to be grown from a sowing in very late summer or early autumn. If this is possible, the result is better than from spring sowings.

Perennials

The seven species are in height order, the smallest first.

A. caucasica (syn. *A. pedemontana*) ♛ is a low-growing plant, up to 30cm (12in) tall, with finely divided, white-woolly leaves. It is found in southern Europe, from Spain to the Ukraine, and is a plant for a rock garden, trough or raised bed.

A. schmidtiana ♛ is about the same height as *A. caucasica*. The hairy, silver leaves, silky to the touch, are palmately bipinnatisect with thread-like segments. Native to Japan and fully hardy, it spreads by rhizomes.

Once established, plants tend to assume an attractive mound-like shape. This is accentuated in the compact dwarf cultivar **'Nana'**, only about 10cm (4in) tall, which is self-evidently a plant for a rock garden or scree bed.

A. pontica ♛ (Roman wormwood) is evergreen and fully hardy, and forms clumps of unbranched, erect stems

up to 80cm (32in) tall. The aromatic leaves, grey-green and densely hairy, are only about 4cm (1½in) long but are finely divided. Accordingly, each stem with its foliage presents a narrowly columnar appearance. Plants spread vigorously by rhizomes and can often be invasive.

A. dracunculus (Tarragon) is not of notable ornamental value, the hairless, green leaves being straightforwardly linear or lance-shaped, and up to 10cm (4in) long. A very hardy plant, up to 1m (3ft) or more in height, it is native to an area stretching from European Russia through Siberia to northern China, and to parts of North America. It spreads by runners.

The cultivar **'Sativa'** is French tarragon, preferred for its flavour to **'Inodora'**, Russian tarragon, which is more vigorous. As French tarragon seldom sets seed, it is propagated by division or cuttings, while Russian tarragon may also be raised from seed if desired. This species is widely used in cooking, and is known to aid digestion.

A. ludoviciana (White sage, Louisiana sage), along with *L. dracunculus*, differs from all the other species described in having more or less undivided leaves. These are silvery-grey-white, up to 10cm (4in) long, and linear to lance-shaped. They are borne on slender, unbranched stems, which reach a height of up to 1.25m (4ft). They are often

Artemisia ludoviciana 'Silver Queen' ♛ is a dwarf version of the species and has toothed leaves.

PLATE XI
Achillea and Other Herbaceous Perennials

Achillea millefolium
'Summer Pastels'

Achillea millefolium
'Summer Pastels'

Achillea
'Feuerland'

Achilllea 'Wesersandstein'

Achillea 'Taygetea'

Achillea
'Credo'

Anaphalis
margaritacea

All plants shown at approximately half lifesize

Achillea
ageratum

Achillea
filipendulina
'Gold Plate'

Solidago 'Laurin'

Achillea ptarmica
'The Pearl'

better for some support. This native of North America and Mexico spreads by underground rhizomes, often rapidly. An individual plant, or even several, may look a little lost in the first season after planting, but in subsequent years established clumps are a superb foil for red- and pink-flowered neighbours. It can become invasive.

var. *latiloba* (up to 60cm/24in) and the varieties **'Silver Queen'** ♔ (75cm/30in) and **'Valerie Finnis'** ♔ (60cm/24in) are all dwarfer than the species and have leaves with attractively toothed margins.

A. vulgaris (Mugwort) is another rhizomatous plant, widespread in Europe, including the British Isles, Aasia and North Africa. Up to 1.5m (5ft) tall, its leaves are dark green and pinnately lobed, with pointed segments. It is often included in herb collections: it has been widely used medicinally, and was once a flavouring for beer, from which comes its common name. Otherwise, its interest to gardeners arises from its varieties **'Variegata'**, with white-flecked foliage, and **'Oriental Limelight'**. Sometimes used as an annual in large patio tubs, the second cultivar has leaves handsomely variegated green and yellow.

A. lactiflora ♔ (White mugwort), a native of western China, is more ornamental as a garden plant because of its inflorescences. It is a clump-forming plant up to 1.75m (6ft) tall, the hairless branched stems clothed by large, deeply cut, dark green leaves. From midsummer onwards, large numbers of tiny, cream-coloured flower-heads are borne in spreading, loose panicles up to 50cm (20in) long. Long-lasting and fragrant, these give the plant in flower a distinctive attractiveness. It associates very well with autumn-flowering asters.

A. lactiflora does best on moisture-retaining soils, and will tolerate partial shade. It sometimes needs some support. **Guizhou Group** has white flowerheads and plants often have purple-flushed stems and leaves.

Shrubby species and cultivars

A. abrotanum (Southernwood) is a hardy and very aromatic shrub of dense growth, widespread through eastern and southern Europe. Its erect, freely branched stems reach a height of around 1m (3ft). The grey-green leaves, which may be deciduous or semi-evergreen depending on environment, are among the most finely divided of the species described here. They are 2- or 3-pinnatisect with thread-like segments. Southernwood spreads by rhizomes, so may be increased by division.

A. absinthium (Common wormwood, Old man, Lad's love) is a hardy, evergreen species with woody-based stems, up to about 1m (3ft) in height. A native of temperate parts of Europe, including the British Isles, and of much of Asia, it has also become naturalized in the Americas. The aromatic, silvery-grey foliage is finely divided. The species is best known for the cultivars **'Lambrook Silver'** ♔ and **'Lambrook Mist'** ♔, both selections by the late Margery Fish. They are both dwarfer than the species, to 75cm (30in), and 'Lambrook Silver' has foliage appropriate to its name. Not easy to propagate; cuttings should be taken in midsummer.

The liqueur absinthe – made illegal in Britain in 1915 – was an extract from the roots of the plant. It is addictive, and poisonous if taken in quantity. The artist Toulouse-Lautrec was one of its known victims.

A. alba, an aromatic subshrub, has stems branching from the base and again may attain 1m (3ft). The semi-evergreen silver-grey foliage is very finely divided, with many of the thread-like segments curling. It is native to southern Europe and North Africa and not hardy enough to overwinter reliably in areas with cold winters.

'Canescens' ♔ is characterized by being dwarfer (up to 50cm/20in) and densely covered by very short, fine, soft hairs.

A study in plant contrast: *Artemisia* 'Powis Castle' and *Heuchera* 'Palace Purple'.

The evergreen *A. arborescens* has woody-based stems, yet again up to about 1m (3ft) tall and with aromatic foliage. The silver leaves are finely divided, with thread-like segments up to 2.5cm (1in) long. The foliage presents a tracery that is particularly delicate, even by the exalted standards of this genus. It is a Mediterranean native, and not reliably winter-hardy. If possible, it should be grown at the foot of a wall with a southerly aspect. **'Faith Raven'** is reputedly hardier.

A. **'Powis Castle'** (syn. *A. arborescens* 'Brass Band') ♛ is almost certainly the most widely planted of all *Artemisia*. An evergreen hybrid, its parents are not certainly known, but are thought to be *A. absinthium* and *A. arborescens*. Jimmy Hancock, then head gardener of Powis Castle, raised and introduced it in the late 1970s. 'Powis Castle' has woody-based stems, which may reach a height of up to 90cm (36in), and feathery, silvery-grey foliage that is divided almost as finely as that of *A. arborescens*. It is usefully hardier than that species, but even so cannot be relied upon to survive winters in colder areas. Where its hardiness is doubtful, it is best positioned at the foot of a wall with a southerly aspect. Moist, fertile soils seem to put it more at risk of succumbing. Hard cutting back at any time is to be avoided: any necessary pruning is best spread out over a period of time.

A. stelleriana (Dusty miller), when out of flower, usually attains a height of no more than 30cm (12in), as the lower parts of its woody-based stems are often prostrate. The thick, silver-white hairy leaves are up to 10cm (4in) long and pinnately lobed, and are not dissimilar to those of *Senecio cineraria*, the universally seen silver-leaved summer bedding plant (p.130). *A. stelleriana* is a native of Japan and Korea, is very hardy and has become naturalized in northern Europe: it is often found in coastal situations on sandy soil. It spreads by rhizomes. The compact cultivar **'Boughton Silver'** (syn. 'Mori's Form') has a semi-prostrate habit and grows only to a height of about 15cm (6in). Both this and the species are excellent as evergreen ground cover and rock garden plants, but need light soil and full sun to be at their best.

SERIPHIDIUM

This is a genus very closely allied to *Artemisia* and sharing the same valuable feature of finely divided, aromatic, grey or silver foliage. Although little seen in cultivation, two species have nevertheless been given the AGM.

Both are easy to grow, and like most *Artemisia* species thrive particularly well on poor, dry alkaline soils in full sun. Cultivation and propagation is as for *Artemisia*.

S. maritimum (syn. *Artemisia maritimum*) (Sea wormwood) ♛ is a British coastal native, common on sea walls. A herbaceous perennial, in cultivation it usually attains 50–75cm (20–30in). Short, pale grey to white hairs cover the strongly aromatic leaves. These are 2- or 3-pinnatisect, with very narrow lobes. The tiny, yellow flowerheads are in panicles with side branches which usually droop.

S. vallesiacum (syn. *Artemisia vallesiaca*) ♛ is a similar plant, native to south-west Switzerland and adjoining parts of France and Italy. It differs from *S. maritimum* only in the details of leaves, flowerheads and inflorescence. In the wild, it grows on dry limestone slopes.

ECHINACEA Purple coneflower

This small genus has a garden character all of its own, as well as sufficient differences from its near relative *Rudbeckia* to convince botanists that it should have a separate identity. The botanical name is from the Greek word for a hedgehog: as those who have handled the flowerheads can testify, the receptacle (see p.24) is covered with stiff, sharp-pointed, dry thin bracts, which are longer than the disc florets. In *Rudbeckia* these bracts are absent or soft.

The genus contains nine species, all from the USA and all hardy herbaceous perennials, but it is on just one – *Echinacea purpurea* – that its horticultural reputation rests. The large, purple-rayed flowerheads of this species, each with its cone, a great orange-bronze central boss, are given still more impact by the reflexing of the rays. Individual flowerheads are long-lasting, and are borne in succession over several months, from midsummer to mid-autumn. Unlike, say, *Rudbeckia fulgida* or the garden hybrids of *Helenium*, the floral display is never a dense, crowded mass making a collective show. Their lesser number gives space to enjoy the character of the individual flowerheads to the full, while in the high season there are still enough to produce a distinctive overall effect from a distance. The appeal is not solely one of colour and form: the flowerheads have a honeyed scent, and are attractive to bees and butterflies. They are long-lasting as cut flowers, and the cones are ornamental in dried-flower arrangements.

The roots of three species, and particularly of *E. angustifolia*, have been used as a source of herbal medication by native Americans for centuries. Modern research has confirmed a range of beneficial properties, such as anti-inflammatory effects and the stimulation of the immune system, and *Echinacea* tincture is now used widely in herbal medicine.

The genus is quite straightforward to grow in well-drained soil: the plants are natives of fairly dry habitats, and accordingly tolerant of less moisture-retentive soil types. They do best in full sun, but if necessary a site with part-day shade is quite acceptable. In exposed situations, the taller species and *E. purpurea* may need support.

Propagate by division in spring, though note that frequent disturbance is resented. Much more productively, plants can be multiplied by cuttings of the thick, black roots in late autumn or early winter. Raising from seed is

The flowerheads of *Echinacea purpurea* reward admiration at close quarters. This cultivar is 'White Swan'.

quite straightforward, though not all individual cultivars of *E. purpurea* come entirely true to colour.

Species and cultivars

E. purpurea, native to the eastern USA, is an erect plant, up to 1.5m (5ft) high, with stiff, sparsely branched, bristly stems. The pointed leaves are also bristly: at the base of the plant they are ovate, while the stem leaves are narrower. The solitary flowerheads are up to 12cm (5in) across, and have about 24 sterile ray florets, up to 8cm (3in) long, reddish-purple and often green-tipped.

The species itself is widely grown, but more often cultivars are chosen, with lesser height and greater flowerhead size. The seed-raised strain **'Magnus'** has very large flowerheads, with deep purple ray florets, twisted in some plants and closer to the horizontal than in the species. Height is about 1m (3ft). **'Rubinstern'** ('Ruby Star') has the same feature of near-horizontal ray florets, is about the same height, and also comes almost entirely true from seed. The colour is carmine-red.

'Robert Bloom' is mauve-crimson, and again about 1m (3ft) tall; **'Leuchtstern'** ('Bright Star') is purple-red and dwarfer, at about 75cm (30in). **'Bressingham Hybrids'** is a seed-raised strain, producing a range of colours from light rose to red. The white-flowered cultivars are dwarfer than the purple: **'White Swan'** is 50–60cm (20–24in), while **'White Lustre'** is rather taller at 75cm (30in). Both come true from seed.

E. angustifolia is a smaller though similar plant, attaining a height of about 60cm (24in). Like the leaves, the ray florets are also much narrower than in *E. purpurea*. About 4cm (1½in) long, they reflex more strongly, and appear almost to hang downwards from the central cone. They vary from light purple to rose-pink. It is this species that has been most used as a herbal medicine.

E. pallida (Pale coneflower) is a larger version of *E. angustifolia*, growing to 1.25m (4ft). Its scented flowerheads have pink, rose or white rays up to 9cm (3½in) long, and a dark maroon cone.

E. paradoxa is the yellow coneflower. Growing to 1m (3ft) or more in height, the plant is almost hairless, with very erect stems which are simple or very little branched. The showy flowerheads have very strongly reflexed, bright yellow ray florets, up to 7cm (3in) long, and a high-domed, chocolate-brown disc.

The flowerhead form of *Echinacea purpurea* contrasts with the dark-stemmed inflorescences of *Eupatorium purpureum*.

EUPATORIUM

E. purpureum is much the most widely seen species in this large and widely distributed genus. The distinguished American horticulturist Dr Allan Armitage has written of this tall and robust plant that it is 'one of the architectural building blocks of British gardens'; and Graham Stuart Thomas wrote that it is 'one of the most imposing of herbaceous plants'. Certainly no-one who visits Beth Chatto's famous garden in Essex when this species is in flower is likely to forget it. There it makes a wondrous backdrop to shorter flowering plants and is, at the same time, a restrainedly colourful division between them and the dark summer greens of tree foliage.

Easy to grow, *E. purpureum* is admired in larger gardens for its long-lasting, slightly domed panicles of numerous purple florets, much visited by butterflies. It is in the same tribe as *Ageratum*, and, different in size and colour though they are, the general character of the inflorescences is quite similar. The pleasingly fuzzy appearance of the flowerheads in both genera arises from the very elongated branches of the styles, which protrude well beyond the ends of the tubular corollas.

Other hardy species, such as the white-flowered *E. rugosum*, share its ease of culture. They are all candidates for large beds and borders, but are seen to best advantage in a wild garden or at its edge. All species will tolerate partial shade. The European native *E. cannabinum* is a good plant for naturalizing in very moist soil conditions, tolerating heavy shade, and is also attractive to butterflies.

Two shrubby species, *E. ligustrinum* and *E. sordidum* are just hardy enough for sheltered positions outdoors in areas with very mild winters. More widely, both add distinction and fragrance in autumn and winter to a cool greenhouse, where they can be grown in large pots.

Propagate all herbaceous species by division or seed, shrubby species by cuttings in spring and summer.

Hardy perennials

All those described flower from midsummer to early autumn.

E. purpureum (Joe Pye weed) forms clumps of stiff, erect stems up to about 2m (6½ft) tall, the terminal inflorescences of tiny, rose-purple florets being up to 15cm (6in) across. The stems themselves are purple at the nodes. The large, finely toothed, lance-shaped leaves are in whorls, usually of 3, 4 or 5: when crushed, they release a vanilla-like scent.

The common name of this eastern North American species commemorates its use as a medicine by a native American doctor, who cured typhus with it.

subsp. *maculatum* has stems mottled and specked purple, rather than blue-green as in the type of the species. **'Atropurpureum'** ♛ has wine-red florets and purple-red stalks.

This species does best in moist, alkaline soil.

E. rugosum (syn. *Ageratina altissima*) (White snakeroot) is of similar character but is rather less tall – not usually over 1.5m (5ft) – and with the upper parts of the stems branching. The inflorescences are up to 6cm (2½in) across, each a cluster of corymbs of pure white flowerheads. This species is harmful to grazing livestock. **'Chocolate'** and **'Braunlaub'** both have brown stems.

E. album, *E. altissimum*, *E. aromaticum* and *E. perfoliatum* are other white-flowered species, the first three preferring drier soils, the last moist ones.

Eupatorium rugosum effectively lightens a dark corner: all species of the genus tolerate some shade.

E. cannabinum (Hemp agrimony, Raspberries and cream) is a European native, commonly found in damp situations in England and Wales. It grows to about 1.25m (4ft) tall, and bears dense panicles, up to 10cm (4in) across, of pink to purple flowerheads on reddish stems. The deeply three-lobed leaves are in opposite pairs on the stems, and have a resemblance to those of hemp (*Cannabis sativa*). It is a plant to commend for gardeners who have a suitably wet place – say the edge of a stream or pool – for its naturalization.

The cultivar **'Flore Pleno'** has purple-pink, double flowers, and can be propagated by division.

Tender perennials

These are both shrubs, native to Mexico, and both have fragrant flowers. Grown in large pots (20–25cm/8–10in), they will perform well in a cool greenhouse where 7–10°C (45–50°F) minimum is maintained in winter. In late spring and summer the plants are best cared for outdoors. After their first flowering season, they can be cut back hard, repotted and grown on for a second year.

E. ligustrinum (syn. *E. micranthum*, *Ageratina ligustrina*) 🏆 grows to about 1m (3ft) tall when grown as a container plant. Its fragrant, white flowerheads are produced in autumn in large inflorescences, borne on slender stems. During the main period of growth – spring and summer – the tips of the shoots are best pinched out two or three times to help induce a bushier habit.

E. sordidum (syn. *E. ianthinum*, *Bartlettina sordida*) is of similar height, but, with stout stems and broader leaves, its habit is quite different. The violet-purple flowerheads, also fragrant, are very reminiscent of the bedding plant *Ageratum*, and are produced in dense corymb-like clusters, mainly in winter. The tips of young shoots are densely covered in short, woolly, golden-red hairs.

LIATRIS

This genus of around 35 North American species includes one, the well-known *L. spicata*, which must surely deserve a place in the top 50 herbaceous perennials. In appearance it is unlike any other well-known members of the daisy family: its flowerheads,

A North American native, *Eupatorium purpureum* is seen here in all its late summer glory.

inflorescences and foliage set it visually far apart from archetypal North American representatives of the family such as *Helenium*, *Helianthus* and *Rudbeckia*. *Liatris* has been accorded a variety of common names, none of which have achieved wide currency as far as I know. Among them are gay feather and blazing star, while snake root and button snake root are descriptive of what is to be seen of the plant when it is dug up.

As herbaceous perennials, *Liatris* species have much to commend them: a distinctive plant form, contrasting with appropriately chosen neighbours both before and during flowering, a long period in bloom, during which they are attractive to bees and butterflies, and good lasting qualities as cut flowers. They have also a pleasingly different interest in flowering detail: unlike almost all other cultivated plants with spike-like inflorescences, the first flowerheads open at the top of the spike, and opening then progresses steadily downwards. Perhaps the greatest criticism that can be levelled against the genus is that its colour range is confined to shades of purple and white. And perhaps even this is scarcely criticism – purpleness always seems to me part of the essential quality of the genus: if genetic modification ever brings us yellows and reds, I shall not give more than two cheers!

The cultivated species are plants well at home in sunny positions in both herbaceous and mixed plantings. Among a plethora of plants with which they associate well are *Coreopsis verticillata* and *Solidago caesia*. All species of *Liatris* are very hardy. *L. spicata* does best on reasonably moisture-retentive soils, though good drainage is important as winter losses may occur if soil lies wet. For gardeners on dry soils, the taller *L. pycnostacha* is likely to prove a better plant.

Propagation may be by seed in the case of the species and *L. spicata* 'Alba', 'Floristan Violett' and 'Floristan Weiss'; plants normally commence flowering the year after sowing. Otherwise, division in spring is usual. Plants grow from corms – swollen subterranean stem bases, which for this genus are commonly misnamed tubers. Slugs and snails may prove a problem as growth commences in spring. During winter, mice and other rodents may eat the corms.

Species and cultivars

All the species described are clump-forming herbaceous perennials. Their rayless flowerheads comprise a large number of very small, tubular florets. They are densely arrayed along the length of the stiff flowering stems, creating an effect like an elongated bottle brush. The flowerheads are purple unless otherwise mentioned.

L. spicata (syn. *L. callilepis*), much the most popular member of the genus, is grown both as the species itself and as cultivars. In sufficiently moist soil, established plants can attain a height of up to 1.5m (5ft), bearing spikes to 70cm (28in) long, though 1m (3ft) tall and spikes of 40–50cm (16–20in) is more usual. The reddish-purple flowerheads are produced from midsummer to mid-autumn. The very narrow leaves, densely furnishing the hairless flowering stems, are up to 40cm (16in) long at ground level, getting shorter higher up.

'Alba', white, differs only in flower colour. 'Kobold' ('Goblin') is notable particularly for its dwarfness, 40–50cm (16–20in), and has bright violet flowerheads. 'Floristan Violett' and 'Floristan Weiss' (purple and white respectively) both come true from seed, and do not normally exceed 1m (3ft) in height.

L. pycnostachya is a similar species with slightly less showy inflorescences. It is rather taller, and commonly needs support to keep the flowering spikes upright. Better on dry soil than *L. spicata*, it is correspondingly more susceptible to winter loss in wet soil.

Two species fairly popular in the USA but little seen in Britain, are *L. aspera* and *L. ligulistylis*. The first is relatively tall, up to 1.75m (6ft), and has spikes less densely furnished with flowerheads. *L. ligulistylis* is only 50–60cm (20–24in) tall, and produces its flowerheads in raceme-like clusters.

SOLIDAGO Golden rod

One of the best known and most easily grown of herbaceous perennials, golden rod nevertheless bears an unfortunate image as a coarse, invasive sort of plant. *S. canadensis* and *S. virgaurea*, the two species naturalized in Britain, undoubtedly contribute to this, being widely seen on waste ground and alongside railway tracks. The great majority of the 150 or so species are native to North America, where the genus as a whole is hardly regarded as worthy of garden space.

Nevertheless, *Solidago* does justify serious consideration in mixed plantings and in wild gardens because of its colour and the characteristic, almost plume-like appearance of its long-lasting inflorescences. Were it difficult to grow, it would undoubtedly be much more

PLATE XII
Foliage Plants

Santolina chamaecyparissus

Artemisia ludoviciana var. *latiloba*

Artemisia virens

Achillea clypeolata

Artemisia alba 'Canescens'

Artemisia 'Powis Castle'

All plants shown at approximately
three-fifths lifesize

Brachyglottis
monroi

Brachyglottis
laxifolius

Helichrysum stoechas
'White Barn'

Senecio cineraria
'White Diamond'

Anthemis punctata
subsp. *cupaniana*

highly prized. A long-lasting cut flower, too, it is now often seen in the popular mixed bouquets sold by florists and their competing retail outlets.

All the species and cultivars described here are very hardy, none require support, and all will thrive in a wide range of soils, in both full sun or partial shade. They are susceptible to powdery mildew, but their natural vigour gives them more capacity than many other genera to tolerate the disease. Propagation of the species is easily achieved by seed. Otherwise, division is the method almost always chosen, although cuttings in spring enable more rapid multiplication to be achieved, if desired. Lifting and dividing every third year is sufficiently frequent, except where it is needed to curb the spread of plants.

Species and cultivars

All are plants of upright habit, with stiff stems furnished with narrow, more or less lance-shaped leaves. Individual flowerheads, in varying shades of yellow, are very small, each with few very short female ray florets. Each inflorescence is a panicle comprising a very large number of flowerheads. The flowering period extends, according to species or cultivar, from midsummer to early autumn.

S. caesia, known in its native USA and Canada as the wreath or blue-stem golden rod, is surely a strong candidate for the title of the plantsman's *Solidago*. Its slender, hairless stems, up to 1m (3ft) tall and bluish-purple, arch over and branch slightly towards their upper ends. They

Solidago caesia attracts admiration from gardeners who are unenthusiastic about more conventional golden rod species.

bear willow-like leaves to their tips. In late summer and autumn the bright yellow flowerheads are produced in small clusters in the leaf axils along much of the entire length of the stems.

S. cutleri (syn. *S. brachystachys*), native to the northeastern states of the USA, is particularly notable for its dwarfness, not exceeding 50cm (20in) and usually shorter. It forms dense tufts of leafy stems and produces short, dense inflorescences of golden-yellow flowerheads in early autumn. Each flowerhead has about a dozen ray florets. The species is a parent of some valuable dwarf cultivars (see Hybrids, opposite).

S. canadensis is a relatively tall species, up to 1.5m (5ft), native to eastern Canada and much of the USA, and naturalized in Europe. The tiny, bright golden-yellow flowerheads are borne in large or very large panicles with one-sided, recurving branches in late summer and early autumn. The leaves on the lower part of each stem die early. This fast-spreading species is a good choice for naturalizing, but is otherwise of particular note as a parent of many less aggressive cultivars.

S. virgaurea is one of the few species native to Europe and Asia and is widely found in Britain. Up to 1m (3ft)

The semi-dwarf *Solidago* 'Cloth of Gold' catching the sun as it comes into flower.

tall, it flowers from midsummer onwards. Individual flowerheads have 6–12 ray florets and are relatively large for the genus, up to 2cm (¾in) across. As with *S. canadensis*, this invasive species is only suitable for naturalizing, but there is a less vigorous variegated form **'Variegata'**, with green and yellow foliage. **subsp.** *alpestris* is much dwarfer than the type, at about 20cm (8in).

'Golden Dwarf' ('Goldzwerg') is a selection, while an ultra-dwarf form, not exceeding 10cm (4in) in height, also exists: **var.** *minutissima*. They are sometimes chosen for rock gardens.

Hybrids

The garden hybrids are of relatively recent origin, many of them the work of Harold Walkden from the 1940s onwards. *S. canadensis*, *S. cutleri*, *S. virgaurea* and possibly × *Solidaster luteus* have been used as parental species. The hybrids vary in habit and flowering period, form of inflorescence and shade of yellow or gold, but most markedly in height. Although all are strong growing, they lack the unwelcome invasiveness of the taller parental species. The selection below is in approximate order of height. The usual flowering time is late summer to early autumn.

'Queenie' ('Golden Thumb')★	30cm (12in)
'Golden Dwarf'	30cm (12in)
'Laurin'	30–40cm (12–16in)
'Goldkind'	50cm (20in)
'Cloth of Gold'	50cm (20in)
'Crown of Rays'	60cm (24in)
'Goldenmosa' ♛	75cm (30in)
'Ledsham'	80cm (32in)
'Lemore'	See × *Solidaster luteus*

★ foliage yellow-green to gold-coloured

× SOLIDASTER

As a rule, plants from different genera totally fail to produce viable seed when cross-pollination – natural or deliberate – occurs. But × *Solidaster* (syn. × *Solidaster hybridus*, × *Asterago* and *Aster luteus*) is one of the rare exceptions (a comparable example in the animal kingdom is the mule). It occurred as a natural hybrid about 1910, in a nursery near Lyons in France. One parent is *Aster ptarmicioides*, but the species of the *Solidago* parent is uncertain. However, the result is a pleasing hardy herbaceous perennial, intermediate in characteristics between the two parents. In practical terms, this means on the one hand a dense inflorescence comprising numerous flower-

heads, but on the other these being large enough – about 1cm (½in) in diameter – to register as individuals of recognizable daisy character, each with 10–12 ray florets.

× *S. luteus* is of value both as a border plant and as a cut flower. The colour of its flowerheads is appealing, the disc florets being the characteristic assertive golden-yellow of *Solidago*, but the ray florets much paler, fading as they age to a soft creamy-yellow. The plant is less vigorous (and less coarse) than its parents, but is a sufficiently good 'do-er' in any reasonable conditions of soil and garden environment. Culture is as for *Solidago*. In common with all intergeneric hybrids, it is sterile, so propagation is by division or cuttings only.

The plant grows to 1m (3ft) – usually rather less – and has a lengthy flowering period from midsummer. The large inflorescences are much-branched panicles and the leaves are narrow and pointed, on the upper part of the stems becoming almost linear.

It is also available through nurseries under the cultivar name **'Lemore'**, and this has received an AGM ♛. It is claimed to be slightly shorter and to have paler-coloured ray florets than the type, of which it may well simply be a selection.

STOKESIA Stoke's aster

The only species of this genus bears pretty flowerheads of markedly cornflower-like appearance, with their elongated, enlarged outer florets finely divided at their tips. Blue, lilac, purple, yellow or white, the flowerheads are up to 10cm (4in) across.

Native to the south-eastern USA, *S. laevis* is a plant for a sunny position at the front of a border or in a large rock garden. Stokesias are good for cutting, though not long-stemmed, except for the cultivar 'Omega Skyrocket'. Good drainage is more than ordinarily important for this plant, especially in colder areas. The species and the cultivars 'Träumerei' and 'Omega Skyrocket' may be propagated by seed. Other cultivars are multiplied by division or root cuttings.

S. laevis has lilac-blue outer florets around a paler centre, creamy-white in the very middle. The foliage is in loose basal rosettes which persist through the winter, while the stems bear their flowerheads 30–40cm (12–16in) above the ground. These are solitary, or sometimes in loose few-flowered inflorescences. The long flowering period peaks in late summer and early autumn, but altogether extends from midsummer to the appearance of the last few flowerheads in mid-autumn.

'**Alba**' is white. '**Träumerei**' ('Dreaming') is also white, but is pink-tinged. '**Blue Star**' has clear pale blue outer florets with a paler centre, as in the species. '**Mary Gregory**' was an introduction of the late 1990s, and has yellow flowerheads. '**Omega Skyrocket**' is of erect habit, and is much taller than other cultivars at about 90cm (36in). The flowerheads are lilac.

VERNONIA Ironweed

A very large genus and widely distributed, *Vernonia* is known in gardens for two hardy herbaceous perennials, native to the USA. Both *V. crinata* and *V. noveboracensis* are tall, stiff-stemmed, clump-forming plants, flowering from late summer onwards. They have loose inflorescences of small discoid flowerheads, which as they fade change to the rusty colours for which the plants have their common American name.

Thriving in almost any soil in a sunny position, they are candidates for wild gardens or large mixed borders. It would be difficult to justify giving them space in small gardens. Self-seeding is likely if deadheading is not practised. Propagation is by seed or division.

V. crinita (syn. *V. arkansana*) grows up to 2m (6½ft) tall (occasionally more) and bears its violet-purple flowerheads in loose, flattened corymbs to 20cm (8in) across.

The similar *V. noveboracensis* also has a white-flowered cultivar '**Albiflora**'.

Rock Garden Daisies

CELMISIA

Almost all of the 60-odd species of this genus are native to New Zealand and almost all have white daisy flowers with yellow discs. Many are small subshrubs or shrubs, while others are tufted herbaceous perennials with large leaves. In the wild most species are mountain natives, so the genus is of particular interest to alpine-garden enthusiasts. Two of those described are also suitable for positions at the fronts of borders. These – *C. spectabilis* and *C. semicordata* – are notable for their stiff, lance-shaped leaves, which are leathery, strongly furrowed by parallel veins and have a silvery sheen on their upper surfaces. The foliage is valuable as a winter attraction as all species are evergreen.

In the British Isles, the genus appears to thrive much more readily in the cooler, wetter parts than in areas such as the south-east and East Anglia. *Celmisia* responds badly to drying out of the soil. In favourable climatic circumstances, it does best with full exposure to the sun, but where the conditions are drier, partial shade is much preferable. A moisture-retentive soil, neutral to acid, is required: plants do well in peat beds. They are hardy, but casualties due to severe frost have been known.

Propagation is by seed, which needs to be fresh for good results, or by cuttings taken in late spring.

All the species described flower in early summer. Flowerheads are solitary, on stems furnished only with bracts. The pure white ray florets are narrow and numerous, so creating a visual effect not found in other white-flowered daisy genera such as *Anthemis*, *Leucanthemum* and *Rhodanthemum*. Variability in detailed characteristics is common, and difficulties in identification have led to some confusions in naming.

Shrubs

C. angustifolia, a subshrub with small, grey leaves, grows up to 25cm (10in) tall with flowerheads to 3.5cm (1½in) across. Individual specimens can spread very widely.

C. ramulosa is a relatively easily grown shrublet, just 20–25cm (8–10in) tall. The flowerheads are up to 2.5cm (1in) across, on short slender stems. **var. *tuberculata*** is the form mainly grown. It has tiny, grey leaves dotted with minute, silvery tubercles.

Very dwarf species

The three plants here are only 5–10cm (2–4in) high.

C. argentea is cushion-forming, with tiny silvery-grey leaves, and stemless flowerheads about 3cm (1¼in) across.

C. bellidioides, a subshrub, is the easiest to grow in this group. A mat-forming plant, it has leaves that are dark green and shiny, and again very small. The short-stalked flowerheads are 2cm (¾in) across.

C. sessiliflora forms loose cushions with small, linear leaves in rosettes, some of which produce a stemless flowerhead up to 2.5cm (1in) across.

Taller herbaceous species

C. semicordata (syn. *C. coriacea*) has flowerheads up to

6cm (2½in) across on stout, white stems up to 40cm (16in) long. Leaves are a similar length, and silver beneath. Those of **subsp.** *stricta* are stiffer and narrower with upper surfaces more markedly silver-coloured. This species is too large for any but the biggest rock garden.

C. spectabilis is similar but rather smaller, with flower-heads up to 5cm (2in) across on stems to 25cm (10in) tall. Leaves are up to 20cm (8in) long. This is a very variable species, with upper leaf surfaces green to silvery-green and lower surfaces felted white, cream or buff.

BELLIS Daisy

The spring-flowering double daisies, seen quite widely in municipal bedding schemes, are cultivated forms of **B. perennis**, the species that infests lawns, albeit prettily. The size and doubleness of the flowerheads of these dwarf daisies are an amazing example of what dedicated breed-ers can achieve, but they are clearly well out of place in a rock garden. Happily, there is a small number of cultivars of the same species that have smaller and more refined flowerheads. They are easily cultivated, readily propagated by division, and make a colourful contribution to a rock garden. They are sterile, so self-seeding is not a nuisance. Of them, the most commonly seen is **'Dresden China'**, a pretty pink with relatively small, double flowerheads and quilled ray florets. **'Miss Mason'** is a pure white double of similar flowerhead size.

Plants of the seed-raised series are almost always treated as biennials. All are 10–15cm (4–6in) tall with white, pink and red flowerheads up to 5cm (2in) across. They include the large-flowered **'Bright Carpet'** and **'Goliath'** series. Quilled ray florets are the special fea-ture of the smaller-flowered **'Pomponette'** series ♔. The **'Tasso'** and **'Habanera'** series are similar, but larger-flowered. **'Habanera White with Red Tips'** is a pleasing variant.

They are easily raised from seed, sown early in the summer preceding flowering. Flower size and doubleness diminish on plants kept as perennials, and they come to look more like the basic species. Deadheading is impor-tant for these cultivars, as their offspring can be weed-like. The sterile cultivars are, of course, free of this defect.

B. rotundifolia is a native of south-west Spain and north-west Africa and is not quite fully hardy. It is a spring-flowering plant, to 20cm (8in) tall, for a sheltered position in a rock garden. **'Caerulescens'** has single,

pale blue flowerheads with a yellow disc, 3–4cm (1¼–1¾in) across.

A very pretty plant, widely mistaken for a cultivated form of the common lawn daisy, is *Erigeron karvinskianus* ♔ (see p.79).

BELLIUM

Bellium is not only similar in name to *Bellis*: it is very closely related, separated botanically by features of no particular gardening importance. There are only four species, all from southern Europe, and of these, only one is much seen. This is the not quite hardy perennial **B. bellidioides**, a native of the Balearic Islands. It is a mat-forming plant, spreading by short, very thin runners, and with solitary flowerheads no more than 2cm (¾in) across. These are close in appearance to miniature lawn daisies, and often have reddish reverses to the white ray florets. This species is sometimes sold under the name *B. minutum*, which is a very small-flowered annual.

A plant for rock garden or alpine house, it needs a warm spot but is not tolerant of dry, poor soils. Propaga-tion is by seed or division.

COTULA and LEPTINELLA

These genera have long been recognized as very closely related botanically, and in most cases their similarities extend to their garden character and uses. Both have small, discoid, button-like flowerheads and attractive, finely divided foliage.

All but one of the six species described are low-growing, spreading perennials, particularly suitable for groundcover when planted in gaps in paving, or in a rock garden or scree bed. The *Leptinella* species tolerate some treading. The odd one out is *L. coronopifolia*, a taller plant of variable habit, for waterside situations such as the edges of ponds. It will grow in shallow water, to a depth of about 15cm (6in).

Both genera are native to the southern hemisphere, the three *Cotula* species to South Africa, and the three *Lep-tinella* species to New Zealand. *Cotula hispida* and *C. lin-eariloba* are hardy only to around $-5°C$ ($23°F$), and may not survive prolonged exposure to lower temperatures. To preserve stock from one year to the next, plants are sometimes lifted and overwintered in a coldframe. Apart from the water-loving *L. coronopifolia*, all the species described do best in full sun on well-drained soils that are no more than moderately fertile. Propagation is by fresh seed or division at almost any time of year. Where winter conditions are unfavourable for the survival of *L. coronopifolia*, which is also only moderately hardy, it may be treated as an annual, sowing in early spring.

Species

C. coronopifolia (Brass buttons) grows to 40cm (16in) tall, depending largely on habit, which varies from erect to semi-prostrate. The bright yellow flowerheads, about 1cm (½in) across, are borne on slender stems in summer. The fresh green leaves are linear, and lobed or toothed.

C. hispida is less than 10cm (4in) tall, with bright yellow to red flowerheads, about 1.5cm (½in) across, which arise from a mat of hairy, finely divided silvery-grey leaves.

C. lineariloba is a tufted, rhizomatous plant with stems attaining a height of 15–20cm (6–8in). It is similar in flower and leaf to *C. hispida*, but the flowerheads may be up to 2.5cm (1in) across.

L. atrata (syn. *Cotula atrata*) is a tufted, creeping plant about 15cm (6in) tall when in flower. The foliage is finely divided, and sometimes purple-flushed. **var. luteola** is more widely grown and has deep crimson flowerheads enhanced by conspicuous creamy-white stigmas. The flowerheads are about 1.5cm (½in) across and open in late spring and early summer.

L. potentillina (syn. *Cotula potentilloides*) is a mat-forming species, not exceeding 20cm (8in) in height, and usually much less, with yellowish flowerheads up to 1cm (½in) across. The pinnately cut leaves of most plants are slightly tinted purple-brown.

L. squalida (syn. *Cotula squalida*) is of similar stature, and is again mat-forming, with tiny leaves that are bronzy-green and attractively divided. The yellow-green flowerheads are very small, about 5mm (¼in) across. This can be an invasive plant and is better avoided in small rock gardens. It is useful for a gravel garden.

ANTENNARIA Cat's ears, Pussy toes

The three species of this genus that are much in cultivation are the alpine-garden enthusiast's everlasting flowers. Like those of edelweiss (below), which also belongs to Gnaphalieae, the tribe of the everlasting flowers, they are too small-flowered and short-stemmed to be in much practical use as such, but they are valuable in other respects. Mat-forming, silver-leaved plants, they are easier to grow than the majority of comparable species. Both for their foliage and their flowerheads, they are attractive in rock gardens, dry stone walls, and informal paving, and are sometimes used as path edging plants. The distinctive flowerheads are in most species and cultivars pink or red.

Slight shade is tolerated, and the plants will thrive in a wide range of freely drained soils, including well-prepared clays. They can become invasive, and may need close watching in small rock gardens. Propagation is by division or seed.

Species and cultivars

All described are more or less white-hairy in foliage and stems. They spread by stolons, and both these and the stems are leafy. The flowering period is late spring and early summer. Flowerheads are small and discoid, with unisexual florets, but the surrounding bracts contribute further colour and greater size.

A. dioica, native to both Europe and North America, is up to 20cm (8in) tall when in flower. The leaves, up to 3.5cm (1½in) long, may be hairless above. (**var. tomentosa** is white-hairy on both surfaces and is commonly available from nurseries.)

Up to eight flowerheads are closely clustered together in each inflorescence. In cultivated plants of the species, the overall colour effect, pink, is contributed jointly by florets and bracts: in **'Alex Duguid'** it is deep pink, and in **'Rubra'** dark red.

A. microphylla, a North American native, is generally similar to *A. dioica*, but has smaller leaves and is sometimes taller. The flowerheads are an attractive pink.

A. parvifolia, again North American, is notable for being densely white-downy overall. Up to 15cm (6in) tall when in flower, with sparsely leaved stems, it has 3–6 elongated flowerheads in each inflorescence. They are about 1cm (½in) across and white or pink.

LEONTOPODIUM Edelweiss

Although the genus is quite large – around 60 species – and mainly Asiatic, in gardens it is known almost solely for a single European species, *L. alpinum*, one of the most universally recognized of all alpine plants. It is, of course, a plant for rock garden or scree bed.

It is also quite easily grown. Fully hardy, its requires full sun, a sharply drained soil low in nutrients (in relatively fertile soils it gains in size but loses in charm), and some protection from winter rains. Acid soils should be limed before planting. Propagation is by fresh seed, or division in early spring. Plants are attractive to slugs and snails.

L. alpinum is a clump-forming dwarf perennial, to 20cm (8in) tall, with grey-green, hairy basal leaves to 4cm (1½in) long. Its star-shaped arrangement of white-felted bract-like leaves radiates around clusters of small, yellowish-white disc florets. With their bracts, the inflorescences may be up to 10cm (4in) across, and are developed in late spring and summer. **'Mignon'** ('Silberstern', 'Silver Star') is dwarfer and has still whiter inflorescences.

LEUCOGENES New Zealand Edelweiss

This small genus of dwarf perennials native to mountain areas of New Zealand is also for rock-garden enthusiasts. Its flowerheads bear a strong resemblance to those of the related *Leontopodium*, being clusters of very small, tubular florets, insignificant in themselves but surrounded by relatively large white-woolly bracts.

Leucogenes species need excellent drainage, but do well in both shady and sunny situations. Protection from winter wet should be provided outdoors, or they can be grown in an alpine house. Propagation is by fresh seed, or by cuttings taken in late summer. The plants are attractive to slugs and snails.

L. grandiceps is a mat-forming plant, up to 15cm (6in) tall. The broad leaves, to 1cm (½in) long, are white-downy, and densely packed on the stems. In early summer it bears yellow flowerheads surrounded by a collar, 3cm (1¼in) across, of about 15 white-felted leaves.

L. leontopodium is rather larger, with more erect stems and narrower leaves up to 2cm (¾in) long. The hairs on these are grey-silver. Its similar flowerheads have collars of 20 leaves and are about 4cm (1½in) across.

× LEUCORAOULIA

Forming small, dense cushions of silver-hairy leaves, packed in tight rosettes, × **L. loganii** is a very attractive natural hybrid that is native to a small mountainous area of New Zealand. Its presumed parents are *Raoulia rubra* and *Leucogenes leontopodium*. It is most readily pot-grown in an alpine house. Outdoors, in a rock garden or a scree bed, it needs a sunny position, sharp drainage and should be protected from winter wet.

Propagation is by cuttings taken in late spring. Plants are very susceptible to powdery mildew.

RAOULIA

This is a genus for rock gardens and scree beds, best known for the species that form large hummocks in their native New Zealand, where they are fittingly known as vegetable sheep. *R. eximia* is the one most famous in this respect, and though very slow growing it can eventually form hummocks up to 1m (3ft) deep. This species is very difficult to cultivate, but among the 20 or so in the genus, two are relatively easy and popular, and are grown for their low, ground-hugging, widespreading evergreen mats of very attractive, fine grey or silvery foliage. Their small, inconspicuous flowerheads are almost stalkless.

They need a sunny position and moisture-retentive soil with excellent drainage, rich in humus but poor in nitrogen. In winter, prolonged wet conditions, like low temperatures without snow cover, often prove fatal. The strategy of overwintering some plants in pots in a cold-frame is a convenient way to insure against losses. Propagation of mat-forming species is easily achieved by division, as the creeping, prostrate stems root freely.

Species

R. australis eventually forms silver-grey mats up to 60cm (24in) across, occasionally more. The tiny, rounded leaves are densely hairy. The yellow flowerheads, only about 5mm (¼in) across, are produced in mid- to late summer. This is the most widely available species.

R. hookeri has white-woolly leaves of similar size and shape. The flowerheads are slightly larger. It is probably the hardier of the two, and does well in poor, fast-draining soils, similar to those in which it is found in the wild.

R. × loganii. See × *Leucoraoulia loganii* (this page).

R. tenuicaulis is another mat-forming species, much less widely available than the two previously described. It is a fine carpeting plant, easy and rapid-growing, with honey-scented, white flowerheads.

R. × petrimia is the easiest of the cushion-forming species and has silver-hairy leaves. It is available only as the cultivar **'Margaret Pringle'**.

17 Some Key Annuals

This chapter contains both true annuals and perennials grown as annuals. Among the 22 genera described are some of the best annuals in any family: I rate *Brachyscome*, *Cosmos*, *Layia* and the smaller-flowered cultivars of *Zinnia* very highly. There are some invaluable plants for containers here, too, with *Bidens* and *Brachyscome* to the fore, but *Asteriscus*, *Sanvitalia*, *Thymophylla* and others meriting attention, as well. A few are notable cut flowers, among them *Cosmos*, the little-seen *Emilia*, *Xeranthemum* and 'Blue Horizon', a tall cultivar of *Ageratum*. Some fine annuals that are members of a genus best known for its perennial species, or in genera that are very closely related to another more important 'perennial' genus, are described in other chapters. For example, *Helianthus annuus* (Sunflowers) and *Coreopsis tinctoria* (Yellow daisies).

Gardeners looking for dwarf plants, or for plants to thrive in sunny, dry conditions will find many interesting choices. And though there are few tall species here – tall plants being lacking among annual plants as a whole – there are the lovely space-filler *Cosmos* and the dramatic *Tithonia* 'Torch' to consider. Annual members of the daisy family in other chapters extend the choice: height is found among the annual sunflowers (pp.38–39), while the experimentally minded could try *Artemisia annua* (p.145) or *Centaurea americana* (p.93).

AGERATUM Floss flower

Ageratum is pleasingly attractive to butterflies. It is almost universally known as a dwarf summer bedding plant, but long-stemmed versions are not uncommonly used in the inexpensive mixed bouquets of cut flowers which are now a supermarket and filling-station commonplace. Long-lasting in a vase, the fluffy, powderpuff-like flower-heads have a distinctive prettiness.

The genus is sizeable, its 44 species all native to Central and South America and to the West Indies. Just two annual species – *A. conyzoides* and *A. houstonianum* – are of garden importance: neither is grown as such, but they are the parents of the familiar blue-, pink- and white-flowered cultivars. The genus is in the same tribe as only two other genera of garden note in cool, temperate countries – *Eupatorium* and *Liatris*.

Horticulturally, treatment as a half hardy annual is almost universal. Unlike some annuals, floss flowers do not do well in prolonged rainless periods, and watering is needed to sustain them in their prolonged flowering period, from midsummer to early autumn. The uses of the various dwarf cultivars are in edge positions in beds and borders, and in containers. If the plants neighbouring them have flowers in pastel colours, the comparatively restrained blues and pinks of *Ageratum* will usually associate with them better than the bright colours of *Lobelia*.

The only taller cultivar currently available, 'Blue Horizon', is a plant for further back in a mixed bed or border, or for a dedicated cut-flowers patch. It may need support.

A. houstonianum (syn. *A. mexicanum*) is the species to which garden cultivars are attributed, although, as noted, *A. conyzoides* is also involved in their parentage. The compact plants have much-branched stems, bearing downy, oval leaves in pairs. Rounded panicles up to 10cm (4in) across each comprise up to 40 flowerheads. They are rayless, but the elongated branches of the styles, protruding well clear of the outer ends of the tubular florets, give the flowerheads their characteristically fluffy appearance.

The blue-flowered cultivars are much the most widely seen, with the F$_1$ hybrids **'Blue Danube'** ♔, mid-blue, and **'Summit Deep Blue'**, both about 15cm (6in) tall, popular examples. The powder-blue **'Blue Mink'** ♔ is taller, at about 25cm (10in). **'Bavaria'** and **'Southern Cross'**, both also 25cm (10in), are remarkable as bicolours, the tube of the corolla visibly white, while the long styles are blue. Pinks and whites (in practice, off-whites) are also available. The purplish-blue **'Blue Horizon'** ♛, at 75cm (30in) tall, is for cut flowers and for use in informal planting.

ASTERISCUS

Though a perennial, *A. maritimus* is not fully hardy, and is almost always propagated (or purchased) anew each year. A dwarf plant of tufted habit, it grows only to a height of around 25cm (10in), and bears deep yellow daisy flowerheads up to 4cm (1½in) across from mid-summer onwards. The ray florets have attractively square-cut, fine-toothed tips, like those of *Rhodanthemum* (p.91). The silky-hairy foliage is greyish-green.

Native to parts of the Mediterranean and the Canary Isles, this is principally used as a container plant, and does well in hanging baskets. In areas with mild winters, it is also an attractive plant for cultivation as a perennial in favoured spots in rock gardens, though it may succumb to prolonged winter wet. Propagation is by cuttings in summer, or by seed sown in greenhouse conditions in late winter.

BIDENS Tickseed

In Britain, this genus was almost unknown to horticulture until the 1990s, yet is now featured annually in half the hanging baskets of the land. There are well over 200 species, distributed worldwide, but just two, *B. aurea* and *B. ferulifolia*, are useful for their summer-long display of small, yellow flowerheads, trailing habit and attractive foliage. They are also good summer groundcover, growing to a height of 30–40cm (12–16in), and look well in gravel gardens. Native to the southern USA, Mexico and elsewhere in Central America, both are perennials, but are almost always effectively treated as half hardy annuals. The genus is closely related to *Coreopsis* and *Cosmos*.

Bidens is famously easy to grow, and although doing best in full sun will also quite happily tolerate considerable shade. Owing to its vigour, it is not suitable for small hanging baskets: if a yellow-flowered trailer is needed for these, try *Thymophylla* (p.170). Even in large containers, care is needed in choosing partners to avoid the tendency of *Bidens* to dominate the entire effect after the first month or two.

Propagation may be by seed, sown indoors in late winter or early spring, or by cuttings. These may be taken in late summer, or in early spring from plants overwintered in a greenhouse: division of these is a further alternative. Young plants should be encouraged to branch by pinching out the growing points. Slugs and powdery mildew may both need control.

B. aurea and *B. ferulifolia* ♛ are very similar, and interchangeable in garden use. Both have slender, trailing, freely branched stems, flowerheads up to 5cm (2in) across with five broad ray florets, and discs given added impact by the black anthers. The rays of *B. aurea* are the longer and relatively narrower of the two. Although I prefer its flowerheads for that reason, the pinnately divided, dark green foliage of *B. ferulifolia* is the more attractive foil for the flowerheads (*ferulifolia* means fennel-leaves).

'Sunshine' is a cultivar of *B. aurea*. *B. ferulifolia* cultivars include **'Golden Goddess'** and the more compact **'Goldie'**, **'Gold Carpet'** and **'Samsara'**.

B. heterophyllus has flowerheads of similar appearance but a quite different garden use. It is another Mexican native, but at least in areas with mild winters, such as those of southern Britain, is usually hardy and can be treated as a normal herbaceous perennial. It grows to 1–1.25m (3–4ft).

BRACHYSCOME Swan River daisy

This genus is among the very few in the daisy family which has a strong claim on the adjective 'pretty'. Other examples are *Erigeron* (p.78) and *Felicia* (p.128), both in the same tribe as *Brachyscome*. They, too, share the particular hard-to-define combination of flower qualities – colour, form, presentation on the plant – which is first thought of as pretty rather than as striking, imposing or otherwise desirable.

The genus is of substantial size, with about 70 species, mostly native to Australia, and it is after the river in the south-west of that country that it is pleasingly named. As a garden plant in Britain, *Brachyscome* is known for one charming fragrant annual species, and for the slender-rayed cultivars mainly used in container gardening.

The floriferous *B. iberidifolia* is a half hardy annual, deserving a wider recognition, as evidenced in the 1990s by the number of cultivars that were then awarded a Fleuroselect Quality Mark. It is also occasionally grown as a greenhouse pot plant, flowering in late winter from a sowing very early the previous autumn. For this, a minimum greenhouse temperature of 7°C (45°F) is needed.

The cultivars and hybrids of *B. angustifolia*, *B. multifida* and other species are becoming increasingly well known for the value of their many-rayed flowerheads in patio containers, window boxes and hanging baskets. The species involved in the parentage of some modern cultivars are perennial. However, in countries with cool climates, their hybrid cultivars are almost invariably treated as annuals and are in practice propagated afresh in greenhouses early each spring by cuttings. In Australia and other places with almost frost-free winters, they are also used as border plants.

Cultivation is easy enough, given a sunny position with some shelter from wind. *Brachyscome* is fairly drought-tolerant. The annual species, *B. iberidifolia*, tends to become floppy as the plants age, and although naturally quite dwarf, it is more attractive if growth is supported by short bushy twigs. Plants respond well to deadheading, using the time-saving practice of shearing the plants back at intervals.

Propagation of *B. iberidifolia* is by seed, as a half hardy annual. Perennial cultivars and hybrids are propagated by cuttings taken from plants overwintered in greenhouses.

Species and cultivars

B. iberidifolia grows to no more than 40cm (16in) in height, each plant spreading widely by the repeated branching of its slender stems. The brilliantly coloured daisy-like flowerheads are up to 4cm (1½in) across and have dark-coloured discs contrasting with, or complementing, the numerous white, blue, violet or purple ray florets. It is most commonly grown as one of its cultivars, all of them dwarfer than the species. The **Bravo Series** (20–25cm/8–10in) has been awarded a Fleuroselect Quality Mark, as have the notably dwarf and compact **'Brachy Blue'** (15cm/6in), and **'Blue Star'** (25cm/10in), which has inrolled, pointed ray florets.

The perennial cultivars are quite similar to *B. iberidifolia* in growth characteristics, but between them they present a much wider range of colours and flowerhead sizes. In the late 1990s, the outcome of breeding work in Australia widened this range further: the cultivars concerned are marketed under the brand name of **Outback Plants**. In the following list, flowerhead diameters are around 4cm (1½in) and plant height 20–25cm (8–10in) unless otherwise stated.

The Outback Plants range includes **'Mauve Delight'**, **'Moonlight'** (white) and **'Mini Yellow'**, with flower-

heads to 2.5cm (1in). Several cultivars in the taller **Jumbo Series** (lilac, mauve and pink) have flowerheads to 5cm (2in) on plants reaching 40–50cm (16–20in) in favourable conditions (but shorter in the intense competition of a densely planted container).

Other cultivars available include **'Blue Mist'**, **'Lemon Mist'**, **'Pink Mist'** and the mauve-pink **'Strawberry Mousse'**.

CALENDULA Pot marigold

As the one common species of *Calendula* so nearly grows itself, the humble pot marigold is very often relegated to the status of a flower for children to grow. This hardly does it full justice, and for those who find the orange colour, with which its flowers are casually identified, altogether too emphatic, there are agreeable creams, yellows and apricots. It is useful as a cheap and cheerful cut flower, as well as a dependable, colourful garden filler.

The genus gives its name to one of the smallest tribes in the daisy family. Other members are *Dimorphotheca* and *Osteospermum*, both African genera, just like most others in the Calenduleae.

C. officinalis, one of 15 or so species of the genus, is known only in cultivation, but is thought to have originated in the Mediterranean area. It has become widely naturalized as an escape almost wherever it has been grown in gardens. Its medicinal uses have been chronicled since ancient times, and were extended on a large scale at least up to the time of the First World War, when it was used to arrest haemorrhaging in wounded soldiers. It has also been and is still used as a colourant for foods as diverse as cheese, rice, buns and cakes, the orange pigment calendulin being found in the ray florets.

Culture might almost be dismissed as child's play indeed, and self-seeded plants are commonplace. It is normally sown where it is to grow in early spring, and will thrive in virtually any soil and any situation where it will get some sun. High fertility, and abundance of moisture and nutrients are unfavourable to free flowering, however. Over almost all of southern England and Wales and in the southern and western USA, sowing *in situ* very early in autumn gives better plants and an earlier start to flowering – usually by late spring. Persistent deadheading is needed to extend the length of the flowering period beyond about two months. *Calendula* is susceptible to black bean aphid and to powdery mildew.

Only *C. officinalis* is much grown, and it is so well known as scarcely to need description. A thick-stemmed, branched, hardy annual, plants attain a height of up to 75cm (30in). The rather fleshy, pale grey-green leaves are aromatic and slightly sticky to the touch. Flowerhead diameter is up to 7cm (3in) in the species, but the semi-double or double blooms of cultivars may be up to 10cm (4in) across. They are all very floriferous.

The most widely available cultivar **'Fiesta Gitana'** ♆ is usually sold as a mixture of yellows and oranges, and is distinguished particularly by its dwarfness (height about 30cm/12in). Most cultivars reach 50–60cm (20–24in). Among the more interesting are: **'Pacific Apricot'**, the colour mixture **'Touch of Red'**, with ray florets finely edged and tipped in red, and the anemone-centred **Kablouna Series**.

CLADANTHUS

In summer, established plants of *C. arabicus* are dense flower-studded bushes of repeatedly branched wiry stems and very finely divided aromatic foliage. Seed is sold under the descriptive cultivar name of **'Criss-Cross'**, since the bright yellow daisy flowerheads, up to 5cm (2in) across, are seen among an intricate open mesh of growth. The distinctive appearance of the plants is caused by the development of four or five new stem branches immediately below each broad-rayed flowerhead as it begins to die.

C. arabicus (syn. *Anthemis arabica*) is native to southern Spain and north-west Africa. It is, nevertheless, hardy enough in milder areas to be sown on light soils in mid-spring where it is to grow. Otherwise it may be treated as a half hardy annual. It needs a sunny position to do well. Plants grow to around 75cm (30in) in height.

COSMOS

Although certainly one of the most universally liked annuals in the daisy family, the popularity of *C. bipinnatus* has been restrained in the past because of the size of the plants. At 1m (3ft) or more tall and of bushy habit, it must have often been passed over by owners of small gardens, despite the appeal of its broad-rayed, clean-coloured flowerheads and the delightful froth of fine lacy leaves which foil them. Happily, shortage of space militates very much less against the dwarf Sonata Series, one of the elite group of seed-raised plants that has been awarded the coveted Fleuroselect Gold Medal.

C. sulphureus is a species of more modest stature than the better-known *C. bipinnatus* and deserves a much wider public than it currently enjoys. The colour range of its cultivars – yellow, orange and red – is quite distinct. The one perennial species of importance in British gardens, *C. atrosanguineus*, provides an echo of the dahlia with its tuberous roots. It is deservedly admired for flowerheads that appear at first glance almost black.

These are the only three species generally cultivated, though there are over a hundred in the genus, natives of the Americas and of Africa. *Coreopsis* and *Dahlia* are closely related and in the same tribe, the Heliantheae. A property they share is that they are good as cut flowers.

Cultivation of all three species is very straightforward, but other plants should be chosen for rich soils as *Cosmos* responds to these with delayed flowering and excessive stem and leaf growth. A sunny, sheltered site is ideal. Flowering usually begins in late summer, a month or so later than most half hardy annuals used as bedding plants.

Seed of the annual species should be sown indoors in mid-spring. The growing points of the fast-growing young plants should be pinched out to encourage branching. The tuberous roots of *C. atrosanguineus* may be replanted where they are to grow in late spring, or started into growth in a greenhouse in early spring, to

Cosmos sulphureus is best known for its dwarf, semi-double cultivars; this is the species itself.

provide shoots for use as cuttings, in just the same way as dahlias. Aphids and slugs can both be troublesome.

Species and cultivars

The three species below are native to Mexico. The single flowerheads usually have eight ray florets and are saucer-shaped.

C. atrosanguineus is a half hardy perennial, most often grown as an annual, although in milder areas the tuberous roots often overwinter successfully outdoors. The plants grow to about 75cm (30cm) tall, and have solitary dark-centred maroon flowerheads, up to 5cm (2in) across, on dark stems. They are chocolate-scented. The leaves are pinnate or bipinnate, but the segments are like those of dahlia, not linear as in the two following species.

C. bipinnatus is the most widely grown of the three, an annual reaching a height of up to 1.25m (4ft). The solitary flowerheads are up to 9cm (3½in) across, with white, pink or crimson ray florets and a yellow disc. The **Sensation Series** is the most widely grown of the taller cultivars, at 1–1.25m (3–4ft). Of similar height, **'Psyche'** is semi-double and **'Sea Shells'** has quilled (tubular) ray florets; both lack the simple charm of the basic flowerhead type. The **Sonata Series** grows only to 60cm (24in) tall. All are usually grown in colour mixtures, but some single colour cultivars are available. These include: **'Daydream'** with ray florets deep pink at the base, fading to pale at the tips; **'Purity'**, white; **'Versailles Tetra'** dark reddish pink; and **'White Sonata'**.

C. sulphureus in gardens is mostly represented by cultivars growing to 25–75cm (10–30in) tall, with semi-double flowerheads usually less than 5cm (2in) across. The colour range is yellow and orange. They are very free-flowering, and are surprisingly little grown. Cultivars include: **'Ladybird'** a 30cm (12in) high, scarlet single; **'Lemon Twist'** a yellow semi-double of 60–75cm (24–30in) high; **'Sunny Gold'** a semi-double of 40cm (16in) tall; **'Sunny Orange-Red'**, also semi-double and 30cm (12in); and the tall, single, orange **'Sunset'**, which reaches 1m (3ft).

'Ladybird' is a free-flowering, dwarf cultivar of *Cosmos sulphureus.*

EMILIA Tassel flower, Flora's paint brush

Two species of this African and Indian genus are in cultivation, but although free flowering, pretty, distinctive and quite easy to grow, they are very seldom seen. Their common names mark the character of the rayless flowerheads, each an upright tuft of brightly coloured, tubular florets splaying outwards from the top of an elongated involucre. This is, of course, also typical of thistle flowerheads, though *Emilia* belongs to the *Senecio* tribe.

Both **E. coccinea** (syn. *E. sagittata*) and **E. sonchifolia** are of upright habit, 50–75cm (20–30in) tall, and produce flowerheads around 2cm (³⁄₄in) across in loose, few-flowered corymbs: scarlet in the first species, purple-red in the second, and both have yellow-flowered forms. The stiff-stemmed inflorescences are good for cut flowers both fresh and dried. They are usually treated as half hardy annuals, but in favourable conditions may be sown where they are to grow.

LAYIA Tidy tips

The one species of this North American genus that is seen in British gardens is a charming annual, characterized by the white tips of the otherwise yellow ray florets. This is the same colour scheme as in the well-known poached egg plant, *Limnanthes douglasii*, also an annual from California; tidy tips is much the more elegant of the two, but unfortunately, it is much less often seen.

Its botanical name is **L. platyglossa** subsp. **campestris** but it is better known under its synonym *L. elegans*. A half hardy annual reaching 40–50cm (16–20in) tall, the solitary flowerheads are around 4cm (1½in) across. Black anthers add to their character. Attractive to butterflies, the flowerheads last well when cut.

Free-flowering when grown in a sunny position, the plant does best on naturally drier soils. Sow it in mid-spring in the position where it is to grow, or treat it as half hardy.

LEUCOPHYTA

An Australian native and a shrub, the one species of this genus is propagated annually for summer use as a low-growing bedding plant and in containers.

L. brownii (syn. *Calocephalus brownii*) is remarkable for its silver-grey stems, wiry, much-branched, and apparently leafless, which give it a unique value in planting associations. Examples of plants to grow with it are heliotrope, tuberous begonias, dark-leaved pelargoniums, and – if you want to grow it – *Salvia splendens*.

It tolerates wind-borne salt, but not frost, and thrives in dry, sunny conditions. Plants do not usually exceed 30cm (12in) in height and can be pinched to make them dwarfer if required. The stems are covered with fine white-woolly hairs, giving them their characteristic colour, and the very narrow leaves are closely pressed to them. The white inflorescences are very small and inconspicuous.

Propagation is by cuttings taken in late summer and overwintered in a frost-free greenhouse. Pinch young plants to encourage branching.

LONAS African ageratum

L. annua (syn. *L. inodora*) is the only species of its genus. Little seen in gardens, the bushy plants, about 50cm (20in) tall, are none the less attractive for their bright golden-yellow flowerheads. These lack ray florets and are individually very small, but are borne in dense clusters, 10cm (4in) or more across. The flowering period commences in midsummer and individual flowerheads are long lasting. The dark green, finely divided leaves provide a good foil for the flower display. The inflorescences make good dried flowers.

A Mediterranean native, *Lonas* needs reasonably good exposure to sunshine. On suitable soils, it may be grown as a hardy annual, sowing where it is to grow in mid-spring. Otherwise half hardy annual treatment is appropriate.

MADIA Tarweed

M. elegans is an erect annual yellow daisy native to the west coast of North America. It is notable for the strongly scented foliage – hence its common name – and for the unusual pattern of flowerhead opening. This is to close in bright sun, but to open in the morning and evening. In a shady position, or in dull weather, flowerheads remain open through the middle of the day.

They are about 5cm (2in) across, and the bright yellow florets each have a brown basal spot, so forming a darker-coloured zone around the disc. Plant height is about 60cm (24in) or more. Seed may be sown in mid-spring where plants are to grow.

MATRICARIA Mayweed, German camomile

The feathery foliage and cheery white-rayed, yellow-disced flowerheads of *M. perforata* and *M. recutita* are among the best-known and most pleasing wild flowers of waste places and post-harvest cornfields. If they were natives of, say, Bhutan, and hard to grow in our climate, they would no doubt be much-prized garden plants, probably specially admired at Wisley! In practice, they are easily grown hardy annuals, usually sown where they are to flower. Both are excellent in wild flower meadows.

M. parthenium. See *Tanacetum parthenium.*

M. perforata (syn. *Chrysanthemum inodorum*, *M. inodora*, *Tripleurospermum inodorum*) is the scentless mayweed. Other than its use for naturalizing, it is notable for its double-flowered cultivar **'Bridal Robe'**, which is an old-fashioned cottage garden annual, with flowerheads about 4cm (1½in) across. The upright plants grow to 30–40cm (12–16in) tall. The flowers last well when cut.

M. recutica (syn. *Chamomilla recutica*), German or false camomile, is very similar, apart from its marked aroma. Both this plant and the perennial *Chamaemelum nobile* (p.144), Roman chamomile, have a long history of use in herbal medicine; some of the claims made for them have been substantiated – in the treatment of ulcers, for example. Camomile tea, which I enjoy, is made with the dried flowerheads of *M. recutica* and is reputedly soothing.

PERICALLIS Cineraria

Few flowering pot plants are more familiar to customers of garden centres and florists' shops than this. Grown on nurseries by the million for sale in late winter and spring, it is the archetypal cheap-and-cheerful plant. A dense spreading dome of brightly-coloured daisy flowers almost completely obscures the foliage for a brief flowering period – six weeks or so in suitably cool conditions. They are sometimes used as spring bedding plants in climates slightly warmer than the British Isles.

The correct scientific name, *Pericallis*, is seldom used outside botanical circles. *Cineraria* is the closely related genus to which the pot plant in question once belonged. Although there are important botanical differences between the two genera, for gardening purposes, it is sufficient to know that the *Cineraria* species are all yellow-flowered and native to mainland Africa, while the fifteen *Pericallis* species have flowers of other colours and are native to the Canary Islands, Madeira and the Azores. Both genera are closely allied to *Senecio*.

Cool greenhouse conditions, with a minimum temperature maintained at 5°C (41°F) are quite sufficient for success. Mere frost exclusion suffices for flowering in mid-spring. Propagation is by seed sown at any time in summer. Flowering starts largely according to sowing date, between midwinter and mid-spring. By mid- or late autumn, plants should be in their final pots, 10–13cm (4–5in) in diameter. Once established, early-sown plants are better outdoors until frosts or rough autumn weather threatens, mainly because pests are then less troublesome than in a greenhouse. Pests often present the main difficulty in growing quality plants: aphids, leaf miner, and, in greenhouses, whitefly and red spider mite, may all require control between seedling emergence and late autumn. Powdery mildew is also a common affliction.

P. × hybrida (syn. *Cineraria cruentus*, *C. × hybridus*, *Senecio cruentus* and *S. × hybridus*) is the gardener's cineraria, and is an artificial product of nineteenth-century breeding in England, involving at least two species in the parentage. It is a true perennial, but is very seldom grown other than as an annual. In flower, plants may attain a height of 75cm (30in) or more, but almost all modern cultivars are shorter. The large, rather coarse, long-stalked leaves form a rosette in young plants. Well-branched stems produce flowerheads in both terminal and axillary corymbs.

All cultivars usually available make plants of 20–30cm (8–12in) in height, and seed is almost always sold in mixed colours. These range through white, shades of pink and of red, copper and blue, and usually include bicolours, in which the white bases of the ray florets create a contrasting zone around the disc. Flowerhead diameters range from 4–8cm (1½–3in). Some better-known series are the large-flowered **British Beauty**, **Jester** and **Spring Glory** and – with smaller flowerheads – **Starlet Mini** and **Star Wars**.

SANVITALIA Creeping zinnia

In the twentieth century, this easy to grow, spreading annual never gained as much popularity in Britain as might have been expected. In Germany, with a similar summer climate, it seems to have been more warmly received. It is an easy-to-grow spreading plant that produces small, yellow- or orange-rayed flowerheads very freely over three months or more.

A member of the sunflower tribe, the genus is closely related to *Zinnia*, and, like it, is native to Mexico and adjacent countries.

S. procumbens, the only species ordinarily cultivated, is a slender-stemmed, opposite-leaved plant, not usually exceeding 15cm (6in) tall, but with a spread of up to three times this. The flowerheads are 2–2.5cm (¾–1in) across, with about a dozen ray florets and a relatively large disc, and flowering starts in midsummer.

Sanvitalia needs a reasonably sunny position but, given that, has no special requirements. It makes a good summer groundcover plant, and is popular for the purpose in Germany's well-tended cemeteries. It is also excellent as a plant for raised beds or containers, trailing pleasingly over the edges. In hanging baskets, it is an obvious yellow-flowered alternative to the ubiquitous *Bidens*. I am sorry that we do not see rather less of this and rather more of *Sanvitalia*. For groundcover, seed may be sown in mid-spring where the plants are to grow, but more commonly plants are raised as half hardy annuals. By repute, they resent root disturbance, so seed should be sown in cell trays or small pots.

'Mandarin Orange' has golden-orange rays and a bold near-black disc. **'Yellow Prince'** is similar, but with yellow rays. **'Aztec Gold'**, **'Irish Eyes'** and **'Little Sun'** also have yellow rays, but the disc is green. The cultivars **'Sprite Orange'** and **'Sprite Yellow'** are turn-of-the-millennium introductions, both of them semi-double.

Sanvitalia procumbens does well both in containers and as an annual groundcover plant. This is 'Little Sun'.

STEIRODISCUS

S. tagetes is a pleasing bushy, dwarf, South African annual with yellow daisy flowerheads up to 2cm (¾in) across. Plants grow to 20–30cm (8–12in) tall, and the foliage adds to their appeal – the dark green leaves are fern-like and pinnately parted into very narrow segments.

Best results are obtained in a sunny position on light soil. Half hardy annual treatment is appropriate.

TAGETES French marigold, African marigold

Here is a genus of paradoxes: it is native neither to France nor to Africa, but comes from Central and South America. More significantly for gardeners, there can be few genera of which so many plants are grown, and few that are disliked by so many people. Colour is one factor in the widespread adverse reaction, as numerous cultivars are marked by the fierceness of their oranges.

For those gardeners who do not wish to dismiss the entire genus out of hand, I would like to add a personal view. This is that some modern cultivars, if they were at all difficult to grow, would be prized by many who do not give them garden room as they are – very easy indeed. Which modern cultivars is very much a question of taste. Personally, I like most cultivars in the single-flowered Disco Series of French marigolds. I also like the

tiny-flowered *T. tenuifolia* (syn. *T. signata*), the plant known widely in the trade and to gardeners quite simply by its generic name. Planted in discreetly small numbers, in the right setting, and in association with the right neighbours, I rate these as fine plants.

Some members of the genus have interesting claims to utilitarian value, as repellent to a variety of pests and to perennial weeds. The practice of growing *Tagetes* in the greenhouse to reduce whitefly problems is best known. There is evidence that some eelworms and some types of slugs are also repelled, and some organic vegetable growers use French and African marigolds for interplanting between and barrier planting around susceptible crops. *T. minuta*, which is not particularly ornamental, is claimed to excrete from its roots herbicidal compounds that repress the spread of such perennial weeds as ground elder, couch grass and bindweed.

Cultivation of the three species that are grown as ornamental plants is very straightforward – as half hardy annuals sown indoors in mid-spring. Six weeks at most is a sufficient raising period, as germination and seedling growth is among the most rapid of any annuals. At the price of a delayed start to flowering, it is also quite possible to sow them in late spring where they are to grow. Once flowering gets under way, deadheading is unnecessary for the Afro-French marigolds and impossible for *T. tenuifolia,* but otherwise is important to help prolong flowering. It is particularly needed for *T. erecta*, the large-flowered African marigold, for a further reason: this is to prevent decaying blooms making the plants seriously unsightly (or *even more* unsightly, if that is your view of these particular plants).

Species and cultivars
Of the 50 or so species, annual and perennial, only three annuals are horticulturally important, and these are grown only as their cultivars. They are all stiff-stemmed, branching plants, bearing flowerheads of orange, yellow and cream. In the French and Afro-French marigolds, reds and mahogany are also much seen. The dark green leaves are pinnately cut and have toothed margins. They are attractive visually, but have a pungent aroma, which is generally disliked.

T. erecta is the African marigold, upright in habit and bearing solitary flowerheads up to 10cm (4in) across. The cultivars are all double-flowered. Heights range from 20 to 50cm (8–20in). Many gardeners regard them as gross,

and the dwarf cultivars as top heavy into the bargain: they need a spacious setting if they are not to look incongruous. The **Inca Series** and **Perfection Series** are much grown. **'Vanilla'** has agreeably cream-coloured ray florets.

T. patula, the French marigold, is the species most seen. Much dwarfer and more spreading than African marigolds, its cultivars range from 15 to 30cm (6–12in) in height, with flowerheads up to 6cm (2½in) across, borne in almost unsurpassed profusion. The ray florets in many cultivars are various shades of red and mahogany, most commonly in bicolour combinations with yellow. In a prodigious choice, the **Safari Series** and the dwarf **Boy Series** are both good double-flowered examples, and the **Disco Series** is single-flowered.

The **Afro-French marigolds** are hybrids between the two previous species. The flowerheads are up to 7cm (3in) across, rather larger than any French marigold, and on somewhat bigger plants, usually attaining 30–35cm (12–14in). All florets are sterile, and in consequence the continuation of their flowering is unaffected by seed setting. Seeds are around five times as expensive as those of French marigolds because they can only be produced by repeating the cross-fertilization process between the parental cultivars. **Solar Series** and **Zenith Series** are both double-flowered.

T. tenuifolia (syn. *T. signata*) is notable for the repeated branching of the plants' wiry stems, the fineness of its very narrow leaves and the vast profusion of single flowerheads, no more than 2.5cm (1in) across. On plants up to about 25cm (10in) tall, they open both above and within the interlacing network of stems and almost thread-like leaves. These plants are near to gracefulness, a term that not even their most enthusiastic admirers would dream of applying to French marigolds, let alone African.

The **Gem Series** and the newer **Luna Series** are the most widely offered. **'Starfire Mixed'** includes some bicolours.

THYMOPHYLLA Dahlberg daisy, Golden fleece
T. tenuiloba is a pretty, fine-leaved, yellow daisy, less seen than it deserves. The solitary flowerheads, about 2cm (¾in) across, are freely borne over a long summer period on dwarf, spreading plants. These grow to a height of

only 15cm (6in) or so, and have much-branched stems with agreeably pungent, finely divided leaves.

A native of Texas and Mexico, this annual species grows best in full sun, and unsurprisingly is drought-tolerant. It makes a very pleasing plant for the edge of a bed, particularly if it is raised, and is also attractive in containers, as well as being a good choice as a temporary filler for a year or two in a newly made rock garden.

It is usually treated as a half hardy annual, but may also be sown in mid-spring where it is to grow.

TITHONIA Mexican sunflower

Tithonia is very closely related to *Helianthus* (p.36), and the species cultivated is an annual with a good deal in common with *H. annuus*. Like it, **T. rotundifolia** (syn. *T. speciosa*) in the wild is a coarse, tall, branching plant with large, simple leaves and stiff-stemmed, solitary flower-heads. However, the orange-rayed flowerheads are more closely similar in appearance to single dahlias than to sunflowers. In a sufficiently spacious setting, it can pro-vide an exotic touch, thanks to the vividness of the flower colour and the unfamiliarity of the plant. The flowerheads are attractive to butterflies.

A native of Mexico and Central America, it is half hardy and better planted out later rather than earlier, as it fails to thrive in cool conditions. Otherwise cultivation is straightforward, but a sunny position and reasonably fer-tile soil are needed. 'Torch', the tallest cultivar currently available, will need support except where the site is very sheltered. The plants are vulnerable to slug damage.

All the cultivars have flowerheads about 8cm (3in) across with broad, orange ray florets – usually 12 to 15 in number – and a yellow disc. The stem just below the flowerhead is characteristically swollen.

'Goldfinger' was the most widely grown cultivar in the late twentieth century, and is up to 75cm (30in) tall. The very similar **'Fiesta del Sol'** was introduced to the British market in 2000, and is claimed to be more com-pact. Having seen it under trial, I think it may well replace 'Goldfinger'. **'Arcadian Blend'** is similar in height to 'Goldfinger', and has a colour range from yellow to orange. **'Torch'** grows to about 1.25m (4ft).

TOLPIS

A native of the Mediterranean area, **T. barbata** is a pleas-ing annual for a sunny position, doing best on light soil. The much-branched, slender-stemmed plants usually attain a height of 40–60cm (16–24in). The attractive light

There is an exotic character to the sun-loving Mexican native, *Tithonia rotundifolia*.

yellow flowerheads, about 4cm (1½in) across, are charac-terized by the broad, square-ended outer florets and the much smaller purple-brown inner ones. Another distinc-tive feature is the widespreading and very narrow outer involucral bracts, which form a pretty circular fringe, most noticeable around the buds and the withered flow-erheads. Midsummer to early autumn is the flowering period. *Tolpis* is closely related to *Hieracium* (p.137).

T. barbata can be treated successfully as a hardy annual. If the site is not sheltered, some low support may be needed.

XERANTHEMUM Immortelle

The name of this genus translates directly from its Greek roots as 'dry flower'. The Ancient Greeks were almost certainly familiar with it, as the one species cultivated is native to south-east Europe and Turkey.

X. annuum is found in the wild in dry habitats, and in gardens is most at home on fast-draining, relatively poor soils. Though most commonly grown for dried flowers, it is a useful plant in its own right for its starry flowerheads, freely produced on plants of graceful habit over a long period from late summer onwards. For drying, flower-heads should be cut just before they become fully open.

It is hardy enough, and fast enough into flower, to be sown where it is to grow in mid- or late spring. A rea-sonably sunny spot should be chosen. Flowering usually commences about three months afterwards. If more convenient, it can be treated as a half hardy annual. Cultivation is usually without problems, though if grown in an unsheltered spot, it may need a little support around the base of the stems.

The plants are erect and wiry-stemmed, in flower attaining a height of 50–75cm (20–30in). The flowerheads are about 4cm (1½in) or just over in diameter and come in various shades of pink and purple, and in white. They are papery to the touch, because what at a casual glance might be taken for ray florets are, in fact, enlarged, petal-like bracts. This is also a feature of many species of *Helichrysum* and the genera of everlasting flowers closely related to it. *Xeranthemum* is botanically far removed, however, and belongs to the cornflower and thistle tribe, the Cardueae. All the true florets are short and tubular and form the central disc. The narrow leaves, rather woolly-haired, are grey and silvery.

ZINNIA

This genus has a poor reputation with many gardeners in Britain, and no doubt in similar climatic conditions elsewhere, although it is very well-liked in the USA. This reputation is partially, but not fully, deserved, because the garden performance of the species and cultivars available varies very widely. Some comparatively small-flowered but very floriferous cultivars do dependably well in most summers and are plants of real and distinctive garden worth. Among them are the hybrid Profusion Series, an outstanding turn-of-the-millennium introduction, and *Z. angustifolia*.

Others – those best known – need a reasonable approximation to the warm, dry conditions of their Mexican homeland to do themselves justice. For their almost sumptuously showy blooms, many of them of great depth and vibrancy of colour, it is small wonder that the large-flowered garden hybrids are so popular in those parts of the USA where warm, dry summers can be expect. For gardeners in Britain and elsewhere in northern Europe, the showiness and colour goes for naught in cool, rainy weather, with flowers and stems brown and collapsed as the omni-present grey mould fungus Botrytis takes hold. For them the alternative is to grow the smaller-flowered species and cultivars, which are far less susceptible to weather-induced problems, and enjoy them for their own particular form of excellence.

Zinnias are primarily thought of as a bedding plant, but they are also long-lasting cut flowers. *Z. peruviana*

and the taller hybrids can be worth growing for that purpose in a sheltered situation.

In cooler climates, cultivation is usually best as a half hardy annual. Zinnias need as full exposure to sun as can be provided, and a sheltered site is required for the taller hybrids. The relatively expensive seeds should be sown indoors in mid-spring, singly in 7.5 or 9cm (3 or 3½in) pots, as the plants are intolerant of root disturbance. Sow seed about six weeks before the last expected frost. A single watering-in immediately after planting out should be given, but no more because of the risk of fungal infection at the stem base. The risk of losses from soil-borne fungi during raising is reduced by watering from below.

In climates with dependably warm springs, and elsewhere in favourable site and soil conditions, sowing where they are to grow can also be successful.

Unfortunately, zinnias are often attacked by aphids.

Species and cultivars

Just four of the 22 species in the genus have contributed to the garden flora, all of them hairy annuals of erect habit with opposite leaves which are more or less stalkless. All flower from midsummer onwards to early autumn. They share with their near-relative *Heliopsis* the unusual feature of having female ray florets.

Z. angustifolia is a fine dwarf plant of bushy habit, characterized by a long-lasting abundance of star-shaped flowerheads about 4cm (1½in) across. These have about eight ray florets, in white, yellow or orange, and a deep golden disc. **'Starbright Mixed'** is the usual seed-company offer, but the white is also available separately, and is the usual choice of the more discerning. Plants attain a height and spread of about 30cm (12in).

The **Profusion Series**, a result of hybridization between *Z. angustifolia* and *Z. elegans*, was introduced from 1998 on. Larger-flowered than *Z. angustifolia*, up to 5cm (2in) across, and with a different colour range, the plants are of similar stature, differing mainly in having broader leaves. The flowerheads also have a larger number of relatively broad ray florets. Colours currently available are cherry-red, orange and white; more are likely to become available. **'Profusion Cherry'** and **'Profusion White'** have both been awarded a Fleuroselect Gold Medal, an almost entirely dependable indication of something outstanding and novel among bedding plants.

Z. peruviana is the least-seen member of the genus. Its height – about 75cm (30in) – and slender habit rule it out for use as a bedding plant, but its individuality gives it worthwhile appeal for gardeners who enjoy growing annuals in informal plant associations. The flowerheads are about 5cm (2in) across, with yellow or red ray florets. Cultivars are **'Bonita Yellow'** and the bright red, dark-stalked **'Red Spider'**.

Z. elegans and *Z. haageana*, neither ordinarily cultivated outside botanic gardens, are the parental species of the garden hybrids, which are available in a very wide range of both flowerhead size and plant height. All are stiff-stemmed with solitary flowerheads, almost all semi-double or fully double, with a colour range embracing white, yellow, orange, pink, red, maroon and purple.

The smallest-flowered – with flowerheads only 3–4cm (1¼–1½in) across and resembling a pompon dahlia – are the only hybrids with good resistance to poor summer weather. Of these, the **'Lilliput'** and **'Sun Bow'** culti-

vars are about 50cm (20in) tall, and the ultra-dwarf **'Thumbelina'**, only 10–15cm (4–6in). Also of relatively weatherproof performance is **'Persian Carpet'**, about 40cm (16in), with flowerheads around 5cm (2in) across in shades of yellow, orange and red, and including some bicolours.

The flowerhead size range of the various large-flowered hybrids is 7–12cm (3–5in), on plants 25–90cm (10–36in) high. As already indicated, these are probably best passed over as inappropriate for cool, damp climates. **'Cactus-Flowered'**, with pointed ray florets, and **'Dahlia-Flowered'** are the archetypal tall zinnias. An assortment of shorter versions and colour variants is available. For example, there is **'Envy'** for lovers of green flowers, while the single-flowered **Whirligig Series** has ray florets tipped by a contrasting colour.

The Fleuroselect Gold Medal winner *Zinnia* 'Profusion Cherry' is not unhappy in cool wet conditions.

18 Shrubs and Climbers

The eight genera assembled in this chapter obviously share their woody habit, but are otherwise widely assorted, both in their botanical relationships and as garden plants. Diverse as they are, they do have some important features in common. The first is that they are all evergreen, and the second is their southerly origin: four genera are from Australia and New Zealand, including the two largest and most horticulturally significant, *Brachyglottis* and *Olearia*; *Euryops* and *Othonna* are African; and *Santolina* Mediterranean. Given this situation, it is unsurprising that many species lack dependable winter hardiness in most of the British Isles and in north-eastern and central USA.

Attractive and distinctive foliage is widespread in these genera, and indeed is the primary reason for growing most species. A feature of some *Olearia* and *Ozothamnus* is fragrance. Showy flowerheads are particularly of note in *Euryops* and the little-grown genus of climbers, *Mutisia*. Many *Olearia* species are also nothing wanting in their floral display.

OLEARIA Daisy bush

In this chapter, *Olearia* stands alone in its wealth of species in cultivation, the foliage interest of many of them, and, for some species, their qualities as hedge plants. It is not just the number of cultivated species that is impressive, but also their appearance when in flower – some species are downright spectacular. The genus is also remarkable for the capacity of its members to thrive in salt-laden winds and on chalky soils. Most species make pleasingly dense growth and some of these are widely used as hedges in milder coastal districts.

The principal limitation on their popularity is lack of hardiness: only five species are able to survive undamaged winter temperatures down to about -10°C (14°F). Occasional exposure to temperatures as low as −15°C (5°F) can be tolerated. Unfortunately, most of the best are only suitable for gardens in mild coastal areas. As ever, there will also be a suitable micro-climate for these species close to a wall with a southerly aspect in many inland gardens.

The genus is named after a seventeenth-century German botanist, whose Latinized name was 'Olearius': the pronunciation is, therefore, *O-lee-area* – so rhyming with 'hairier'. A common but incorrect pronunciation rhymes with 'drearier'.

O. phlogopappa is an Australian native, but all other species described here are from New Zealand. All species are evergreen, and most eventually reach 1.5–2m (5–6½ft), with a similar or rather greater spread. The flowerheads of most are white, and borne profusely in many-flowered corymbs in late spring and summer.

All need a sunny position to give their best: avoid spots where much of the foliage is shaded most of the time by neighbouring buildings, trees or shrubs. Most species are fast growing, but are slow to develop a straggling habit: if they do, they respond to hard cutting back in spring by regenerating from near the base. Where frost damage has occurred, prudence dictates that pruning should wait until the potential for regrowth from the older wood is clear to see. Propagation is easiest by semi-ripe cuttings, taken in summer, although in early autumn more mature shoots removed with a heel will also root successfully.

Hardy species
These species can survive winter temperatures to −10°C (14°F).

O. × *haastii* is the most widely seen species. A rounded bush when established, it also makes a good hedge, even in atmospherically polluted urban environments. The leaves are smaller than in most species, up to 2.5cm (1in) long, as are the fragrant flowerheads, rather less than 1cm (½in) across. These are cream, and not particularly attractive. Flowering is in mid- and late summer.

O. nummulariifolia has relatively large flowers, up to 2cm (¾in) across, although each flowerhead has few ray florets, and thus lacks individual showiness. They are borne in midsummer at the ends of the shoots, either singly or in clusters of two or three. The leathery leaves are very small, up to 1cm (½in) long only, but furnish the branches densely.

O. 'Waikariensis' (syn. *O. oleifolia*) is compact and produces its small flowerheads, each with very few, broad ray florets, in many-flowered panicles, in mid- to late summer.

O. macrodonta ♔ is among the most vigorous species, and, with *O. × haastii*, is the one most widely grown. As a specimen shrub, it is upright and may eventually exceed 3m (10ft) in height. The whole plant has a musky fragrance. Each flowerhead has many ray florets, and borne as they are in large corymbs, their effect is showy. The flowering period is mid- to late summer.

It is suitable as a hedge plant and is sometimes known as New Zealand holly on account of its characteristic large, toothed leaves, up to 10cm (4in) long.

O. ilicifolia is similar in most respects to *O. macrodonta*, but is rather more spreading in habit, and has narrower leaves. The individual flowerheads are larger, but the corymb-like inflorescences are a little smaller.

Less hardy species

Gardeners in areas where temperatures, even in relatively hard winters, can be more or less counted on to remain above −5°C (23°F) have a very wide choice of species. In this group, the hardiest are *O. × scilloniensis* ♔ and *O.* 'Talbot de Malahide', while the most useful for hedges are *O. paniculata* and *O. traversii*. *O. capillaris* is a compact, small-leaved species of particular appeal where space is limited, as it does not usually exceed 1.25m (4ft) in height.

O. 'Henry Travers' (syn. *O. semidentata* hort) ♔ is of particular remark for the size and colour of its solitary flowerheads, up to 5cm (2in) across, each with many lilac ray florets surrounding a purple disc.

O. × mollis 'Zennoriensis' ♔ is notable for its striking foliage. The dark olive-green leaves are sharply toothed, up to 10cm (4in) long, but little over 1cm (½in) wide at most, and tapering to a fine point. Young stems are covered with dense, brown hair. Flowerheads are

borne in large corymbs in late spring. An outstanding plant for mild maritime conditions. At the time of writing, a young specimen is doing well at Wisley, where winter temperatures below −5°C (23°F) are common.

O. paniculata is a large shrub distinguished by the fragrance of its inconspicuous, rayless flowerheads in late autumn and early winter. It is successful as a hedge plant in mild areas and has large, olive-green, wavy-edged leaves.

O. phlogopappa (syn. *O. gunniana*), like 'Zennoriensis', is also among the earlier-flowering species. In loose corymbs, the flowerheads are relatively large, up to 3cm (1¼in) across. Ray florets in the species are white, but there are two fine cultivars, **'Comber's Blue'** and **'Comber's Pink'**. The leaves are grey-green.

O. × scilloniensis ♔ again flowers early, in late spring, is of compact habit and is particularly floriferous. The flowerheads are large, up to 6cm (2½in) across. A further commendation of this natural hybrid, found in 1910 on Tresco in the Scilly Isles, is that it is more frost-resistant than most species, tolerating occasional temperatures down to −10°C (14°F). The cultivar 'Master Michael' is blue-flowered.

O. stellulata (syn. *O. × scilloniensis* hort) is again early-flowering – late spring – and is of small to medium size and rather lax in habit.

O. solandri is grown particularly for the flowerheads, which open very late for this genus, from late summer onwards. Although they are individually insignificant, small, solitary and pale yellow, they are very strongly fragrant. It is sometimes chosen as a wall shrub and has a dense and upright habit. The very small, narrow leaves are no more than 1cm (½in) long, and mostly in clusters.

O. 'Talbot de Malahide' (syn. *O. albida* hort) is a late-flowering shrub for larger gardens, attaining a height of up to 3m (10ft). The large and very dense corymbs (up to 10cm/4in across) of small flowerheads are borne in late summer and early autumn. It is of similar hardiness to *O. × scilloniensis*.

O. traversii is a fast-growing, vigorous species, used almost entirely for tall hedges and windbreaks in coastal areas with mild winters. It commonly attains 6m (20ft), and in its native New Zealand it can grow considerably taller, and achieve a trunk diameter of over 50cm (20in). The rayless flowerheads are inconspicuous.

BRACHYGLOTTIS

One of the very few large genera in the entire daisy family that is known in horticulture for its shrubs, *Brachyglottis* shares much in common with *Olearia*. They are both almost entirely New Zealand in origin, both evergreen, both lime tolerant, both wind-resistant, and both thrive in coastal situations.

Oddly enough, the two genera belong to different tribes and are, therefore, not particularly closely related within the family. There are other differences, too: all the better-known cultivated species of *Brachyglottis* are yellow-flowered, while most *Olearia* are white. Flowerheads are a less significant reason for growing *Brachyglottis* species anyway, as it is the foliage of the cultivated species that makes them garden-worthy. Stems, young shoots, young foliage and the undersides of older leaves all have a characteristic dense covering of white hairs, giving entire plants a silver-grey cast.

The cultivar 'Sunshine' is among the most universally seen shrubs; despite its name, it is for its foliage that it is grown. It deserves its place in larger gardens, complementing a prodigious range of shrubby and herbaceous plants, particularly those with pink or red foliage or flowers, such as red valerian, *Centranthus ruber*. In winter, it can almost be counted as a focal attraction in its own right: the crisp white margin, that runs around the edges of the grey-green leaves so noticeably in this season of the year, provides interest and character at close quarters. As with those other silver-leaved, yellow-flowered members of the daisy family, *Santolina chamaecyparissus* and *Senecio cineraria*, it is arguable whether the flowerheads add to its garden-worthiness. It is the character of the neighbouring plants that should be allowed to determine the argument. Hard pruning in spring will promote shoot growth and foliage display at the expense of flowering, and this is the treatment I recommend.

For small gardens, 'Sunshine' is a questionable choice because of its size and vigour. *B. monroi* ♔ is a commendable alternative, as is *B. compacta*, provided in each case that its hardiness is sufficient.

All the species described here will thrive without difficulty in a suitable location in any well-drained soil. They are drought-tolerant, and do well in windy coastal situations. The Dunedin Group, including the ubiquitous 'Sunshine', is reliably hardy in winter conditions to −15°C (5°F), and may survive lower temperatures still. Other species may not survive prolonged periods of low winter temperatures, particularly in soil that lies wet. Pruning may be carried out if flowers are not wanted, but otherwise deadheading and the removal of damaged and sprawling growth after flowering suffices. Propagation is most easily achieved by semi-ripe cuttings taken in mid- to late summer.

Species and cultivars

Brachyglottis is a member of the *Senecio* tribe and in the past all the species described here were placed within the genus *Senecio*. They are still commonly catalogued under their former names.

Dunedin Group was first recorded early in the twentieth century at the Dunedin Botanic Garden in New Zealand. It is the result of inter-specific hybridization, between *B. compactus* and *B. greyi*, or possibly the closely similar *B. laxifolius*, and is hardier than either parent. **'Sunshine'** ♔ is the selection by which the group is known, and is so common as scarcely to need description. Unless curtailed by severe annual pruning, plants are likely to reach 1.5m (5ft) high with a larger spread. The ovate leaves are up to 7cm (3in) long. Flowerheads, up to 3cm (1¼in) across, are borne in loose panicles over a long period from midsummer onwards. There is also a little-seen yellow-variegated cultivar, **'Moira Reid'**.

B. compacta at maturity is up to 1m (3ft) tall. The growth is dense, the wavy-edged leaves smaller than those of 'Sunshine', and the flowerheads are usually in few-flowered racemes. It is hardy where temperatures seldom fall below −5°C (23°F), but is less dependable elsewhere.

B. greyi is a rather taller shrub than 'Sunshine', with larger leaves. It is hardy only in favoured positions in areas with mild winters. Most of the plants offered by nurseries under this name are in fact of 'Sunshine'.

B. monroi ♔ is in Britain second only to 'Sunshine' in both popularity and hardiness, and is a dependable survivor wherever lowest winter temperatures remain above −10°C (14°F). Of dense growth, it reaches up to 1m (3ft) in height, and has leaves up to 4cm (1½in) long with hairless, olive-green upper surfaces and notably wavy-edged margins. The flowerheads are up to 2cm (¾in) across, in terminal corymbs.

B. bidwillii is smaller and slower growing than any of the species above. Sometimes chosen for large rock gardens, it seldom attains more than 75cm (30in) and is characterized by thick, shining dark green leaves up to 1.5cm (½in) long. These are carried on stout stems, densely hairy when young. The flowerheads are inconspicuous.

B. rotundifolia (syn. *B. reinoldii*) is larger than the other species described, growing up to 3m (10ft) and occasionally more. The rounded leaves, borne on stout stems, are leathery, glossy above and up to 13cm (5in) long. Growth is dense and very wind-resistant: it is a good shrub for exposed coastal gardens. The yellowish flowerheads lack ray florets and are inconspicuous. It is comparable in hardiness to *B. greyi*.

The distinctive *Euryops tysonii* is not so well known as other species in the genus.

EURYOPS

Just three species of this genus are widely available in Britain. Nevertheless, two have received the AGM, and the popularity of one of these – *E. pectinatus* – has raced forward with its widespread adoption as a patio plant. All the species have yellow daisy flowers and foliage attractive for colour, form or both.

There are almost 100 *Euryops* species, almost all shrubby. The genus is in the same tribe (and sub-tribe) as *Senecio*. Distribution in the wild is confined to the African continent and Arabia. The species commonly cultivated are South African natives.

As already mentioned, *E. pectinatus* makes an attractive plant for patio containers, and for the purpose is best treated like many other half hardy herbaceous perennials grown for a single season's flower display outdoors. Propagation is by taking cuttings annually in summer; the resulting young plants are overwintered in cool greenhouse conditions for planting out in spring. Plants raised in this way are also sometimes used as summer bedding, and will grow more vigorously than in containers

because of their unrestricted root run. *E. chrysanthemoides* may be used for the same purposes. They are suitable for coastal gardens, as they are resistant to wind and salt.

These two species and *E. virgineus* will tolerate frosts down to about −5°C (23°F). Where lower temperatures are expected, they are plants for large containers in cool greenhouses and conservatories, where all will flower through the winter, given sufficient warmth and light.

Species and cultivars
Ray florets and discs are yellow in the following species.

E. acraeus ♀ (syn. *E. evansii* hort) stands alone for its hardiness and dwarfness, features used to best advantage as a rock-garden plant. A native of high mountain country, it is more or less fully hardy, particularly where soil drainage is excellent. It makes a dense bush up to 50cm (20in) tall and as wide. The much-branched stems have closely spaced, small, linear leaves, rather leathery and silvery grey-blue. A fine show of lemon-yellow flowerheads, up to 3cm (1¼in) across, is produced in late spring and early summer. The plant is very attractive for its foliage when out of flower.

E. pectinatus ♀ is of upright growth, reaching about 50cm (20in) when grown for a single season in a container, but otherwise up to twice that height. The long-stalked, buttercup-yellow flowerheads are usually solitary, but sometimes in twos and threes. They are up to 6cm (2½in) across and are borne from early summer to autumn, under glass continuing through the winter.

The grey-green foliage is an attraction in its own right, just as it is for *E. acraeus*, though the individual leaves are quite different. Up to 10cm (4in) long, they are deeply lobed, with very narrow individual segments (the Latin *pectinatus* means comb-like). **'Jamaica Sunshine'** is a selection.

E. chrysanthemoides is of similar character to *E. pectinatus*. It is slightly dwarfer, has a more densely branched habit, narrower leaves with wider lobes, and slightly smaller flowerheads, more freely produced.

E. virgineus is a much-branched shrub of similar stature to *E. pectinatus*. It produces clusters of very small, few-rayed flowerheads on short stalks at the tips of its erect stems. These are densely furnished with very small, finely lobed leaves.

E. tysonii has foliage reminiscent of the monkey puzzle tree (*Araucaria araucana*). The leathery, pointed leaves are closely spaced on the thick, more or less upright stems. At least as hardy as *E. pectinatus*, it is a small shrub of 75cm (30in) high with a greater spread. The solitary flowerheads, to 2.5cm (1in) across, are borne on short, thin stalks in the axils of the leaves.

OTHONNA
One species only of this large African genus has come into cultivation – a native of Algeria and Tunisia.

O. cheirifolia, a dwarf shrub bearing yellow daisy flowerheads, is quite widely grown, probably not so much for its rather unspecial blooms as for its characteristically exotic habit. Although hardy enough to be grown outdoors in suitable locations, it is sometimes included in greenhouse collections of cacti and succulents, where it very much looks the part.

The freely branched, spreading stems grow to a height of about 40cm (16in). The fleshy, grey-green leaves, up to 8cm (3in) long, are stalkless and narrow, with blunt ends. Upwardly poised, they clothe the stems densely. The solitary flowerheads, up to 4cm (1½in) across, with disc and florets both yellow, are produced in summer. It is a plant for a sunny, sheltered spot where soil drainage is very free: a large rock garden or bank suit it well. Where the soil is wet for prolonged periods in winter, it is more susceptible to dying out in periods of hard frost.

Propagation is by cuttings taken in summer. The plant is attractive to aphids.

OZOTHAMNUS
This genus of about 50 species of shrubs, that are closely related to *Helichrysum*, makes a small but distinctive contribution to gardening. The distinction – and three AGMs must speak loud when so few species are in cultivation – owes much to foliage characteristics and, in *O. ledifolius*, *O. hookeri* and *O. thyrsoideus*, fragrance. That the contribution is small is largely because of limited hardiness: of the five or six species currently available, *O. selago*, and probably *O. ledifolius* and *O. coralloides*, can be counted on to survive where temperatures do not fall below −10°C (14°F) for more than the occasional night. The remainder are only suitable for more favoured areas near the sea, and for particularly sheltered garden positions elsewhere. The genus, like *Brachyglottis* and *Olearia*, is native to Australia and New Zealand.

All the plants described here are listed as *Helichrysum* species in older books and some nursery catalogues, and correspondingly labelled in some gardens. They are small-leaved evergreens, with small, white or cream flowerheads that lack ray florets. Two of the species – *O. coralloides* and *O. selago* – are dwarf enough to be very appropriate as rock-garden plants. Both of these require excellent drainage. Like the others, which range from 1–3m (3–10ft) in eventual height, they need a sunny, sheltered spot to do themselves justice. In such an environment, the fragrance of some species can be appreciated to the full. Propagation is by seed or semi-ripe cuttings taken in mid- to late summer.

Species and cultivars

These are described in order of hardiness. This coincides approximately with that of height, except in the case of *O. hookeri*.

O. selago is the dwarfest and hardiest species, a slow-growing, much-branched, dense little shrub with aromatic foliage. Its eventual height is about 40cm (16in). The very small, shiny, triangular leaves are closely pressed to the upright shoots. Small, cream flowerheads are produced in summer.

O. coralloides ♛ is a similar plant in general character, though it may be a little less hardy. The appearance of the shoots is quite different, however. Each looks like an intricately patterned, green and white cylinder due to the larger, fleshier and white-woolly leaves, which are closely pressed to the upright stems. Flowerheads are similar to those of *O. selago*, but may not be seen in cool climates.

O. ledifolius ♛ (Kerosene bush) is of very dense, freely branched and upright growth, and attains a height of around 1m (3ft). The youngest parts of the stems and the undersides of the narrow, dark green leaves are distinguished by their clearly visible yellow-downy covering. The small, white flowerheads are produced in early summer, in corymbs up to 5cm (2in) across. Brick-red bracts enfold them before they open, adding to the attractiveness of the plant in late spring. The sweet aroma of the plant comes from a sticky exudate of the older leaves. This is inflammable, and is the explanation for its American common name, which is not descriptive of the aroma, fortunately: Graham Stuart Thomas has described

this as an 'entrancing mixture of beeswax and hot strawberry jam'.

O. rosmarinifolius is of larger stature and more graceful habit than *O. ledifolius*, being up to 2m (6½ft) and sometimes higher. It is also rather less hardy. Its upright, freely branching shoots are slender and closely furnished by narrow, dark green, rosemary-like leaves, up to 4cm (1½in) long. Shoot tips and young leaves beneath are white-woolly. The white flowerheads, opening in early to midsummer, are similar in colour and size to *O. ledifolius*. Also similarly, the flowerheads before opening are enfolded by conspicuous colourful bracts, in this case rich red. **'Silver Jubilee'** ♛ has silver-grey leaves.

O. hookeri and **O. thyrsoideus** (Snow in summer) are significantly less hardy than the preceding species, and are most of interest to gardeners in coastal areas with mild winters. *O. hookeri* attains a height of about 2m (6½ft), *O. thyrsoideus* about 3m (10ft). Both are white-flowered and fragrant. *O. thyrsoideus* has slender branches and spreading linear leaves while *O. hookeri* has small, scale-like leaves, closely pressed to the stems, after the fashion of *O. selago*. They are woolly below.

CASSINIA Golden heather, Silver heather

While descriptive of the plant's appearance, the common names of *C. leptophylla* are misleading: *Cassinia* is not a heather, being closely related to *Ozothamnus*, and like it, also native to Australia and New Zealand.

C. leptophylla is the best-known species. Like some of the more popular species of its relative, *Ozothamnus*, it is winter-hardy where winter temperatures do not fall below −5°C (23°F). The plant responds well to hard pruning as necessary to preserve a compact habit.

The most widely grown subspecies, subsp. *fulvida* is said to be marginally hardier than the type, and than subsp. *vauvilliersii*. It is often used as a hedge in seaside gardens.

Propagation is by seed or semi-ripe cuttings.

C. leptophylla itself is not often grown. It is a small, evergreen shrub, which eventually reaches about 2m (6½ft). Of dense growth habit, the erect, slender, hairy stems are crowded with very small, dark green, narrow leaves, only about 5mm (¼in) long and downy beneath. The white flowerheads, without ray florets, and also very small, are produced in summer in many-flowered, flattish, terminal, open clusters, up to 5cm (2in) across.

Lavender cotton, *Santolina chamaecyparissus*, makes an attractive dwarf shrub but is sometimes used for a low hedge.

subsp. *fulvida* (Golden heather) has longer and relatively broader leaves, up to 8mm (⅜in) in length. More significantly, both their undersides and the young stems are yellow-downy. They are also sticky to the touch.

subsp. *vauvilliersii* is very similar but is usually grown as its variety ***albida*** (Silver heather), which has white down where the subspecies itself has yellow.

'Ward Silver' has silver-grey upper leaf surfaces.

SANTOLINA Lavender cotton, Cotton lavender

One of the most widely known of all silver-leaved plants is *S. chamaecyparissus*, a dwarf shrub with a botanical name quite out of proportion in length to its own humble stature. All the species of its fairly small genus are found in the wild in or close to the Mediterranean area. They are typically plants of poor, very freely drained soils on sites fully exposed to the sun. All are small, evergreen shrubs; all those in cultivation have finely divided leaves and all are aromatic to a greater or lesser extent.

It is as foliage plants that they are of primary interest, though small, solitary button-like flowerheads are produced on long, leafless stalks in summer. These lack ray florets, and the extent to which their appearance contributes to the attractiveness of the plants is debatable. In

Santolina as in other genera, I dislike the foiling of strong yellow flowerheads by silver-grey foliage. Fortunately, there are cultivars with pale yellow flowerheads. This is a much more friendly tint: I commend to you *S. chamaecyparissus* 'Lemon Queen' and *S. pinnata* 'Edward Bowles' and 'Sulphurea'. The bright yellow flowerheads of *S. rosmarinifolia* do look well, though, because the foliage against which they are foiled is dark green.

S. chamaecyparissus was used extensively in the past as an edging plant for flowerbeds, partly because it responds well to clipping. To preserve the austere formality of the miniature hedges that resulted, the flowerheads were removed. Few gardeners would use the plant in this way today, though it still finds a place as edging for herb gardens and in recreations of Elizabethan knot gardens. More often the three species described below are used informally, in sunny positions at or near the edges of beds and borders. They can be used to good effect as groundcover plants, and the dwarfer cultivars have a place in large rock gardens.

All are fairly hardy, but may succumb to a winter combination of low temperatures, exposure to wind and persistently wet soil. They perform best on fast-drained, rather poor soils: on richer, more moisture-retentive ones, growth may easily lose the dense, compact quality that enhances their visual effect. This should be promoted by annual cutting back in spring: they are capable of sprouting well from old wood. Nevertheless, plants usually need replacing every five to seven years.

Propagation is usually – and easily – by semi-ripe cuttings taken in late summer; raising from seed is also easy. There are no commonly occurring pest or disease problems of note.

Species and cultivars

Those described are variations on a basic central theme of a small evergreen bush of dense growth, cultivated for its divided, aromatic foliage. The variations are in plant size, leaf colour, leaf form and flowerhead colour.

S. chamaecyparissus (syn. *S. incana*) ♔ (Lavender cotton, Cotton lavender) is native to the Pyrenees, southern France and north-west Italy. It makes a rounded bush of a height up to 50cm (20in), but with a wider spread as it ages. Both the young shoots and the aromatic foliage are densely covered in short, grey to white hairs. The leaves are up to 4cm (1½in) long and are pinnatisect, with very short segments. The flowerheads, produced in summer, are up to 2cm (¾in) across, and deep bright yellow.

'Lambrook Silver' differs from the species in the silver tinting of the foliage. **'Lemon Queen'**, of compact habit and less spreading than the species, has very pale yellow flowerheads. **var. nana** ♀ and **'Small-Ness'** are both very dwarf, up to 20cm (8in) only in height.

S. pinnata, native to the same areas of Europe, differs primarily in being more or less hairless. Other dissimilarities are the mid-green leaves, with longer, threadlike segments, and the creamy-white flowerheads. It is also rather taller, up to about 75cm (30in). **subsp. neapolitana** ♀ has young stems and leaves covered with short white hairs. The flowerheads are bright yellow. Its cultivar **'Edward Bowles'** shares the same leaf colour, but has creamy-white flowerheads, while in **'Sulphurea'** they are pale yellow.

S. rosmarinifolia, native to Spain, Portugal, southern France and north-west Africa, often has stems that are horizontal in their lower parts. The dark green, hairless leaves are very aromatic. The uppermost ones are undivided and linear, as in rosemary. Lower on the stems, they are pinnatisect, with the very short segments well spaced from one another. The flowerheads are bright yellow.

subsp. canescens has young shoots and leaves densely covered with short white to grey hairs. Its cultivar **'Primrose Gem'** ♀ has paler-coloured flowerheads.

MUTISIA Climbing gazania

The species of this South American genus have the rare distinction among cultivated daisies in being climbers; only three other climbers are found in this book – all species of *Senecio*. The climbing habit is, in fact, not a rarity in the family, but is largely confined to genera native to warm areas of the globe.

The three species listed below are all showy plants bearing solitary flowerheads in summer and autumn. Each leaf terminates in a tendril, an uncommon arrangement in garden plants and probably best known in the glory lily, *Gloriosa rothschildiana*.

In cultivation *Mutisia* needs the support of a net or trellis. None of the species is quite fully hardy, and outdoors they need the protection of a wall of southerly aspect. They are, otherwise, plants for a cool greenhouse or conservatory. As full exposure as possible to sun is desirable, but the roots are better in shade. Propagation is by cuttings in summer, or by layering.

Species

M. decurrens is a slender-stemmed shrub, growing to 3m (10ft), with orange flowerheads, sometimes exceeding 10cm (4in) across. In the wild it is found in dry, rocky places.

M. ilicifolia reaches a similar height and has pale pink flowerheads, to 6cm (2½in) across, with yellow discs.

M. oligodon is a straggly shrub, attaining a height of 1.5m (5ft) at most. Its long-stemmed flowerheads, to 7cm (3in) across, have pretty pink ray florets and a yellow disc.

The south European shrub, *Santolina pinnata* subsp. *neapolitana* ♀ contrasts with the Australian everlasting *Craspedia globosa*.

Appendix I *Glossary of Terms*

Achene A small, dry fruit with a tight, thin wall that does not open to release the seeds when dry. The characteristically one-seeded fruits of plants in the daisy family are achenes, although the term *cypsela* is also used for these.

Anther The terminal pollen-bearing portion of a *stamen*.

Bipinnatifid see pinnatifid.

Bipinnatisect see pinnatisect.

Bract A leaf-like structure that has a protective function. In the daisy family, bracts surround the base of the flowerhead, forming an involucre. They have the same relative position and relationship to the flowerhead as does the *calyx* to the *corolla* in most other plant families. The bracts are often in several rows, and are particularly conspicuous in many members of the thistle tribe, Cardueae, and the tribe of the everlasting flowers, Gnaphalieae.

Calyx (**calyces**) In most families of flowering plants, the outermost part of a flower, immediately within which is the *corolla*. It consists of sepals, which may be separate or fused. In Compositae, the calyx is absent, but its place is often taken by the *pappus*.

Capitulum (**capitula**) A head of densely clustered flowers or florets, stalkless or nearly so, as is typical of flowerheads of the daisy family.

Composite As used in this book, an adjective derived from the plant family name Compositae.

Compound Of leaves, divided into separate leaflets as in the pinnate leaves of, for example, Dahlia.

Corolla This consists of petals that in Compositae are fused either to form a tube, with five more or less symmetrical lobes or teeth at the outer end, or to form a *ray floret*.

Corymb A flat-topped or convex *inflorescence* in which the outer flowerheads open first.

Cultivar A variety that has arisen in cultivation, either by deliberate selection or breeding, or by chance.

Cypsela See achene.

Disc The central part of a *radiate* flowerhead, formed by the short tubular disc florets.

Disciform A type of *composite* flowerhead in which the outer florets differ from those in the centre, but do not radiate outwards (see p.24).

Discoid The simplest type of *composite* flowerhead, in which the similar or identical florets are tubular (see p.24).

Dissected A general term for the description of leaf blades that are cut in any way, e.g. pinnatisect.

Elliptic Of the shape of leaf blades, elongated with the margins of the two halves of the leaf, one on each side of the midrib, symmetrically curved in outline (see also lanceolate and ovate).

Family A natural grouping of genera distinguishable from others by shared reproductive characters. The usual ending of a family name is -aceae, e.g. Ranunculaceae (Buttercup family).

Floret A flower that is very small and usually part of a densely packed inflorescence.

Form (or **Forma**) (abbr. f.) A naturally occurring population that differs from the type species only in one or two minor characters, e.g. flower colour.

Genus (**genera**) Usually a group of species with distinctive characters in common, particularly in relation to the flower. A single species that is highly distinctive constitutes a genus in its own right.

Group A group is intermediate between a *species* and a *cultivar*. The individual plants within a group are closely similar, and distinct from other individual plants within the species, but nevertheless show too much variation from one another to be regarded as members of the same cultivar. The best-known example in the daisy family is *Achillea ptarmica* The Pearl Group.

Half hardy Damaged by exposure to temperatures below 0°C (32°F). See also tender.

Hardy Tolerant of the lowest temperature likely to occur in the garden conditions under consideration. In Europe, 'frost hardy' is taken to mean tolerant of temperatures down to −5°C (23°F), and 'fully hardy' to −15°C (5°F).

Hybrid A plant with genetically dissimilar parents, most commonly of different species.

Inflorescence The flowering stem and the flowers (and *bracts*, if present) that are borne on it. In the daisy family, the flowerheads are inflorescences in their own right. The term is, nevertheless, applied to the stem and the flowerheads arising from it, provided that there is more than one.

Involucre See bract.

Lamina Leaf blade.

Lanceolate Of leaf shape, spearhead shaped, with a length 3–6 times as great as the width, tapering to a pointed tip.

Latex Milky fluid, often white, found in the cells of plants of the lettuce tribe, Lactuceae, and of many other genera, e.g. Euphorbia.

Ovary The base of the female reproductive organ of the flower. It contains ovules, which after fertilization develop to form seeds.

Ovate Of leaf blades, egg-shaped, therefore widest below the middle and rounded at both ends.

Panicle A branched inflorescence that comprises short *corymbs* or *racemes* all of which arise from a main central stem. In the daisy family, panicles are rounded or pyramidal.

Pappus A whorl or tuft of scales or bristles, surrounding the base of each floret in many members of the daisy family (see. p.26).

Pedicel The stalk of a flower.

Perfect A floret with both *stamens* and *pistil*.

Petiole The stalk of a leaf.

Phyllary An alternative name for an involucral *bract*.

Pinnate A type of *compound* leaf, including four or more leaflets in two matching rows, one on each side of a central stalk, the *rachis*.

Pinnatifid Of leaves, with the leaf blade divided almost to the midrib into broad segments. In bipinnatifid leaves the initial divisions are again divided in the same fashion.

Pinnatisect As for *pinnatifid*, but into narrower segments. In bipinnatisect leaves the initial divisions are again divided.

Pistil The female reproductive organs of the flower, comprising the *ovary*, the *style* and the stigma.

Raceme Type of *inflorescence* characterized by a single unbranched stem, and bearing an indefinite number of stalked flowers. The flowers at the base of the stem usually form and open first, though *Liatris* is an exception (see also spike).

Rachis The axis – or principal stem or stalk – of a *compound inflorescence* or compound leaf.

Radiate The form of flowerhead characterized by outwardly spreading *ray florets* surrounding the short tubular florets of the centre (or disc).

Ray floret (**ray**) An outer floret in a radiate flowerhead, with one side of its *corolla* lengthened and enlarged.

Receptacle In Compositae, the enlarged end of the stem on which the flowerhead develops.

Rhizome A creeping stem that grows either on the soil surface or shallowly below it. Lateral stems develop from a rhizome, either along its length or at its apex.

Rosette A growth formation of leaves in herbaceous perennial plants, all of them arising at or very close to ground level from a single central point, and radiating outwards from it.

Runner A prostrate stem on which plantlets and roots develop.

Segment Of a deeply divided leaf or *corolla*, a part that is distinguishable from the rest although joined to it and merging with it at its base.

Sepal See calyx.

Simple Of leaves, not divided into leaflets.

Solitary Of flowerheads, each borne singly on a separate stem.

Species The basic unit of classification of living organisms. All individual plants in a species share a number of features, particularly in the flower, which distinguish them from members of all other species and are usually capable of cross-fertilization. Since cross-fertilization between members of different species in most cases cannot take place, the characteristics of individual species are preserved.

Spike A form of *inflorescence* sharing all the features of a *raceme* except that the flowers are without stalks (sessile).

Stamens The male reproductive organs of a flower. Each stamen consists of a stalk, the filament, and one or more *anthers*. In Compositae each stamen has two anthers.

Stigma The outermost part of the *pistil*. This is the part that receives pollen.

Stolon See runner.

Stoloniferous Producing *stolons* (*runners*).

Style The part of the *pistil* between the *ovary* and the *stigma*. It is characteristically slender.

Sub-species (abbr. subsp) A population found in the wild within a *species*, differing substantially in a number of characters from the type species as described. A sub-species is usually found in a separate location from the type species.

Subtend To be inserted directly below. Hence, each daisy flowerhead is subtended by an *involucre*.

Tender Susceptible to damage by exposure to temperatures below 5°C (41°F).

Tribe A group of genera within a family sharing characteristics which indicate that their relationship is particularly close.

Type Plants that are identical or closely similar to the *species* as originally described, are said to belong to the 'species type', or the 'type of the species'. *Sub-species*, *varieties* and *forms* differ from the type.

Variety (abbr. var.) A population occurring naturally within a *species*, differing in a very small number of characters from the type species. Unlike a sub-species, a variety usually shares, at least in part, the same distribution in the wild as the type species (see also sub-species and form).

Appendix II *Daisy Classification*

All the genera described in this book are listed below, grouped into the tribes to which they belong. Three of the tribes are not mentioned by name elsewhere: these are Arctoteae, Mutisieae and Vernonieae.

Tribe Anthemideae

Achillea
Ajania
Anacyclus
Anthemis
Argyranthemum
Artemisia
Chamaemelum
Chrysanthemum
Cladanthus
Coleostephus
Cotula
Ismelia
Leptinella
Leucanthemella
Leucanthemum
Lonas
Matricaria
Nipponanthemum
Rhodanthemum
Santolina
Seriphidium
Tanacetum
Ursinia

Tribe Arctoteae

Arctotis
Gazania

Tribe Astereae

Aster
Bellis
Bellium
Boltonia
Brachyscome
Callistephus
Celmisia
Erigeron
Felicia
Grindelia
Heteropappus
Heterotheca
Kalimeris
Olearia
Townsendia

Tribe Calenduleae

Calendula
Dimorphotheca
Osteospermum
Tripteris

Tribe Cardueae

Amberboa
Carlina
Carthamus
Centaurea
Cirsium
Cynara
Echinops
Galactites
Leuzea
Onopordum
Serratula
Silybum
Xeranthemum

Tribe Eupatorieae

Ageratum
Eupatorium
Liatris

Tribe Gnaphalieae

Ammobium
Anaphalis
Antennaria
Bracteantha
Cassinia
Chrysocephalum
Craspedia
Helichrysum
Leontopodium

Leucogenes
Leucophyta
Ozothamnus
Pteropogon
Raoulia
Rhodanthe
Schoenia

Tribe Helenieae

Arnica
Eriophyllum
Gaillardia
Helenium
Layia
Madia
Tagetes
Thymophylla

Tribe Heliantheae

Bidens
Coreopsis
Cosmos
Dahlia
Echinacea
Helianthella
Helianthus
Heliopsis
Melampodium
Rudbeckia
Sanvitalia
Silphium
Tithonia

Tribe Inuleae

Asteriscus
Buphthalmum
Inula
Pulicaria
Telekia

Tribe Lactuceae

Andryala
Catananche
Cicerbita
Cichorium
Hieracium
Lactuca
Microseris
Pilosella
Sonchus
Tolpis
Urospermum

Tribe Mutisieae

Gerbera
Mutisia

Tribe Senecioneae

Brachyglottis
Doronicum
Emilia
Euryops
Ligularia
Othonna
Pericallis
Petasites
Senecio
Sinacalia
Steirodiscus

Tribe Vernoniae

Stokesia
Vernonia

Appendix III *Where to see Daisies*

Because of the wealth of horticulturally important genera in the daisy family, almost all gardens open to the public offer good opportunities to see some of them. For daisy displays open for public viewing in North America, please check with the American Association of Botanical Gardens and Arboreta at 351 Longwood Rd, Kennett Square, PA 19348, or check their web site at www.aabga.org/. In Britain National Collections and Botanic Gardens are of special appeal to gardeners with a particular interest in the family.

National Collections

The National Council for the Conservation of Plants and Gardens (NCCPG) co-ordinates and administers the National Plant Collections Scheme in the British Isles. It publishes an annual directory of collections, which can be obtained from larger garden centres and nurseries or from NCCPG, The Pines, Wisley Gardens, Woking, Surrey GU23 6QB. In the year 2000 the daisy family genera included in the scheme were as shown below.

Achillea

Anthemis tinctoria

Argyranthemum

Artemisia

Aster (autumn-flowering)

Aster amellus, A. cordifolius and *A. ericoides*

Aster novi-belgii

Brachyglottis

Celmisia

Chrysanthemum: Charms and Cascade, Korean hybrids and Rubellum hybrids

Coreopsis

Dahlia

Doronicum

Echinacea

Erigeron

Helianthus

Helichrysum (dwarf varieties)

Heliopsis

Inula

Leucanthemum × superbum

Ligularia

Olearia

Osteospermum

Rudbeckia

Santolina

Tanacetum (garden pyrethrum)

Botanic Gardens

An original function of Botanic Gardens was to maintain a comprehensive, labelled collection of plants formally arranged by their families – in family beds, as they are customarily called. In some present day botanic gardens this tradition is maintained, and the daisy family, the largest of all, is usually strongly represented.

Examples of where visitors can easily gain an overview of the daisy family include the following Botanic Gardens in the British Isles:

Cambridge University Botanic Garden
The Chelsea Physic Garden, London
Cruickshank Botanic Gardens, Aberdeen
National Botanic Gardens, Glasnevin, Dublin
Royal Botanic Gardens, Kew
St. Andrews Botanic Garden
University of Dundee Botanic Garden
University of Oxford Botanic Garden

Appendix IV *Where to buy Daisies*

Seeds
The following companies offer a wide selection of seeds of species and cultivars within the daisy family.

Europe
B & T World Seeds, Paguignan, 34210, Olonzac, France

Chiltern Seeds, Ulverston, Cumbria, LA12 7PB

Jelitto Staudensamen GmbH, Postfach 1264, D - 29685 Schwarmstedt, Germany

Thompson & Morgan Ltd, Ipswich, Suffolk IP8 3BU

USA
Burpee Seeds, 300 Park Ave, Warminster, PA 18974

Jelitto, 125 Chenoweth Ln, Louisville, KY 40207

Park's Seeds, 1 Parkton Ave, Greenwood, SC 29647-0001

Prairie Nursery, P.O. Box 306, Westfield, WI 53964-0306

Seedhunt, P.O. Box 96, 200 Casserly Rd (Watsonville), Freedom, CA 95019-0096

Thompson & Morgan, P.O. Box 1308, 22 Farraday Ave, Jackson, NJ 08527-0308

Plants
Nurseries that have made a speciality of an individual genus in the daisy family and those that stock a particularly wide selection of members of the family are listed below. Numbers in brackets preceding the nursery name indicate the field of interest as follows: 1) Hardy herbaceous perennials; 2) Alpine and rock garden plants; 3) Shrubs; 4) Argyranthemum; 5) Aster; 6) Celmisia; 7) Chrysanthemum; 8) Dahlia

UK
8) Aylett Nurseries Limited, St Albans, Herts AL2 1DH

6) Ballyrogan Nurseries, Newtownards, County Down, Northern Ireland BT23 4SD

1) Beeches Nursery, Saffron Walden, Essex CB10 2HB

1) Beth Chatto Gardens Ltd., Colchester, Essex CO7 7DB

3) Burncoose & South Devon Nurseries, Redruth, Cornwall TR16 6BJ

8) Butterfields Nursery, Bourne End, Bucks SL8 5JJ

1) Cally Gardens, Castle Douglas, Scotland DG7 2DJ

7) Collinwood Nurseries, Macclesfield, Cheshire SK10 4QR

1) Cotswold Garden Flowers, Evesham, Worcs WR11 5EZ

3) Duchy of Cornwall Penlyne Nursery, Lostwithiel, Cornwall PL22 OHW

1) Four Seasons, Norwich, Norfolk NR16 1JT

1) Green Farm Plants, Farnham, Surrey GU10 5LZ

1) Hall Farm Nursery, Gainsborough, Lincs DN21 5UU

7, 8) Halls of Heddon, Newcastle-upon-Tyne, NE15 OJS

7) Home Meadows Nursery Ltd., Woodbridge, Suffolk IP12 4RD

4) Lower Icknield Farm Nurseries, Aylesbury, Bucks HP17 9TX

1) Manor Nursery, Saffron Walden, Essex CB10 2UT

2) Mendle Nursery, Scunthorpe, Lincs DN16 3RF

1) Monksilver Nursery, Cottenham, Cambs CB4 8TW

5) Old Court Nurseries, Malvern, Worcs WR13 6QE

1, 2) Perhill Nurseries, Great Witley, Worcs WR6 6JT

3) Perryhill Nurseries, Hartfield, East Sussex TN7 4JP

1, 2) Rumsey Gardens, Waterlooville, Hants PO8 OPD

1) Stillingfleet Lodge Nurseries, Stillingfleet, Yorkshire YO19 6HP

7) Woolmans Plants Ltd., Evesham, Worcs WR11 5EN

USA
1) Bluestone Perennials, 7211 Middle Ridge Rd, Madison, OH 44057-3096

1) Carroll Gardens, 444 E. Main St, Westminster, MD 21157

1) Crownsville Nursery, P.O. Box 797, Crownsville, MD 21032

1) Fieldstone Gardens, 620 Quaker Road, Vassalboro, ME 04989-9713

1) Forestfarm, 990 Tetherow Rd, Williams, OR 97544-9599

7) King's Mums, P.O. Box 368, 20303, E. Liberty Road, Clements, CA 95227

1) Niche Gardens, 111 Dawson Road, Chapel Hill, NC 27516

2) Siskiyou Rare Plant Nursery, 2825 Cummings Road, Medford, OR 97501

1) Sunlight Gardens, 174 Golden Lane, Andersonville, TN 37705

1) Woodside Gardens, 1191 Egg & I Road, Chimacum, WA 98325

Appendix V *Daisy Societies*

While there are no societies for enthusiasts of the daisy family as a whole, there are societies for those specifically interested in chrysanthemums and dahlias, as well as some that include members of the daisy family in a wider field of interest.

UK

Alpine Garden Society, AGS Centre, Avonbank, Pershore, Worcestershire WR10 3JP

The Hardy Plant Society, Little Orchard, Great Comberton, Pershore, Worcestershire WR10 3DP

The National Chrysanthemum Society, George Gray House, 8 Amber Business Village, Amber Close, Tamworth, Staffordshire B77 4RD

The National Dahlia Society, 19 Sunnybank, Marlow, Buckinghamshire SL7 3BL

USA and Canada

American Dahlia Society, 1 Rock Falls Ct, Rockville, MD 20854

National Chrysanthemum Society, 10107 Homar Pond Drive, Fairfax Station, VA 22039-1650

Canadian Chrysanthemum and Dahlia Society, 142 Grand River Bend, Scarborough, ONT M1B 1GS, Canada

Hardy Plant Society, Mid Atlantic Branch, 491 Dowlin Forge Road, Exton, PA 19341

Hardy Plant Society of Oregon, 1930 NW Lovejoy Street, Portland, OR 97201

Northwest Perennial Alliance, P.O. Box 85565, University Station, Washington 98145

North American Cottage Garden Society, P.O. Box 22232, Santa Fe, NM 87502-2232

Appendix VI *Further Reading*

Alpine Garden Society, Beckett, K. (editor) *Encylopedia of Alpines* (Volumes 1 and 2) (AGS, 1994)

Armitage, A. *Armitage's Garden Perennials* (Timber Press 2000)

Bean, W. J. *Trees & Shrubs Hardy in the British Isles* (Volumes 1–4) (John Murray, 8th edition 1976–1980)

Bremer, K. *Asteraceae* (Timber Press, USA, 1994)

European Garden Flora Volume 6 (Cambridge University Press, in preparation)

Harper P. *Time-Tested Plants* (Timber Press 2000)

The Hillier Manual of Trees & Shrubs (David & Charles, 6th edition 1991)

Jelitto, L. & Schacht, W. *Hardy Herbaceous Perennials* (Timber Press, USA, 3rd edtion, 1990)

National Chrysanthemum Society *Wallace Brook's World of Chrysanthemums* (NCS, 1998)

Everett, T. H. (editor) *New York Botanical Garden Illustrated Encyclopaedia of Horticulture* (Volumes 1–10) (Garland Publishing, 1982)

Picton, P. *The Gardeners' Guide to Growing Asters* (David & Charles and Timber Press, 1999)

Rowlands, G. *The Gardeners' Guide to Growing Dahlias* (David & Charles and Timber Press, 1999)

Royal Horticultural Society *New Dictionary of Gardening* (Volumes 1–4) (Macmillan, 1992)

Index

ACKNOWLEDGEMENTS

The photographs for this book were taken at Bourton House, Colegrave Ltd., the Hiller Garden, Moles Seeds Ltd., Old Court Nurseries, Pershore College, Red Gables, Evesham and the University of Oxford Botanic Garden. The co-operation of all individuals and organizations concerned is gratefully acknowledged.

I am greatly indebted to many people for their advice, assistance, encouragement and interest, and would like particularly to record my gratitude to the following:

Denis O'Brien Baker of Home Meadows Nursery Limited; Sylvia Baldwin of Lower Icknield Farm Nurseries; John Davies of the Hardy Plant Society, Nottingham; Mr & Mrs Peter Heaton, Christopher Norris, and Paul Picton of Old Court Nurseries, all of them holders of NCCPG collections; Richard Ball of Four Seasons; Bruce Harnett of Kernock Park Plants; Mark Lunghusen of Outback Plants in Australia; Kevin Marsh of Beeches Nursery; Dr Brian Meredith of Cotswold Garden Flowers; Rolf Offenthal of Solitärstauden in Germany; Julie Ritchie of Hoo House Nursery; Geoff Salisbury of the Hiller Garden; Joe Sharman of Monksilver Nursery; Mark Smith of Yoder Bros Inc, USA; Carl Soerensen of Cape Daisy in Denmark; Duncan Straw of Perhill Plants; David Tristram of Walberton Nurseries; Jack Williams of the Paul Ecke Ranch, California, USA; Jos van Popering of Sakata Seed Europe BV; Stuart Lowen of Colegrave Ltd.; Dr Elisabeth Sahin of K Sahin Zaden BV; Rowena Hall of Thompson & Morgan (UK) Ltd; Dr Nicholas Hind of the Royal Botanic Gardens, Kew; Sue Minter of Chelsea Physic Garden; Dr Tim Upson of Cambridge University Botanic Garden; Timothy Walker of the University of Oxford Botanic Garden; George Parker and Stephen Taffler of the Hardy Plant Society; staff of the library of Pershore College and of the Lindley Library; Bob Hares of Pershore College; Linda Jones and Piers Trehane of the Royal Horticultural Society; Professor Allan Armitage of the University of Georgia, USA; Paul Williams; Anna Mumford and Ali Myer of David & Charles, and editor Jo Weeks.

Last, but by no means least, my wife Deirdre, who typed the entire script, prepared the index, made innumerable suggestions for improving the text and provided the patient support without which this book might never have reached completion. The responsibility for any errors is, of course, my own.